ACCOUNTING
for
BUSINESS
CONSOLIDATIONS

Important Disclaimer

This publication is sold with the understanding that (1) the authors and editors are not responsible for the results of any actions taken on the basis of information in this work, nor for any errors or omissions; and (2) the publisher is not engaged in rendering legal, accounting or other professional services. The publisher, and the authors and editors, expressly disclaim all and any liability to any person, whether a purchaser of this publication or not, in respect of anything and of the consequences of anything done or omitted to be done by any such person in reliance, whether whole or partial, upon the whole or any part of the contents of this publication. If legal advice or other expert assistance is required, the services of a competent professional person should be sought.

Legislation reproduced

Commonwealth legislation herein is reproduced by permission, but does not purport to be the official or authorised version. It is subject to Crown copyright. The *Copyright Act 1968* permits certain reproduction and publication of Commonwealth legislation. In particular, sec. 182A of the Act enables a complete copy to be made by or on behalf of a particular person. For reproduction or publication beyond that permitted by the Act, permission should be sought in writing from "The Secretary, Attorney-General's Department, Canberra, A.C.T. 2600".

3783 AUS

ACCOUNTING *for* BUSINESS CONSOLIDATIONS

by
Darryl K. Swindells

CCH AUSTRALIA LIMITED
Incorporated in N.S.W.
THE INFORMATION PROFESSIONALS
Cnr. Talavera & Khartoum Roads, North Ryde
P.O. Box 230, North Ryde, N.S.W. 2113
Phone: Sydney 888 2555

About CCH Australia Limited
The Information Professionals

The CCH group, with world wide activities in North America, Australia, New Zealand, Asia and Europe is almost certainly the world's largest legal publisher.

CCH Australia Limited, while a wholly owned subsidiary of Commerce Clearing House, Inc. of Chicago, Illinois, USA, enjoys an independence of operation not common in such international corporate relationships.

CCH Australia Limited commenced in Australia in 1969, and in 1973 established a branch in New Zealand which now operates as Commerce Clearing House New Zealand Limited. In that time it has published an extensive local line of highly efficient loose-leaf subscription services and bound books covering a wide range of topic areas essential to accountants, lawyers, business people and employee organisations. It also markets the publications of its CCH affiliates from the USA, Canada, Europe and Asia.

The essence of all CCH publications is accuracy, authority, practicality and an ease of reference achieved by the presentation of information in a highly readable form and by the use of excellent indexes and other locators. CCH is pre-eminent in the field of loose-leaf publishing, providing not only an in-depth analysis of the topic in question but an unmatched dedication to keeping you promptly informed of new developments and helping you understand them.

While CCH is probably best known for its publications in taxation, business law and other areas such as family law, it has expanded activities beyond its traditional sphere to become true information professionals. CCH Australia Limited entered the field of electronic publishing in 1984 with its first legal data base. In the educational area CCH Australia Limited provides material for students of legal and commercial studies, computer education, economics, commerce and the various social sciences.

In the area of accounting, CCH publishes the *Australian Accounts Preparation Manual*, in association with The Institute of Chartered Accountants in Australia and the Australian Society of Accountants. This loose-leaf service is specially designed for members of the accounting profession.

A dedicated management team, highly qualified editorial staff, a most efficient printing organisation, over 75 years of publishing know-how and the personal interest of your local CCH area manager stand behind each CCH publication.

National Library of Australia Cataloguing in Publication Data

Swindells, Darryl K., 1956-
    Accounting for business consolidations.

Includes index.
ISBN 1 86264 238 9.

1. Financial statements, Consolidated.
I. Title.

657.3

Cover design and execution by Peta Lewin.

© 1990 CCH Australia Limited

All rights reserved. No part of this work covered by copyright may be reproduced or copied in any form or by any means (graphic, electronic or mechanical, including photocopying, recording, recording taping, or information retrieval systems) without the written permission of the publisher.

Wholly set up and printed in Australia by CCH Australia Limited

Foreword

Simplicity is the keynote of this excellent work by Darryl Swindells.

In this, as we are so often told, increasingly complex world the author has sought to deliver to the reader his philosophy for approaching the often daunting task of consolidating group accounts in a logical and practical presentation.

I believe he has achieved his objective and that this work will be of great assistance to the learner and a reference source for the experienced.

In the high pressure world of public accounting practice Darryl is the "guru" of his seniors, peers and young accountants on the subject of consolidation. In our firm the seal of approval is "I checked it with Darryl".

I congratulate Darryl on making the effort to convey through the work his extensive experience of the consolidation process for the benefit of accounting practitioners.

Robert A. Lamond F.C.A.
Chairman Audit and Accounting
KPMG Peat Marwick
Australia

Preface

Consolidated group accounts are becoming an increasingly significant reporting medium in today's rapidly changing financial environment.

This has been recognised, and accelerated, by the issue in 1986 by the National Companies and Securities Commission of a class order relieving directors of wholly owned subsidiaries of Australian companies from the requirements of the Companies Code relating to the preparation of accounts of those subsidiary companies, and by changes to the *Income Tax Assessment Act*, also in 1986, effectively to allow income tax to be paid on a wholly owned group basis.

Both the Commonwealth Government and the Australian accounting bodies are moving in the direction of reducing the proliferation of "off balance sheet" reporting, and towards including more companies, and entities other than companies, in consolidated accounts.

Business enterprises can be operated through a wide variety of frameworks, such as companies, trusts, partnerships, etc. Consolidation accounting is concerned with the process of reporting for a combination of business enterprises irrespective of the framework, legal or informal, used within an enterprise.

Consolidation accounting is simply the restatement of a collection of financial statements which have been prepared from an individual entity point of view to a set of financial statements prepared from a group point of view. This is a logical exercise which requires an appreciation and understanding of the "group point of view", and identification of differences between financial statements prepared on these two bases. Once this appreciation is gained, the development in accounting terms of adjustments required to "individual" financial statements is straightforward, and no further information or experience is needed to enable consolidated financial statements to be prepared.

For simplicity this text has been prepared using an approach with a few manufactured "rules". These, explained in detail in the text, are:

(1) The "first" consolidation adjustment is the elimination of inter-entity investments.

(2) The "second" consolidation adjustment is the allocation of minority interest.

There is no real requirement to follow this approach. Consolidation adjustments are designed to achieve an end — the portrayal of a group financial position. This end can be arrived at in numerous ways, any of which must be considered correct if the same result is achieved.

However, the adoption of a standardised approach simplifies the explanation of adjustments necessary in relation to more complex consolidation issues, and forms a sound basis from which to develop an approach to solving even the most complex problems.

The material has been arranged in a logical order. It includes examples of various situations and their solutions, as well as guidance as to how errors in consolidation can be easily detected.

The statutory requirements for group accounts in Australia are briefly covered, as well as relevant accounting standards of the Accounting Standards Review Board, The Institute of Chartered Accountants in Australia and the Australian Society of Accountants.

This book has been written bearing in mind the needs of students having their first "tussle" with consolidations, Professional Year students, and accountants in both public and private practice, including those with an advanced knowledge who need an easy reference.

Acknowledgements

This book would not have been written without the immense support of Mr John Buttle, a Partner of KPMG Peat Marwick. John's encouragement to people to perform at levels above their own perceived limits has been enjoyed by many including myself. His challenging enthusiasm provided the motivation to make this book a reality.

My thanks also go to Bruce Sutton of KPMG Peat Marwick for his constant readiness to discuss technical issues and to challenge my perceptions, and to Bob Lamond for agreeing to write the foreword to this book.

Finally, and most importantly, my thanks to my wife, Mandy, whose willingness to act as both mother and father of our children, Rachel and Danielle, has allowed me the time for this work.

Darryl Swindells
May 1990

About the Author

Darryl Swindells is a Senior Manager with KPMG Peat Marwick, Chartered Accountants, in Sydney, and has many years of experience in the specialised field of consolidations. He has been actively involved with the Professional Year Programme of The Institute of Chartered Accountants in Australia. He has acted as consultant on both practical and theoretical consolidation issues to many corporations in Australia, New Zealand and the U.K.

Contents

	Page
Foreword	v
Preface	vii

Chapter

1	General principles of consolidations	1
2	Basic principles	4
3	Goodwill on consolidation	13
4	Date of acquisition	27
5	Profit and loss accounts	30
6	Intra-group debt	33
7	Intra-group investments	39
8	Equity accounting	57
9	Minority interest	67
10	Dividends	80
11	Intra-group inventory movements	90
12	Intra-group fixed asset movements	100
13	Equity accounting prior to consolidation	114
14	Piecemeal or creeping acquisition	118
15	Sale of shares	123
16	Subsequent issue of shares by subsidiary	155
17	Preference shares	176
18	Reduction in shareholders' funds of subsidiary	182
19	Indirect interests	190
20	Adjustments to pre-acquisition situation	199
21	Statements of sources and applications of funds	208
22	Overseas subsidiaries	213
23	Current Australian statutory requirements for companies	218
24	Cross holdings	226

Appendix

A	Example covering various aspects of consolidation	231
B	Example consolidated financial statements	238
Index		307

1

General principles of consolidations

Not only for companies ———— ¶101
Group entity ———————— ¶102
Elimination of inter-entity
    transactions ———————— ¶103

¶101 Not only for companies

"Consolidation" is the aggregation of financial information concerning a number of individual entities which operate together as a "group", to show the financial position of the group. Consolidation is not only applicable to companies, although the legal corporate framework is by far the most common. More meaningful financial reporting of any group of entities is obtained through consolidation. This applies equally to groups comprising any mixture of companies, trusts, unincorporated joint ventures, business undertakings, etc. where a common element of control exists.

For ease of reference throughout this work reference is made to "companies". This should be taken as referring to any type of business entity.

¶102 Group entity

Consolidated accounts do not reflect the financial position of a legal entity, nor are they the sum of a number of legal entities. They relate to a notional entity which, more effectively than any other means, indicates to holding company shareholders the extent of their investment.

This "notional entity" concept is central to an understanding of the information presented by consolidated accounts.

Many situations facing the preparers of consolidated accounts which may appear complex when viewed individually become more simple when considered "from a group point of view". The raising of the question "what has the group done?" will allow the true nature of a transaction or a series of transactions to be clarified. Throughout this work this question will be raised often, as an aid to problem solving. Indeed, any student or accountant involved in consolidation should keep this question foremost in their thoughts, and should not stray from the consideration of each and every situation "from a group point of view".

¶103 Elimination of inter-entity transactions

Financial statements of a single entity show the results of transactions between that entity and others.

Consolidated financial statements, being the financial statements of a combination of entities, must also be prepared on that basis. The consolidated accounts will show the results of transactions between the combined entity and others.

Financial statements of a single entity do not include the results of transactions within an entity, and consolidated financial statements do not include the results of transactions within the combined entity, or "group".

Consolidated accounts are prepared using the rationale that transactions which take place between group companies (hereafter referred to as "inter-company" or "intra-group" transactions) have not taken place. Although there is no dispute that such transactions are genuine as far as they relate to the individual companies involved and must be accounted for as such, it is nevertheless also true that in the group context they are synonymous with transfers between branches or between departments of a segmented business. As a consequence the financial effects of all inter-company transactions are eliminated in preparing consolidated profit and loss accounts and balance sheets.

When making a decision as to whether a transaction should be included in consolidated financial statements, the question should always be asked "what has the group done?".

If the answer to this question is that the financial position of the overall group has not been altered as a result of the transaction, then it is not a transaction between the group and others and should not be included in consolidated accounts.

As an inter-company transaction has occurred between a member of the group and another entity, it will have been included in the financial statements of that member. As that other entity is also a member of the group, the transaction is not to be included in the group accounts and should be "notionally" removed from the accounts of that first member

GENERAL PRINCIPLES OF CONSOLIDATIONS

prior to completion of the group accounts. This is necessary as group accounts are most easily prepared using a simple aggregation of individual financial statements of members of the group, making adjustments to those aggregated accounts where necessary.

The transactions which have been reported on by member entities but which are not to be reported on by the group are commonly referred to as "intra-group transactions", and their notional removal is referred to as "elimination".

For ease of explanation, throughout this text reference will be made to "inter-company" transactions. This should be read, if applicable, as a reference to "inter-entity" transactions.

2

Basic principles

Which entities to be consolidated — ¶201
How to consolidate ——————— ¶202
Gathering information ————— ¶203
Consolidation adjustments ———— ¶204
Elimination entries ——————— ¶205
Disclosure adjustments ————— ¶206
Consolidation worksheets ———— ¶207
Consolidation review checklist —— ¶208

¶201 Which entities to be consolidated

The first task of any preparer of consolidated accounts is to determine the entities which will be consolidated.

Current Australian companies legislation requires the consolidation of a "holding" company with all of its "subsidiary" companies.

Overseas and international accounting standards require the consolidation of a "parent" entity and its "subsidiary" entities.

A preparer of consolidated financial statements must first decide under which rules the accounts will be prepared. This may include reference to companies legislation, accounting standards — both local and overseas, stock exchange listing rules, trust deeds and partnership or other agreements.

Once the "rules" are known, determination of the make-up of the group can begin.

Such "rules" are, in the main, based on a definition of control of a subsidiary, where control is evidenced by either:

BASIC PRINCIPLES

(1) ownership; or

(2) control.

Whichever criterion for inclusion applies, the mechanics involved in preparing consolidated financial statements do not change.

In some circumstances the overriding aim of the preparation of financial statements, i.e. to provide information, will require preparation of consolidated accounts even though no statutory, stock exchange or accounting standard requirements specify that this must be done.

The following example of an operating trust provides an indication of good reporting in respect of such a situation. This trust is one of the few trading trusts currently listed on the Australian Stock Exchange. The group organisational chart is set out below:

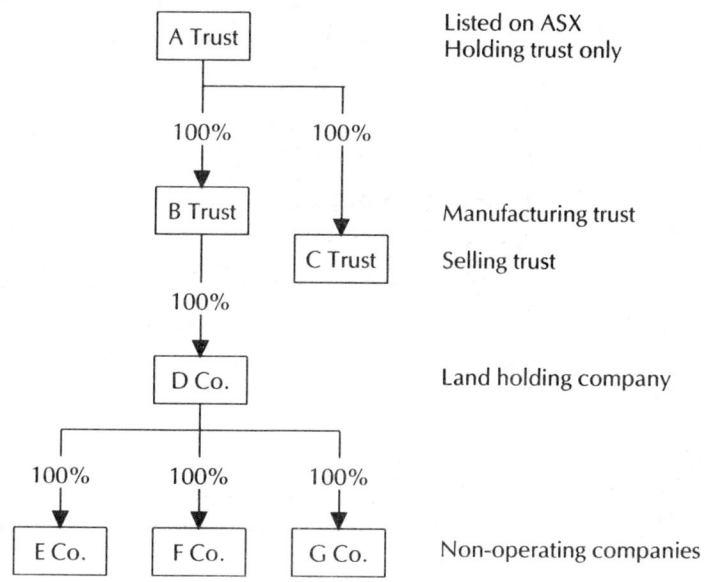

```
                    ┌─────────┐      Listed on ASX
                    │ A Trust │      Holding trust only
                    └────┬────┘
                ┌────────┴────────┐
              100%              100%
                │                 │
                ▼                 ▼
           ┌─────────┐      
           │ B Trust │           Manufacturing trust
           └────┬────┘      ┌─────────┐
                │           │ C Trust │  Selling trust
              100%          └─────────┘
                │
                ▼
           ┌─────────┐
           │  D Co.  │           Land holding company
           └────┬────┘
       ┌────────┼────────┐
     100%     100%     100%
       │        │        │
       ▼        ▼        ▼
   ┌──────┐┌──────┐┌──────┐
   │ E Co.││ F Co.││ G Co.│     Non-operating companies
   └──────┘└──────┘└──────┘
```

The ultimate holding entity in this group is the listed trust (the "A Trust"). The only activity of the A Trust is to hold units in two subsidiary trusts, "B Trust" and "C Trust". The balance sheet of A Trust shows investments in subsidiary trusts as its only assets. This provides little information to readers of A Trust's, B Trust's and C Trust's financial statements.

All manufacturing and distribution is performed by B Trust and C Trust, with certain assets held in the subsidiary companies.

Neither current legislation nor stock exchange rules require consolidated accounts for the A Trust group to be prepared, other than in respect of D Company and its subsidiary companies. However, in the interests of presenting adequate information to unitholders, consolidated financial statements are prepared for A Trust and all its subsidiary trusts and companies.

¶201

¶202 How to consolidate

The consolidation process can be seen as involving the following stages:

(1) obtain financial statements and other required information for each company in the group;

(2) note that information on a consolidation worksheet;

(3) determine which transactions need to be eliminated, prepare journal entries to eliminate those transactions and note these on the consolidation worksheet;

(4) prepare journal entries which may be necessary to better disclose the financial position of the group;

(5) aggregate the information on the consolidation worksheet.

Each of these stages is discussed in more detail below.

¶203 Gathering information

The usual source of information is the financial statements of each entity in the group. However, in order properly to disclose the financial position of the group it will usually be necessary to gather more information from each member of the group than that disclosed in its financial statements. This will include details of transactions between group members during the reporting period (usually one year) and any other information which may be necessary.

In practice, the identification of information required should be made well in advance to enable member entities to obtain and collate the information for the group accounts.

Group accounting policies

The accounts of various entities will be prepared using certain accounting policies for which alternates may exist, e.g. tax-effect accounting may be followed by some entities and not by others.

In order for group accounts to convey meaningful information to users of those accounts the accounting policies adopted in the preparation of those accounts should be consistent.

To reduce the adjustments required to be made by the preparer of the group accounts it is suggested that, where possible and practical, all member entities within that group should follow the same accounting policies. Where this cannot be done, sufficient information will be required to be provided to the preparer of those group accounts to enable adjustments to be made at the consolidation level (i.e. on the consolidation worksheet).

Standardised reporting format

The preparer of group accounts will be more easily able to obtain information from the accounts of member entities if the accounts of each of

BASIC PRINCIPLES

those member entities are prepared using the same format. It may not be possible in certain situations for the "main" financial statements of each member to be prepared using a standard format, e.g. member entities may be incorporated overseas and may be required by local legislation to follow a specified format in the accounts which they are required to prepare in accordance with that legislation. Nevertheless, it is recommended that such entities be asked to also prepare information in the format required to facilitate preparation of the group accounts.

¶204   Consolidation adjustments

Consolidation journal book

In practice, consolidation entries are often noted on the consolidation worksheet with memorandum notes to support entries.

As will be seen throughout this text many consolidation journal entries, especially those relating to elimination of investments in subsidiary companies, are carried forward and repeated each year. It is therefore essential that accurate detailed information is maintained to support each consolidation entry. This is best achieved by the maintenance of a separate consolidation journal book.

Each component of journal entries separate

Each component of every elimination journal entry can be determined independently. The use of "balancing figures" in consolidation journal entries is to be discouraged. If a component of an entry is merely the balancing figure for the other parts of the entry, an error in any of those other parts would not be detected but would be perpetuated. The conclusion may be drawn that the entry is correct because it balances, and this would be an incorrect conclusion.

¶205   Elimination entries

Whenever an accountant is faced with a consolidation problem, the first step in solving that problem will be the preparation of journal entries.

Consolidation journal entries do not affect the accounts of any entity within the group being consolidated. Consolidation entries are said to be "outside the books" and should be maintained in a separate journal book.

However, components of elimination entries should be notionally allocated to particular entities in the group. This will simplify many aspects of consolidation, such as allocation of minority interest (Chapter 9), elimination of unrealised profits (Chapters 11 and 12) and determination of contributions to group profit by each member of the group.

Journal entries should include a note of the particular entities affected by each component. It may not be appropriate to allocate a whole journal entry to a particular group member. Each component of a journal entry must be considered and notionally allocated to a group entity, e.g. "Dr operating profit before income tax — Company A".

¶205

One aim of elimination entries is to eliminate double counting. When the overall group point of view is considered, the question should be asked "has anything been double counted?". For example, investments in subsidiary companies need to be eliminated because the holding company's investment as shown in the holding company's accounts is represented by the assets and liabilities of the subsidiary company. To include in group accounts both the investment and the assets and liabilities would be "double counting", and accordingly the investment needs to be eliminated.

Another aim of elimination entries is the removal of transactions which have been reported on by members of the group and which can be said not to have occurred from a group point of view, i.e. inter-company transactions.

Journal entries for each individual reporting entity are recorded in separate journal books or computer files. The same concerns as to maintenance of detail apply to consolidation entries and such entries should be maintained in a separate journal book or computer file — anywhere that a permanent record can be maintained.

As will be seen in Chapter 15, when subsidiaries are sold the initial acquisition information must be known in order to enable proper recognition of profits and losses on sale.

As many of the entries do not change from year to year, a set of standing consolidation entries can be maintained. Each such entry must provide sufficient detail to enable its accuracy to be maintained.

Another common error in practice is to summarise journal entries and refer to prior years' accounts or working papers as support for the entries. This can cause unsolvable problems should the information from any preceding year be lost or destroyed.

A tendency that has been observed in practice is to aggregate standing consolidation entries for the elimination of investments in a number of subsidiary companies. This should be avoided as the information required to de-consolidate a particular subsidiary may not be available from an aggregated entry.

¶206 Disclosure adjustments

Accounting policies and formats

The accounting policies and reporting formats of certain members of the group may not be the same as required by the group. Accordingly, adjustments may need to be made to the information noted on the consolidation worksheet to ensure consistency of reporting.

A simple example of a situation requiring adjustment is the disclosure of motor vehicles owned by member entities. Some may include in their financial statements a separate amount for the cost of motor vehicles owned, whereas others may include such information within a caption such as "plant, equipment and motor vehicles".

BASIC PRINCIPLES 9

Minority interests

Chapter 9 reviews in detail the concept of minority interest, and notes that separate disclosure is recommended for minority shareholders' ownership interests in the equity of the group. Adjusting entries are necessary to facilitate the required disclosure.

¶207 Consolidation worksheets

A standard tool of consolidations accountants is the consolidation worksheet. This is simply a schedule which facilitates aggregation of the information to be reported on by a group.

Group accounts are most easily prepared by simply aggregating information in respect of each group entity and adjusting where necessary. A consolidation worksheet is a simple tool to assist in this process.

Consolidation worksheets can be manually prepared or computer prepared and usually take either of the following formats:

1. With minority interest column

Details	Source of information	Consolidation journal entries	Minority interest	Group
	Co. A | Co. B | Co. C | Co. Z	Debit | Credit		

2. Without minority interest column

Details	Source of information	Consolidation journal entries	Group
	Co. A | Co. B | Co. C | Co. Z	Debit | Credit	

The type of information required in the group accounts is noted in the "Details" column (e.g. issued capital, operating profit) and the actual value of the information is shown for each possible source.

Elimination and reallocation entries are shown in the debit and credit columns.

If a minority interest column is used, amounts to be shown as relating to minority interests are shown in that column.

The use of a minority interest column is not recommended. The double entry method of accounting is the basis for all accounting theory and practice. Any transaction or adjustment therefore requires both a debit and a credit. This leaves nothing to be shown in a "Minority interest" column.

Proponents of the use of this column use it to show the allocation of information from an area to the minority interest disclosure. It is considered that this is best done through journal entries rather than through "adjustments". Throughout this text all consolidation worksheets will take the format noted at (2) above.

¶207

Consolidation worksheets can range from simple one-page schedules to complex multi-paged and multi-columned schedules.

The mathematics involved in the use of consolidation worksheets are relatively simple, being confined to additions and subtractions. As such, consolidation worksheets lend themselves readily to computerisation which reduces the time involved in the aggregation process and can reduce the possibility of errors being made.

A detailed discussion of minority interest is included in Chapter 9.

Aggregation

Once all information is noted on the consolidation worksheets, including elimination and allocation entries, the worksheets are simply added across to arrive at the total group "picture".

¶208 Consolidation review checklist

Consolidated financial statements represent a portrayal of the financial position of a group at a point in time. The only reason for preparation of consolidation journal entries is to convert the aggregation of individual group members' financial statements to show the group picture rather than a collection of individual pictures.

There are a number of factors which will be present in all group accounts. These can be used to review the results of consolidation journal entries to ensure that the outcome is as intended. A checklist as shown below is a useful "quick check" to be applied when preparing consolidated accounts. There are no exceptions to these "rules":

1. Investments in subsidiaries must be $nil.
2. Issued capital attributable to shareholders of the group holding company must equal issued capital of the holding company of the group.
3. Retained earnings brought forward to the current year must equal the prior year closing balance.
4. Group dividends paid must equal group holding company dividends paid.
5. Retained earnings in the balance sheet and closing retained earnings in the profit and loss account must be equal.
6. Minority interest must be able to be reconciled.

If all inter-company transactions have been recognised and each of these "tests" is "passed", the consolidated accounts will invariably show a true portrayal of the group financial position.

1. *Investments in subsidiaries must be $nil*

All investments in subsidiaries are represented in the group accounts by assets and liabilities of subsidiary companies. All such investments must be eliminated to avoid double counting.

BASIC PRINCIPLES

2. Issued capital attributable to shareholders of the group holding company must equal issued capital of the holding company of the group

All issued capital of subsidiaries is either:

(a) acquired by the group holding company or a subsidiary thereof and is therefore eliminated against the cost of that capital; or

(b) "owned" directly by minority shareholders and therefore included in minority interest in group shareholders' funds, in whatever fashion this is disclosed.

3. Retained earnings brought forward to the current year must equal prior year closing balance

This is true by definition. However, whereas individual entity financial statements are prepared from the prior year's financial statements, group accounts are invariably prepared by aggregating and adjusting current year financial statements. The matching of group retained earnings brought forward to the prior year's closing balance is therefore not a "fait accompli", and consolidation adjustments often need to be made for this to occur.

4. Group dividends paid must equal group holding company dividends paid

All dividends paid or proposed by subsidiaries should be eliminated. This will be the case irrespective of whether a subsidiary is wholly, partly or indirectly owned. Dividends paid by subsidiaries are either:

(a) paid to another group company and eliminated against dividends received; or

(b) paid to a minority shareholder who will have been shown as having an interest in those profits and therefore the dividend paid eliminates that interest.

5. Retained earnings in the balance sheet and closing retained earnings in the profit and loss account must be equal

If consolidation entries are prepared using the methodology proposed in this book, retained earnings in the balance sheet will be determined from the closing balance of the profit and loss account.

However, if journal entries are (incorrectly) made directly against retained earnings in the balance sheet, the two balances will need to be checked to ensure that they equate.

6. Minority interest must be able to be reconciled

Minority interest in the balance sheet should be reconciled to the proportional interests in subsidiary companies' net assets at balance date, e.g. a minority interest in the balance sheet relating to a subsidiary may equal 40% of a subsidiary's net tangible assets ("NTA").

¶208

Adjustments made on consolidation and notionally attributed to the net assets of a subsidiary company will affect this reconciliation. The "adjusted" net asset of the subsidiary should be used in the reconciliation, for example:

	$
Net assets of subsidiary	1,000
Less: Profit recognised by the subsidiary on sale of inventory to another group company, eliminated as unrealised from a group point of view	10
Adjusted net assets	990
Minority share, i.e. 40% of $990	396

This reconciliation will involve a review of each consolidation journal and the preparation of "adjusted" NTA figures where necessary for each subsidiary.

The reconciliation will also include minority interest in post-acquisition NTA movements of indirectly owned subsidiaries (see Chapter 19).

Computerised consolidation worksheets

Each of the six checklist items can be incorporated into computerised consolidation software. The "failure" to meet any of the six conditions noted above can be programmed to be highlighted so that appropriate adjustments can be made to the consolidation journal entries which have been prepared.

¶208

3

Goodwill on consolidation

What is goodwill?	¶301
Goodwill is an asset	¶302
Why amortise goodwill?	¶303
Amortisation of goodwill	¶304
Straight-line amortisation not essential	¶305
Goodwill write-off	¶306
Negative goodwill/discount on acquisition	¶307
Discount on acquisition — future periods	¶308
Elimination of discount on acquisition against fixed assets	¶309
Adjustment to discount on sale of adjusted assets	¶310

¶301 What is goodwill?

The accounting treatment of goodwill has been the subject of much accounting debate in recent years. Goodwill is defined in Approved Accounting Standard ASRB 1013: Accounting for Goodwill as "the future benefits from unidentifiable assets".

Goodwill on consolidation arises when a company acquires an interest in a subsidiary company and the purchase consideration for that acquisition exceeds the fair value of the net assets of that subsidiary.

ASRB 1013.31 specifies for companies that goodwill "shall be measured as the excess of the cost of acquisition ... over the fair value of the identifiable net assets acquired". Such excess payments will usually be made with an expectation that a benefit will flow as a result of the acquisition — this benefit may be future profits to be earned by the acquirer as a result of the past transactions of the entity being acquired; for example, a company has a certain standing in the business community such that its profitability can be expected to continue with no input of expertise or any other input from outsiders. A buyer of that company may be willing to pay the seller an amount equal to a number of years' expected profits in the belief that profits from future years will flow to the new owner.

Goodwill may also be paid to keep a competitor from acquiring an advantage, thus allowing the acquiring company to maintain its own future profitability.

Decisions as to accounting for goodwill cannot be made using general assumptions. To do so can lead to false conclusions as to the accounting treatment to be applied. It appears that much of the public criticism and comment in recent times relating to goodwill has its source in generalised assumptions as to what goodwill represents in particular cases. Had the writers of such comment had a full understanding of the nature of and reasons for goodwill paid by particular groups, the public debate might have been considerably reduced.

Determination of the accounting method to be applied to goodwill requires an understanding of why the goodwill was "paid" and of what "future benefits" are expected from that payment. The matching concept of accounting will then supply the answer as to what is the appropriate treatment to be applied to that goodwill.

The matching concept involves the recognition in the profit and loss account of related income and expense items during the same period, e.g. if a payment is made in one year for a service to be supplied in the following year, under the matching concept the payment would be shown as an expense in the profit and loss account during the year in which the service is received.

The matching concept seeks to eliminate the reporting of an expense in one year and related income in another year.

In applying the matching concept to goodwill "future benefits" should be defined in terms of the profit and loss account, i.e. what benefits are expected to be recorded in future profit and loss accounts and in which years are those benefits expected to be realised? Having identified the periods during which future benefits are expected to be realised, the application of the matching concept requires that the goodwill (i.e. "future benefits") paid be matched in the profit and loss account with the expected

¶301

GOODWILL ON CONSOLIDATION 15

receipt of those benefits; goodwill should be "written off" as an expense in the profit and loss account to match the expected benefits paid. The net result in the profit and loss account will be the difference, if any, between the expected benefit for each year and the actual benefit received in each year.

By way of illustration, consider the following example:

Company A acquired all of the issued share capital of Company B for $100,000 on 1 January 19X0. The fair value of the net assets of Company B at the date of acquisition is $60,000. Company A has paid $40,000 goodwill on the expectation that Company B will earn $10,000 profit per year for each of the next four years.

Company A would account for the goodwill in the consolidated accounts of the Company A group as follows:

Date	Value of goodwill in balance sheet $000	Profit & loss account $000
1. 1.X0	40	—
31.12.X0	30	Dr 10
31.12.X1	20	Dr 10
31.12.X2	10	Dr 10
31.12.X3	—	Dr 10

Goodwill has been recognised as an expense in the years in which future benefits are expected to be realised.

The group cannot be said to have earned profit when the source of that profit is the work of the previous owners of an acquired subsidiary. A group cannot "buy" profit, it can only earn profit. Amortisation of goodwill against the periods of realisation of profits "paid for" results in the group accounts showing no profit or loss (provided of course that realised profits are equal to expected profits). This is the real situation, as the group itself has earned no profit. The group will only earn profit if profit in excess of that expected and "paid for" is earned by the group.

¶302 Goodwill is an asset

The value applied to each asset in a balance sheet must be considered when preparing financial statements. The same applies to goodwill when preparing consolidated financial statements.

At each balance date a review should be made of the "recoverability" of goodwill, through the realisation of future benefits, and any excess of the current value of goodwill over those future benefits should be written off or expensed immediately. The value attributed to the asset "goodwill" at any point in time must not be in excess of the value of expected future benefits.

¶303 Why amortise goodwill?

A number of accountants and other business people consider that in certain circumstances goodwill may be able to be carried forward as an asset indefinitely. This approach assumes that the future benefits to flow

¶303

from the asset known as goodwill will also be realised indefinitely, i.e. that the benefits realised each year are such a small proportion of the total benefits to be realised that amortisation is not warranted.

Acceptance of this argument requires acceptance that projections of the realisation of future benefits can be made far into the future. In practical terms this is rarely, if ever, possible; hence the imposition in accounting standards of a maximum amortisation period.

¶304 Amortisation of goodwill

Current accounting standards both in Australia and overseas require that goodwill should not be carried forward indefinitely but should be amortised in the profit and loss account using a pre-determined program, or plan, to match the amortisation with the realisation of expected benefits. Each such accounting standard specifies a maximum period for such amortisation; this period varies from country to country. The aim of setting a maximum period for amortisation appears to be a desire to "force" the matching concept to be applied within reasonable limits, i.e. current Australian accounting standards and approved accounting standards specify a maximum amortisation period of 20 years, which assumes that in determining future benefits to flow from the payment of goodwill projections will not be made more than 20 years into the future.

The time limit imposed by accounting standards must be recognised as being a maximum only and should not be assumed to be the appropriate amortisation period. The assumption that goodwill is required to be amortised over 20 years is a common misconception. A proper evaluation must be made and the amortisation period determined accordingly.

¶305 Straight-line amortisation not essential

Amortisation of goodwill should not necessarily be on a "straight-line" basis, i.e. the same amount each year. Goodwill should be amortised in accordance with a pre-determined plan. However, there is no necessity for this plan to assume "straight-line" realisation of expected future benefits.

Amortisation on a straight-line basis assumes that future benefits will be the same each year. If this is not the case, amortisation should not be charged ("expensed") to the profit and loss account on a straight-line basis.

¶306 Goodwill write-off

As noted in ¶301, goodwill on acquisition represents the excess of consideration paid over the fair value of assets acquired. The consideration paid would be shown in the holding company's accounts, under the historical cost convention, at cost. On consolidation, the investment is matched against the fair values of net assets acquired with any remaining amount (i.e. any "excess") transferred from "investment" to "goodwill".

The value of the investment in the holding company's accounts needs to be considered at each balance date. Should the asset be considered not to be recoverable either out of future dividends or from a distribution of the assets of the subsidiary company, the asset value should be adjusted to the amount considered recoverable, with the amount not considered recoverable written off to the profit and loss account. If this is done, an argument exists that the goodwill on consolidation may also decrease. For example:

> Company A paid $10 goodwill in an investment of $110 on acquisition of 100% of Company B. At the end of year one, Company A considered that the assets of Company B would realise $100 on distribution and that no future increase in the value of those assets was expected. Company A would therefore write down its investment in Company B by $10. On consolidation the investment to be eliminated would be only $100, hence no goodwill and no amortisation of goodwill.

Whilst this approach results in the correct final profit and loss account result, it does not take into consideration that the write-down of Company A's investment in Company B is a transaction within the group and needs to be eliminated on consolidation. This would result in the investment being restated to $110 and the $10 goodwill component amortised as appropriate and probably all in the one year. The final consolidated presentation should be amortisation of goodwill of $10, rather than write-down of investment in the subsidiary of $10.

¶307 Negative goodwill/discount on acquisition

As noted in ¶306, goodwill on consolidation is the excess of the cost of an investment over the fair value of net assets acquired.

Where the fair value of net assets acquired exceed the cost of an investment, "negative goodwill" or "discount on acquisition" results. This could arise in a variety of ways, for example:

(1) asset values are overstated; or

(2) a bargain purchase has been made.

Where the fair value of net assets acquired is less than their book value, consideration should be given to the need to write down those assets in the books of the subsidiary acquired. This would result in there being no difference between the cost of the assets and their book values.

Where a bargain purchase is made and can clearly be identified as such, the discount on acquisition should be recognised in the profit and loss account during the period in which the discount is realised, for example:

> Company A pays $100 to acquire 100% of the issued share capital of Company B. The only asset of Company B is inventory with a book value, based on cost, of $120. Company B has no liabilities. The shareholders of Company B had to sell their shares in Company B to generate cash for other ventures.
>
> In order to apply the matching concept on consolidation, consider what has happened from a group point of view. The group (now comprising Company A and Company B) has acquired inventory at a cost of $100. This inventory should be shown in the group accounts at $100. Any profit on sale of the

inventory to be recorded in the group accounts will be determined by reference to the cost to the group of that inventory, i.e. $100. Should the inventory be sold for $130 in the year following the year of acquisition, Company B would record a profit of $10 and the group accounts would recognise a profit of $30.

The merits of this approach are recognised in Approved Accounting Standard ASRB 1013: Accounting for Goodwill, and in Statement of Accounting Standards AAS 18 of the same title. Both of these accounting standards require, on consolidation, that any discount on acquisition be applied to reduce the book value of non-monetary assets to the cost of those assets to the group.

Should the assets of the subsidiary company acquired consist only of monetary items, and a true bargain purchase can be said to have been made, the matching concept would require that the discount be recognised as a profit in the year in which the bargain was received by the group.

Part acquisitions

The aim of reducing book values of assets in order to eliminate a discount on acquisition is to show the assets at cost to the acquiring group. Where less than 100% of a subsidiary is acquired, the amount by which assets are to be reduced is the "gross" amount of the discount. For example, the discount received on the acquisition of a 75% interest in an asset would be expected to be less than the discount received on the acquisition of a 100% interest in the same asset. If the 75% discount was $3 on an asset with a book value of $10, the 100% discount would be expected to be $4.

When an adjustment is made on consolidation to reduce the book value by the discount, and the discount is not "grossed up", the resultant book value of the asset will depend upon the percentage acquired, e.g.:

	75% acquired $	100% acquired $
Book value	10	10
Discount	3	4
"Cost to the group"	7	6

This treatment is not appropriate in the context of the entity concept of consolidations adopted in this book. The group has acquired all of the asset, even though the holding company has only acquired a 75% interest.

The book value of the asset in the group accounts should not depend on the holding company's percentage ownership. The discount should be shown as $4 irrespective of whether 75% or 100% is acquired. If only 75% is acquired the apparent discount of $3 should be increased to $4, with the increase debited to minority interest in the balance sheet.

The following example illustrates the application of this approach, and the effect of the word "gross".

¶307

Example 3.1

Company B has only one asset, a truck, which has a net book value of $100,000. Net assets of Company B were $100,000 on the day Company A acquired 80% of the issued shares of Company B for a consideration of $50,000. The discount on acquisition in Company A group's accounts would be:

	$
Net assets of Company B	100,000
Proportion acquired 80%	
Net assets acquired	80,000
Consideration	50,000
Discount on acquisition	30,000

Consider the value placed on the truck by Company A, and the resultant amount paid by Company A.

Had Company A purchased 100% of Company B, it presumably would have been prepared to pay proportionally more than $50,000. Company A was willing to pay $50,000 for 80% of Company B. Company B's only asset is a truck, and in paying $50,000 for 80% of Company B, Company A effectively pays $50,000 for 80% of that asset.

Consider the amount Company A would have had to pay to acquire 100% of the asset. If a $50,000 investment gave Company A ownership of 80% of Company B, we would expect ownership of 100% of Company B to cost $62,500 (i.e. $50,000 ÷ 80% × 100%).

The cost to the group of the truck should be recorded as $62,500.

The discount on acquisition will therefore be eliminated as follows:

Dr discount on acquisition	$30,000	
Cr truck		$37,500
Dr minority interest (B/S)	$7,500	

	$
Net assets of Company B	100,000
"Assumed" consideration for 100%	62,500
"Assumed" discount on acquisition	37,500
Minority interest 20%	
Minority share of "assumed" discount	7,500

Depreciation charges

Adjustment to book values of assets on consolidation will necessitate adjustment to group depreciation charges. Chapter 12 provides examples of adjustments necessary.

¶308 Discount on acquisition — future periods

A discount on acquisition will effectively be recognised in the profit and loss account on subsequent disposal or use of assets acquired. If the

¶308

book value of inventory acquired, for example, is reduced to eliminate a discount, the inventory will have a reduced cost to the group. On sale of the inventory, the group profit on sale will be higher than the subsidiary company profit on sale. For example:

> Cost of inventories to the subsidiary company is $100; and after elimination of a discount on acquisition, the cost to the group is shown as $90. If the inventory is sold one month later for $120, the profit on the sale for the subsidiary is $20, yet the profit on the sale recorded by the group is $30. The additional $10 represents the realisation of the discount as a profit.

¶309 Elimination of discount on acquisition against fixed assets

If a discount on acquisition is eliminated against the book value of fixed assets, the group depreciation will be less than the subsidiary company depreciation, because the group book value of the assets is lower than that shown in the subsidiary company accounts.

A question arises as to how to reduce the book value of fixed assets, since book value involves both cost and accumulated depreciation. Possible methods are:

(1) Reduce the "cost" by the amount of the discount.

(2) Increase the "accumulated depreciation".

(3) Alter both cost and accumulated depreciation proportionally.

(4) Reduce the "accumulated depreciation" to $nil and alter the "cost to the group".

Each of the four alternatives achieves the desired effect. However, alternative (3) is favoured, as it follows the approach adopted for other assets.

Example 3.2

H Company acquired 60% of S Company on 30 June 19X5 at a cost of $600. The balance sheet of S Company as at that date was as shown on the following worksheets.

GOODWILL ON CONSOLIDATION

	H Co.	S Co.	Eliminations Debit	Eliminations Credit	Group
	$	$	$	$	$
Issued capital	1,000	500			
Asset revaluation reserve		500			
Retained earnings	1,000	400			
	2,000	1,400			
Investment in S Co.	750				
Other assets — inventory	1,300	950			
— land		600			
Other liabilities	(50)	(150)			
	2,000	1,400			
Operating profit	340	200			
Income tax expense	140	100			
	200	100			
	200	100			
Retained earnings 1.7.X4	800	300			
Retained earnings 30.6.X5	1,000	400			

What consolidation entries are required at 30 June 19X5?

Suggested Solution to Example 3.2

Journal Entries

			$	$
(a)	Dr Issued capital (60% of $500)		300	
	Dr Asset revaluation reserve (60% of $500)		300	
	Dr Operating profit (60% of $200)		120	
	Cr Income tax expense (60% of $100)			60
	Dr Retained earnings brought forward (60% of $300)		180	
	Cr Investment in S Co.			750
	Cr Discount on acquisition			90
	Elimination of investment by H Co. in S Co. as at 30 June 19X5			
(b)	Dr Issued capital (40% of $500)		200	
	Dr Retained earnings brought forward (40% of $300)		120	
	Dr Minority interest (P/L) (40% of $100)		40	
	Dr Asset revaluation reserve (40% of $500)		200	
	Cr Minority interest (B/S) (40% of $1,400)			560
	Allocation of minority interest			

¶309

(c) Dr Discount on acquisition   90
      Cr Inventory   92
      Cr Land   58
    Dr Minority interest (B/S)   60

Grossing of discount:

60% = $90 therefore 100% = $150

Allocation of discount:

	Book value	% of total book value	% applied to discount	New book value
	$	%	%	$
Inventory	950	61.3	92	858
Land	600	38.7	58	542
	1,550	100	150	1,400

Consolidation Worksheet at 30.6.X5

	H Co.	S Co.	Eliminations Debit	Eliminations Credit	Group
	$	$	$	$	$
Issued capital	1,000	500	[a]300 [b]200		1,000
Asset revaluation reserve		500	[a]300 [b]200		
Retained earnings	1,000	400	460	60	1,000
Minority interest			[c]60	[b]560	500
	2,000	1,520	620	2,500
Investment in S Co.	750			[a]750	—
Other assets — inventory		950		[c]92	2,158
— land		600		[c]58	542
Other liabilities	(50)	(150)			(200)
Discount on acquisition			[c]90	[a]90	
	2,000	1,400	90	990	2,500
Total of eliminations			1,610	1,610	
Operating profit	340	200	[a]120		420
Income tax expense	140	100		[a]60	180
	200	100	120	60	240
Minority interest	—	—	[b]40		40
	200	100	160	60	200
Retained earnings 1.7.X4	800	300	[a]180 [b]120		800
Retained earnings 30.6.X5	1,000	400	460	60	1,000

¶309

GOODWILL ON CONSOLIDATION

¶310 Adjustment to discount on sale of adjusted assets

When an asset which has previously been adjusted to reflect a discount on acquisition has subsequently been sold outside the group, certain entries are required.

As the asset has a lower book value in the group accounts, as a result of the reduction in the book value to eliminate some or all of the discount, the profit on sale as shown in the group accounts must be higher than that shown in the individual company's accounts.

Example 3.3

Using the information shown in Example 3.2 in ¶309 above, assume that one month after acquisition the inventory on hand at acquisition date was sold outside the group for a consideration of $1,000. Assume also that this was the only transaction entered into by the group during the month.

Balance sheets and profit and loss accounts of H Company and S Company as at 31 July 19X5 would be as follows (assuming a tax rate of 40%):

Accounts as at 31.7.X5

	H Co.	S Co.	Eliminations Debit	Eliminations Credit	Group
	$	$	$	$	$
Issued capital	1,000	500			
Asset revaluation reserve	—	500			
Retained earnings	1,000	430			
	2,000	1,430			
Investment in S Co.	750				
Other assets — inventory	1,300	—			
— land		600			
Other assets		830			
Other liabilities	(50)				
	2,000	1,430			
Operating profit	—	50			
Income tax expense	—	20			
	—	30			
Retained earnings 1.7.X5	1,000	400			
Retained earnings 31.7.X5	1,000	430			

Prepare consolidation journal entries and worksheet as at 31 July 19X5.

Suggested Solution to Example 3.3

Consolidation Journal Entries 31.7.X5

		$	$
(a)	Dr Issued capital (60% of $500)	300	
	Dr Asset revaluation reserve (60% of $500)	300	
	Dr Retained earnings (60% of $400)	240	
	Cr Discount on acquisition		90
	Cr Investment in S Co.		750

Elimination of Investment in S Co.

Note:
This entry is based on the elimination entry in Example 3.2(a) above. The entry to retained earnings brought forward above is reconciled to the profit and loss account components of entry (a) in Example 3.2 above as follows:

From Example 3.2:

Dr Operating profit	120	
Cr Income tax expense	(60)	
Dr Retained earnings brought forward	180	
	240	

		$	$
(b)	Dr Issued capital (40% of $500)	200	
	Dr Asset revaluation reserve (40% of $500)	200	
	Dr Retained earnings brought forward (40% of $400)	160	
	Dr Minority interest (P/L) (40% of $30)	12	
	Cr Minority interest (B/S) (40% of $1,430)		572

Allocation of minority interest

		$	$
(c)	Dr Discount on acquisition	90	
	Cr Inventory		92
	Cr Land		58
	Dr Minority interest (B/S)	60	

Initial elimination of discount on acquisition

		$	$
(d)	Dr Inventory	92	
	Cr Operating profit		92
	Dr Minority interest (P/L)	36.8	
	Cr Minority interest (B/S)		36.8

To reflect additional group profit on sale of inventory

Note:
There is no income tax effect of this entry as the profit is a "permanent difference". No tax entry was made at the time of writing down the inventory, and none is required at the time of recognition of the "group" profit. No future tax asset or liability exists as the inventory has no further part to play in relation to the group.

¶310

GOODWILL ON CONSOLIDATION

	H Co.	S Co.	Eliminations Debit	Eliminations Credit	Group
	$	$	$	$	$
Issued capital	1,000	500	ᵃ300		1,000
			ᵇ200		
Asset revaluation reserve		500	ᵃ300		
			ᵇ200		
Retained earnings	1,000	430	448.8	ᵈ92	1,073.2
Minority interest			ᶜ60	ᵇ572	548.8
				ᵈ36.8	
	2,000	1,430	1,508.8	700.8	2,622
Investment in S Co.	750			ᵃ750	—
Other assets — inventory	1,300	—	ᵈ92	ᶜ92	1,300
— land		600		ᶜ58	542
Other assets		830			
Other liabilities	(50)				780
Discount on acquisition			ᶜ90	ᵃ90	—
	2,000	1,430	182	990	2,622
Total of eliminations			1,690.8	1,690.8	
Operating profit	—	50		ᵈ92	142
Income tax expense	—	20			20
	—	30		92	122
Minority interest	—	—	ᵇ12		48.8
			ᵈ36.8		
	—	30	48.8	92	73.2
Retained earnings 1.7.X5	1,000	400	ᵃ240		
			ᵇ160		1,000
Retained earnings 31.7.X5	1,000	430	448.8	92	1,073.2

Consider the results of the consolidation entry.

(1) *Inventory*

The fair value of inventory in the group accounts is the same as the value in the holding company's accounts. This is expected, as the subsidiary company now has no inventory.

(2) *Land*

The book value of land in the group accounts is lower than in the subsidiary company accounts by the amount of the discount allocated to the land. This reflects the lower cost to the group of the land.

(3) *Minority interest*

A reconciliation of minority interest in the group balance sheet shows that the amount disclosed for minority interest is as follows:

¶310

		$
Net assets of S Co. per S Co. accounts		1,430
Minority interest 40%		572
Less: Minority share of discount remaining		
Inventory	$nil	
Land	$58	
	$58	
	40%	23.2
Minority interest in balance sheet		548.8

¶310

4

Date of acquisition

Selection of date ¶401
Long-term effect ¶402

¶401 Selection of date

Determination of the date on which an acquisition takes place can have a significant impact on consolidated financial statements. All profits, losses and other movements in shareholders' funds in a subsidiary which occur prior to acquisition date will not be reported on by the group.

The determination of the date of acquisition is often not straightforward.

> **Example 1:** An offer is made on 1 July 19X5 to buy shares in a company listed on a stock exchange. The offeror already owns 30% of the shares in that company. The closing date for acceptances is given as 31 August 19X5.
>
> At various times during that two-month period acceptances are received, payments are made and new share certificates are issued. At some time during that period a share will be issued which gives the offeror in excess of 50% of the shares on issue and (by virtue of sec. 7(1)(iii) of the Companies Code) establishes a subsidiary relationship.
>
> **Example 2:** An offeror reviews a target company's financial statements and operations as of 31 March 19X8. On the basis of this review an offer is made to the target company's shareholders on 1 May 19X8 and is accepted on 8 May 19X8.
>
> **Example 3:** An offer is made and verbally accepted on 1 April 19X3. Contracts for sale are signed on 20 April 19X3 and share transfer forms stamped on 28 April 19X3. The new owner's name is entered in the register of members of the subsidiary company on 2 June 19X3.

In each of these examples, what is the acquisition date?

¶401

Consider the question from a group point of view. What is the significance of "pre-acquisition"?

The group accounts will report transactions entered into by all members of the group. Profits or losses on those transactions will be recorded in the group accounts and the shareholders of the group will be held accountable, or will be entitled to take credit, for those results. The basis for this approach is that all decisions concerning these transactions have been made by "the group".

Any results reported by a company arise from decisions made by current shareholders. Only those transactions in a subsidiary company which were controlled by the group should be reported on by the group.

The date of acquisition should be the date on which responsibility for decision-making in *practical terms* passes to the group.

In Example 2 above, the offer price was based on activities undertaken by the subsidiary to 31 March 19X8. One would assume that practical control would not have passed to the acquiring group until after the offer was accepted, i.e. some time after 8 May 19X8. The offeror is therefore "at risk" for decisions made by the former shareholders during the period from 31 March 19X8 to some time after 8 May 19X8. Should the target company suffer significant losses during that period, the acquiring company will effectively receive less than expected when the offer was made and therefore will be paying more goodwill (or receiving less of a discount) than anticipated.

¶402 Long-term effect

Choice of an acquisition date has no long-term effect on the results of the group. This is best illustrated by an example:

Company H acquired 100% of the issued shares of Company S at a cost of $1,000. Company H made its offer on 31 March 19X3 and the offer was accepted on 30 April 19X3. Net assets of Company S at each of these dates and the goodwill determined using possible acquisition dates were as follows:

	31.03.X3 $	30.04.X3 $
Net assets	900	700
Investment cost	1,000	1,000
Goodwill	100	300

Note: trading loss of $200 in April 19X3.

Assume goodwill is amortised over five years and that the subsidiary does not trade after 30 April 19X3. Company H prepares group accounts as at 31 March each year.

DATE OF ACQUISITION

The effect on the group accounts of the selection of one of these two dates as the acquisition date is as follows:

		Group profit (loss) 31.03.X3 $	30.04.X3 $
31.3.X4	Loss of subsidiary	(200)	—
	Goodwill amortisation	[1](20)	[3](55)
31.3.X5	Loss of subsidiary	—	—
	Goodwill amortisation	(20)	[2](60)
31.3.X6	" " "	(20)	(60)
31.3.X7	" " "	(20)	(60)
31.3.X8	" " "	(20)	(60)
31.3.X9	Total profit (loss) of the group	—	[4](5)
		(300)	(300)

Note:

1. One year's amortisation = total goodwill ÷ 5
   = 100 ÷ 5
   = 20.

2. One year's amortisation = total goodwill ÷ 5
   = 300 ÷ 5
   = 60.

3. Eleven months' amortisation = 60 ÷ 12 × 11
   = 55.

4. One month's amortisation = 60 ÷ 12 × 1
   = 5.

Whilst this example shows that, in the long term, choice of an acquisition date has no effect on reported group results, it also demonstrates the significant impact that can be made on the reported results of the group during each year until all goodwill is amortised. As Australian accounting standards and approved accounting standards (see ¶301) require goodwill to be amortised over a period not exceeding 20 years, appropriate care must be taken in the determination of the acquisition date.

¶402

5

Profit and loss accounts

General	¶501
Minority interest in the profit and loss account	¶502

¶501 General

"Retained profits" in the balance sheet represents the balance of that item at a point in time. Profit and loss accounts are simply statements of movements in retained profits during the period covered by a set of financial statements. Accordingly, all movements in retained earnings must be disclosed in the profit and loss account. Journal entries should therefore not be made directly to retained profits in the balance sheet. Journal entries should be posted to the individual accounts which are disclosed in the profit and loss account. Were an entry to be made directly against retained profits in the balance sheet, the sum of the accounts in the profit and loss account would not equate to the retained profits in the balance sheet. This principle applies equally to consolidation accounting.

Some authorities suggest that consolidation journal entries should be made only in the balance sheet, and that "adjustments" should be made to items in the profit and loss account to "balance" this account with the balance sheet. This is considered to be contrary to the principles of double entry bookkeeping, and it results in unnecessary complications and difficulties in the preparation of group accounts.

Adherence to the policy of using consolidation entries relating to the individual profit and loss account items ensures that a proper classification of items is effected, and that "adjustments", or "one-sided journal entries", are not required.

Also, at all times retained profits or accumulated losses in the balance sheet will agree with the balance of the profit and loss account, as the

PROFIT AND LOSS ACCOUNTS

source of the balance sheet retained profits or accumulated losses will be the closing balance of the profit and loss account. If an item is taken from a source and not adjusted it will always agree with that source.

The requirement to include correct profit and loss account classification in journal entries also requires appropriate consideration to be given to the nature of each transaction at the time its inclusion on consolidation worksheets is contemplated. This is in practice much easier than reviewing consolidation entries to determine what adjustments need to be made within the profit and loss account in order to equate the bottom line of the profit and loss account with the balance sheet retained earnings.

¶502 Minority interest in the profit and loss account

As explained at Chapter 9, the minority interest shown in a group balance sheet is the sum of the minority interest in the share capital, reserves and retained earnings of the subsidiary companies included in the group accounts. The amount of retained profits shown in the balance sheet is therefore the holding company's shareholders' share of the retained profits of the group. It follows that the balance of the profit and loss account should include only the holding company's share of the group's profits.

The operating profit, income tax expense and extraordinary items shown in the group profit and loss account should include all such items for the group as a whole, so that the result of the operations for the group can be seen.

In order to effect the objective that the balance of the profit and loss account relates only to the holding company's share of retained profits, the minority's share of retained profits of subsidiary companies will need to be deducted from the operating profit after income tax and extraordinary items. Schedule 7 to the Companies Regulations requires this to be disclosed as follows:

Group Profit and Loss Account for the Year Ended 30 June 19X7

	$
Operating profit or loss	x,xxx
Income tax attributable to operating profit or loss	x,xxx
Operating profit or loss after income tax	x,xxx
Profit or loss on extraordinary items	(xxx)
Income tax attributable to profit or loss on extraordinary items	(xxx)
Profit or loss on extraordinary items after income tax	(xxx)
Operating profit or loss and extraordinary items after income tax	x,xxx
Minority interests in operating profit or loss and extraordinary items after income tax	xxx
Operating profit or loss and extraordinary items after income tax attributable to members of the holding company	x,xxx

¶502

Retained profits or accumulated losses at the beginning of the financial year	x,xxx
Aggregate of amounts transferred from reserves	x,xxx
Total available for appropriation	xx,xxx
Dividends provided for or paid	xxx
Aggregate of amounts transferred to reserves	xx
Other appropriations	xx
	xxx
Retained profits or accumulated losses at the end of the financial year	xx,xxx

The opening balance of retained earnings, brought forward from the previous year's balance sheet and profit and loss account, will not require any deduction of the minority's share, as this will have been done in prior years.

Transfers to and from reserves and appropriations will require adjustment to reallocate the part of those items in which minority shareholders have an interest, for the same reason as explained above in relation to operating profit. This adjustment will not be shown in the balance sheet or profit and loss account, as such forms of presentation do not include statements of movements in reserves. In the interest of full disclosure, the allocation of movements to and from reserve accounts should be shown in the notes supporting the profit and loss account and balance sheet, for example:

Note — Movement in general reserve

		$	$
	Opening balance		x
Add:	Transfer from retained earnings	x	
Less:	Minority interest therein	x	x
	Closing balance		x

As a statement of movements in minority interest is not normally shown, the amounts of transfers, etc. relating to minority interest are not shown separately in the group accounts but are grouped together on one line in the balance sheet. However, it is considered good practice for accountants to prepare a statement of movements in the minority interest figure shown in the balance sheet to ensure that adjustments made during consolidation have been correctly processed.

¶502

6

Intra-group debt

General	¶601
Commercial bills	¶602
Contingent debt	¶603

¶601 General

Any amounts owing by one member of a group to another member of the group do not relate to transactions outside the group. Such balances therefore need to be eliminated. Consider the following:

Example 6.1

H Company acquired 100% of the issued capital of S Company on 31 December 19X0 for $300 at which time the net assets of S Company were valued at $300. Set out below are abbreviated balance sheets and profit and loss accounts for H Company and S Company as at 31 December 19X5.

Accounts as at 31.12.X5

	H Co. $	S Co. $	Debit $	Credit $	Group $
Issued capital	100	100			
Reserves	100	100			
Retained earnings	100	200			
	300	400			
Investment	300	—			
Amount owing to H Co.	—	(100)			
Amount receivable from S Co.	100	—			
Other assets		500			
Other liabilities	(100)				
	300	400			
Operating profit	100	—			
	100	—			
Retained earnings brought forward	100	200			
	200	200			
Dividends paid	100	—			
Retained earnings	100	200			

What consolidation entries are required as at 31 December 19X5 in respect of inter-company debt?

Suggested Solution to Example 6.1

Journal Entries

		$	$
1.	Dr Payable by S Co. to H Co.	100	
	Cr Receivable by S Co. from H Co.		100

Elimination of inter-company indebtedness

		$	$
2.	Dr Issued capital of S Co.	100	
	Dr Reserves of S Co.	100	
	Dr Retained earnings brought forward of S Co.	100	
	Cr Investment in S Co.		300

Elimination of investments in S Co., acquired on 31.12.X0

Note: this entry is explained in detail in Chapter 7 (¶701-¶703).

¶601

INTRA-GROUP DEBT

Accounts as at 31.12.X5

	H Co. $	S Co. $	Debit $	Credit $	Group $
Issued capital	100	100	²100	—	100
Reserves	100	100	²100	—	100
Retained earnings	100	200	100	—	200
	300	400	300	—	400
Investment	300	—	—	²300	—
Amount owing to H Co.	—	(100)	¹100	—	—
Amount receivable from S Co.	100	—	—	¹100	400
Other assets		500			
Other liabilities	(100)	—	—	—	—
	300	400	100	400	400
Operating profit	100	—	—	—	100
	100	—	—	—	100
Retained earnings brought forward	100	200	²100	—	200
	200	200	—	—	300
Dividends paid	100	—	—	—	100
Retained earnings	100	200	100	—	200

¶602 Commercial bills

Most inter-company debt is directly offset by corresponding inter-company receivables. However, this does not hold true for commercial bills of exchange.

A bill of exchange is defined by the *Bills of Exchange Act 1909* as:

"an unconditional order in writing, addressed by one person to another, signed by the person giving it, requiring the person to whom it is addressed to pay on demand, or at a fixed or determinable future time, a sum certain in money to or to the order of a specified person, or to bearer."

The entity agreeing to make the payment specified in the order will usually be either a bank ("bank accepted bills") or an entity with a good credit rating. This bank or other entity is known as the acceptor.

The entity making the order is "the drawer" of the bill and will be responsible for reimbursing the acceptor.

The entity to which payment is to be made will be shown on the bill as the "payee", and it is the payee who holds the bill.

¶602

The payee may hold the bill until the payment date specified in the bill, at which time the acceptor will pay the full face value of the bill to the payee on presentation of the bill. Alternatively, the payee may prefer to receive payment on an earlier date and may find another entity willing to buy the bill from the payee; this new owner of the bill will be entitled to collect the full face value of the bill on the date specified on the bill and will pay to the payee an amount less than that face value in recognition of the time value of money. This practice is known as "discounting" the bill.

The original payee retains a liability to reimburse the new owner if the original acceptor does not honour its commitment in respect of the bill. The financial statements of the payee will disclose this contingent liability.

To illustrate the effects of discounted bills of exchange consider the following situation:

Example 6.2

On 21 January 19X6 Company H sells inventory to its subsidiary, Company S, for a consideration of $10,000. Company S "pays" for these goods by giving to Company H a bank accepted bill of exchange, payable in 180 days.

Company H then discounts (i.e. sells) the bill to an outside entity at a discount of $1,000.

Assume that Company S sells the inventory outside the group on 28 June 19X6 and that no profit was made by Company H on the sale to Company S.

How will this be treated in the accounts of Companies H and S, and in the group accounts of Company H, as at 30 June 19X6?

The accounts of Company H will show:

	$	$
Dr Receivable from S Co — bill	10,000	
Cr Inventory		10,000
Dr Cost of goods sold	10,000	
Cr Sales		10,000

Recognition of sale of inventory:

	$	$
Dr Cash	9,000	
Dr Operating profit	1,000	
Cr Receivable from S Co — bill		10,000

Bill discounted

The balance sheet of Company H will show cash of $9,000, and a contingent liability of $10,000 in relation to the bill will be disclosed "off balance sheet".

Contingent liabilities are not "recognised" in balance sheets — they are disclosed by way of notes to balance sheets.

The accounts of Company S will show:

	$	$
Dr Inventory	10,000	
Cr Payable to bank		10,000

Receipt of inventory, on issue of bill

¶602

INTRA-GROUP DEBT

What has happened from a group point of view? The group has a liability to pay the bank, and has received cash and given a discount.

No contingent liability exists from a group point of view. Company H's contingent liability will become a real liability if neither the bank nor the drawer of the bill honour their commitments as shown on the bill. From a group point of view the liability to the bank is a "real" liability and therefore the group cannot also have a "contingent" liability for the same debt.

Consolidation adjustment required:

Delete contingent liability from accounts of Company H.

¶603 Contingent debt

It is common practice for a company within a group (e.g. Company A) to provide security to a financier or other party for advances to or to support the performance of another company within the group (e.g. Company B). For example, Company B may borrow from a bank, and Company A may guarantee the repayment of the loan by Company B.

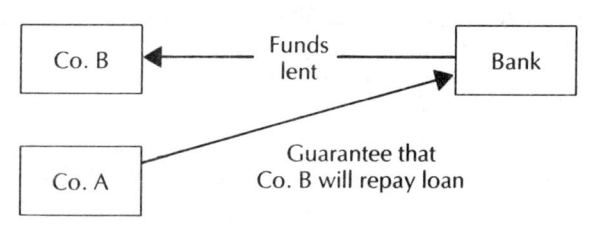

```
  Co. B  ◄──── Funds ────  Bank
                lent        
                           ↗
  Co. A  ──── Guarantee that
              Co. B will repay loan
```

Company B: Liability to repay
Company A: Contingent liability

Also, Company B may enter a contract to construct a building for a third party, and Company A may guarantee the performance of company B in respect of that contract. This is often done either by Company A's directly guaranteeing the performance of Company B, or by Company A's bankers' issuing a guarantee for which Company A agrees to pay should that bank guarantee be called.

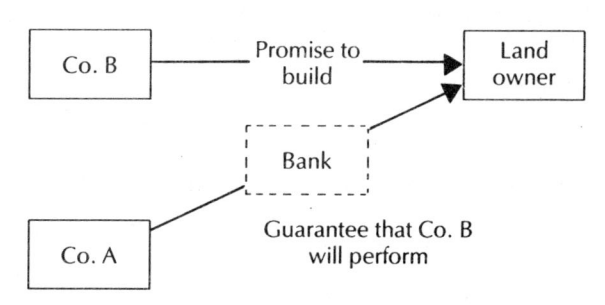

```
  Co. B  ──── Promise to ────  Land
              build            owner
                              ↗
              ┌─ ─ ─ ─┐
              ¦ Bank  ¦
              └─ ─ ─ ─┘
  Co. A  ──── Guarantee that Co. B
              will perform
```

Company B: No accounting recognition
Company A: Contingent liability

¶603

In each of these situations Company A has not incurred a liability by simply making the guarantee. Company A has, however, a contingent liability, because a liability may accrue to Company A as a result of events over which Company A has no control. From an individual entity point of view Company A cannot, for example, control the performance of Company B in its construction activities. Should Company B fail to perform its duties under the construction contract, the bank would be called upon to release funds to the party for which Company B failed to perform. The bank would then call on Company A for those funds, triggering a liability of Company A. Company A has not been involved in the failure to perform, yet it has incurred a liability. The making of a guarantee, and the placing of Company A in a position where a liability may arise from actions over which Company A has no control, results in a contingent liability of Company A. The realisation of the liability is "contingent" upon the actions of another party. Company A would then record, by way of note only, a contingent liability in its financial statements.

In the situation where Company B receives a loan, it would record in its financial statements the liability for repayment of that loan. In the case of a construction contract, Company B's only obligation is to perform as required by the contract. It therefore would record no liability. A guarantee of self-performance is neither a liability nor a contingent liability.

Now consider what will be shown in consolidated financial statements if Company A and Company B are members of a group. What has the group done?

In the case of a loan as in the example above, the accounts of Company B will show a liability for repayment of the loan. The accounts of Company A will show a contingent liability for its guarantee that Company B will repay the loan. The group should therefore record its liability to repay the loan. The group will not record a contingent liability for two reasons. First, the group has already recorded an actual liability to repay the loan. Secondly, the repayment of the loan depends upon the activities of the group. Therefore, no contingency exists over which the group has no control.

Similarly, in the case of bank guarantees for contract performance, the accounts of Company A will show a contingent liability for its guarantee to its bankers, and the accounts of Company B will record no liability. From a group point of view, a group member has entered into a contract. Guarantee of performance by the group (through Company A) is a guarantee of self-performance. The performance of contractual obligations is controlled by the group; therefore at group level no contingent liability exists.

¶603

7

Intra-group investments

General	¶701
"First" consolidation journal entry	¶702
Wholly owned subsidiary — acquisition at balance date	¶703
Elimination in subsequent years	¶704
Acquisition during a year	¶705
Share issue for acquisition	¶706
Asset values at date of acquisition	¶707
Non-corporate entities	¶708

¶701 General

As noted in Chapter 1, consolidation elimination entries are required to eliminate double counting. Investments by one group entity in other group entities as disclosed in individual company accounts are representations of the cost of an interest in the assets and liabilities, or shareholders' funds, of the investee. To include both the investment (from the investor's financial statements) and the net assets acquired (from the investee's financial statements) would be double counting.

The shareholders' funds of the investee at the date of acquisition were not "earned" by the investor company, but by the shareholders from whom the investee acquired the investment. It therefore follows that the consolidated accounts of the investor's group cannot show those shareholders' funds as being "earned" by the group and available for distribution by the group. Such shareholders' funds are considered to be "pre-acquisition", and are eliminated against the amount paid for them by the group, i.e. the cost of the investor's investment.

¶702 "First" consolidation journal entry

Where an investment is held in a subsidiary, in preparing consolidated accounts the investment needs to be eliminated against the shareholders' funds, or net assets, acquired in making that investment. Where the investment is in a wholly owned subsidiary, the investment represents the cost of the group's acquisition of all net assets of the subsidiary at the acquisition date. Any excess (deficiency) of the cost of the investment over the net assets acquired is shown as goodwill (discount) on acquisition (see Chapter 3).

To simplify explanations of elimination entries, the use of a "standard" methodology in preparing consolidation adjustments will be followed in this text. The use of this approach is not mandatory. Any combination of journal adjustments which produces the result that the group accounts show the true group situation is acceptable. However, practice has shown that the establishment of a simple set of "rules" enables a clear understanding of consolidations.

The "first" elimination entries to be noted when preparing consolidated financial statements are those to eliminate investments in subsidiary companies. The form of the other elimination entries suggested later in this text assumes that the first journal entry has been prepared. Indeed, in circumstances where all subsidiaries are 100% owned and no intra-group transactions have taken place, the first journal entries will be the only consolidation adjustments required.

¶703 Wholly owned subsidiary — acquisition at balance date

Consider the following situation:

Example 7.1

Elimination of Wholly Owned Subsidiary

H Company acquired 100% of the issued capital of S Company as at 31 December 19X0 at a cost of $400. At that time the net assets of S Company consisted of:

	$
Issued capital	50
Reserves	50
Retained earnings	100
	200

Prior to the acquisition, H Company's other assets consisted only of cash.

Set out below are abbreviated balance sheets and profit and loss statements for H Company and S Company as at 31 December 19X0.

INTRA-GROUP INVESTMENTS

Accounts as at 31.12.X0

	H Co.	S Co.	Debit	Credit	Group
	$	$	$	$	$
Issued capital	100	50			
Reserves	100	50			
Retained earnings	400	100			
	600	200			
Investment	400	—			
Other assets	200	200			
	600	200			
Operating profit	100	100			
Income tax expense	—	50			
	100	50			
Retained earnings brought forward	300	50			
Retained earnings	400	100			

What consolidation journal entries are required as at 31 December 19X0?

Suggested Solution to Example 7.1

Journal Entry

	$	$
Dr Issued capital of S Co.	50	
Dr Reserves of S Co.	50	
Dr Operating profit of S Co.	100	
Cr income tax expense of S Co.		50
Dr Retained earnings brought forward of S Co.	50	
Cr investment in S Co.		400
Dr Goodwill on acquisition of S Co.	200	

Elimination of investment in S Company

¶703

Accounts as at 31.12.X0

	H Co.	S Co.	Debit	Credit	Group
	$	$	$	$	$
Issued capital	100	50	50	—	100
Reserves	100	50	50	—	100
Retained earnings	400	100	150	50	400
	600	200	250	50	600
Investment	400	—	—	400	—
Goodwill	—	—	200	—	200
Other assets	200	200	—	—	400
	600	200	200	400	600
Total of eliminations			450	450	
Operating profit	100	100	100	—	100
Income tax expense	—	50	—	50	—
	100	50	100	50	100
Retained earnings brought forward	300	50	50	—	300
Retained earnings	400	100	150	50	400

Consider the results shown in the suggested solution.

Prior to the acquisition the H Company group had no other subsidiary companies — its only other asset was cash. We must consider "What has the group done?" (the group now comprises H Company and S Company). This question can be answered for each account.

Issued capital

Has the group changed its issued capital? This could only be done through the issue of more shares, which has not occurred. Therefore the group has not changed its issued capital and the group issued capital is the same after the acquisition as it was before, i.e. when the "group" consisted solely of H Company.

Has the group increased its issued capital by acquiring the issued capital of S Company? The answer is "No!". The group purchased that issued capital, it did not earn the right to display S Company's issued capital as its own.

The issued capital acquired is said to be "pre-acquisition" and any pre-acquisition capital, reserves or retained earnings will have been "earned" by the previous shareholders who would have taken "credit" for the earning of those shareholders' funds in the financial statements of S Company and possibly in the group of which S Company was a member. Once a particular company or group has reported the earning of shareholders' funds, those shareholders' funds cannot be reported as being earned by another group which was not involved as a related reporting entity at that time.

¶703

Reserves

The reasoning applied to issued capital also applies to reserves of whatever description, e.g. capital profits reserve, general reserve, asset revaluation reserve, share premium reserve. All reserves existing at the time of acquisition were earned "pre-acquisition" by the previous shareholders of S Company and are therefore not to be reported as reserves of the H Company group. H Company group acquired the reserves by buying them rather than by earning them.

Retained earnings

Retained earnings are part of shareholders' funds in exactly the same fashion as are reserves and issued capital. All retained earnings at acquisition date were not earned by the acquiring company, and are therefore not to be reported as earned by the acquiring group.

One feature of retained earnings is that movements in this balance are prominently shown in the financial statements, in the profit and loss account. In order to determine the amount of retained earnings which is pre-acquisition we need to consider each item of movement shown in the profit and loss statement.

Consider "Operating profit before income tax of S Company" for the year ended December 19X0. Who made the decision and controlled the transactions which resulted in that profit? H Company only acquired its interest in S Company on 31 December 19X0, so we would assume that all of the operating profit before income tax of S Company for that year had been earned not by the decisions and under the control of H Company, but by the decisions and under the control of the previous shareholders of S Company. Therefore, all of the operating profit before income tax of S Company for the year ended 31 December 19X0 is considered pre-acquisition.

Income tax expense is directly related to operating profit before income tax. The definition of income tax expense in Approved Accounting Standard ASRB 1020: Accounting For Income Tax (Tax-effect Accounting) and Australian Accounting Standard AAS 3 of the same title is "the amount of income tax which would be payable on the pre-tax accounting profit adjusted for permanent differences". Permanent differences are items in the operating profit which have no bearing on income tax to be paid by an entity.

Any change in operating profit before income tax will also result in a change in income tax expense, unless that change in operating profit before income tax represents a "permanent difference".

As income tax expense is directly related to operating profit before income tax, the characteristics of operating profit before income tax also apply to income tax expense. If operating profit before income tax is pre-acquisition, the related income tax expense will also be pre-acquisition. Therefore, in the above example all income tax expense for the year ended 31 December 19X0 is pre-acquisition.

¶703

Retained earnings brought forward is simply the balance of retained earnings at the end of the preceding year and at the beginning of 19X0. This balance represents the accumulated earnings from all activities of S Company up to that date, after any distribution of those earnings as dividends or transfers to reserves.

The treatment considered for the current year operating profit also applies to prior years' accumulated operating profits, or "retained earnings brought forward".

If all profits earned by S Company prior to 31 December 19X0 are pre-acquisition, and retained earnings brought forward represent the accumulation of those profits for the period to 1 January 19X0, then of course all retained earnings brought forward as at 1 January 19X0 are "pre-acquisition" in relation to the acquisition by H Company on 31 December 19X0.

When preparing the consolidation journal entry to eliminate the investment by H Company in the pre-acquisition shareholders' funds, or net assets, of S Company, the journal entry should be structured so that the eliminations can be specifically made against the correct account balances, i.e. against operating profit before income tax, income tax expense, retained earnings brought forward, issued capital, etc.

Some authorities suggest that consolidation journal entries should only be made in the balance sheet, with adjustments made to the profit and loss account to equate the result of the profit and loss account with the balance sheet. It is considered that this is not the best approach for a number of reasons.

First, the whole philosophy of bookkeeping and accounts preparation is based on the double entry system; the use of adjustments, or "one-sided journal entries", is not in accordance with this philosophy.

Secondly, journal entries are to be made against general ledger accounts, and financial statements are prepared from the balances shown in those general ledger accounts. A profit and loss account is prepared from general ledger accounts. Retained earnings in the balance sheet is the product of the profit and loss account; it is not a general ledger account itself until after the profit and loss account has been reported on and closed off. Therefore we cannot do journal entries to retained earnings in the balance sheet.

Thirdly, the making of entries directly against retained earnings on the balance sheet would require later analysis of each of those entries to determine which components of the profit and loss account were affected, and the adjustment of such components. It is preferable to consider each elimination entry only once. Therefore, at the time of initial consideration of an elimination entry, all factors relating to that entry, including the particular components of the profit and loss account affected, should be reviewed to avoid having to cover the same matter again at a later point in the consolidation process.

¶703

Investment in subsidiary

The H Company group cannot have an investment in itself. Therefore we would expect all investments by group companies in other group companies to be eliminated. As can be seen from the suggested solution to Example 7.1, the group investment in subsidiaries is $nil.

Goodwill

Goodwill has been defined as the excess of consideration paid over net assets acquired (see Chapter 3). The entry to eliminate the investment in a subsidiary company shows all components of net assets acquired, and the difference between the sum of these and the cost of the investment is shown as goodwill.

This can be checked as follows, to ensure that all pre-acquisition components have been included in the entry:

	$
Cost of investment	400
Less: Net assets of S Co. at date of acquisition	200
Goodwill	200

Goodwill shown in the elimination entry as $200 is therefore correct.

Net assets of group

The overall position of the H Company group should also be considered. Immediately prior to the acquisition the net assets of the H Company group, which consisted at that time of only H Company, were $600. Would we expect the net assets of the H Company group to change? The only transaction entered into by the group was the acquisition of shares in S Company. The group has done nothing to increase its current net worth, although one would expect that the decision to acquire shares in S Company was made in the expectation that the net worth of the group would increase in the future.

Therefore we would expect the net assets of the group not to have altered. The suggested solution shows net assets of H Company, and therefore of the H Company group, as $600 immediately prior to the acquisition, and as $600 immediately subsequent to the acquisition, which is the result expected.

¶704 Elimination in subsequent years

At any time after an acquisition of shares in a subsidiary company, the preparation of consolidated accounts will require the elimination of that investment against the net assets acquired. We have considered in ¶703 (Example 7.1) a situation where H Company acquired 100% of the issued capital of S Company on 31 December 19X0. We will now consider the elimination entry required one year later.

Example 7.2
Elimination of Investment in Wholly Owned Subsidiary
One Year after Acquisition Date
Accounts as at 31.12.X1

	H Co. $	S Co. $	Debit $	Credit $	Group $
Issued capital	100	50			
Reserves	100	50			
Retained earnings	400	360			
	600	460			
Investment in S Co.	400	—			
Other assets	200	460			
	600	460			
Operating profit	—	500			
Income tax expense	—	240			
	—	260			
Retained earnings brought forward	400	100			
Retained earnings	400	360			

The accounts of H Company as at 31 December 19X1 show that H Company has made no profit or loss during the year ended 31 December 19X1, and the net assets of H Company have not changed during the year.

The accounts of S Company as at 31 December 19X1 show that S Company earned an operating profit after tax of $260 during the year ended 31 December 19X1.

What elimination entry is required?

Suggested Solution to Example 7.2
Consolidation Entry to Eliminate Investments

	$	$
Dr Issued capital of S Co.	50	
Dr Reserves of S Co.	50	
Dr Retained earnings brought forward of S Co.	100	
Cr Investment in S Co.		400
Dr Goodwill	200	

Elimination of investment in S Company

¶704

INTRA-GROUP INVESTMENTS

Accounts as at 31.12.X1

	H Co.	S Co.	Debit	Credit	Group
	$	$	$	$	$
Issued capital	100	50	50	—	100
Reserves	100	50	50	—	100
Retained earnings	400	360	100	—	660
	600	460	200	—	860
Investment in S Co.	400	—	—	400	—
Goodwill	—	—	200	—	200
Other assets	200	460	—	—	660
	600	460	200	400	860
Total of eliminations	—	—	400	400	
Operating profit	—	500	—	—	500
Income tax expense	—	240	—	—	240
	—	260	—	—	260
Retained earnings brought forward	400	100	100	—	400
Retained earnings	400	360	100	—	660

Consider the results shown in the suggested solution.

Net assets of H Company group

The net assets of the H Company group as at 31 December 19X1 were $600. As at 31 December 19X1 the net assets of the H Company group are $860, an increase of $260.

What has the group done during the year? The group (by way of S Company) has made an after tax profit of $260, which increases retained earnings of the group, and therefore net assets, by $260. The group has done nothing further which would be expected to affect its net worth.

Profit and loss components of elimination entry

Note that the components of the elimination entry as at 31 December 19X0 (see ¶703, Example 7.1) which related to the profit and loss account were:

	Dr(Cr)
	$
Dr Operating profit before tax	100
Cr Income tax expense	(50)
Dr Retained earnings brought forward	50
	100

In the profit and loss account of S Company for the year ended 31 December 19X1 all the prior years' profit and loss entries have been

¶704

accumulated into the "retained earnings brought forward" caption. Therefore this caption will include all of the profit and loss account components for the year ended 31 December 19X1.

The original elimination entry (i.e. the entry made immediately following the acquisition of shares in S Company) targeted specific accounts. As the profit and loss account components previously targeted have been "moved" to retained earnings brought forward, the elimination entry needs to be "moved" also.

As can be seen, the 19X1 elimination entry shows a debit to retained earnings brought forward of $100, being the sum of the 19X0 profit and loss account components of the elimination entry.

Retained earnings brought forward

As its name implies, the balance of retained earnings brought forward in the group profit and loss account must be the same as the closing balance in the prior year's profit and loss account. Compare the group profit and loss account for the year ended 31 December 19X1 with that for the year ended 31 December 19X0 and it can be seen that this is the case. The 19X1 opening balance of $400 is the same as the 19X0 closing balance.

Goodwill

The goodwill as at acquisition date also has not changed — the elimination entry at 31 December 19X1 shows $200 goodwill on acquisition, as did the journal entry at 31 December 19X0. Of course, goodwill would be amortised during the year ended 31 December 19X1 to the extent considered necessary, by the journal entry:

Dr Operating profit before tax
 Cr Goodwill

In order to simplify the example, this entry has not been shown in the suggested solution to Example 7.2 above.

¶705 Acquisition during a year

How is the elimination affected when an acquisition is made other than at the end of a year? The application of consolidation principles does not change. We must consider "What has the group done during the year?". The investment made in the subsidiary company must be eliminated against the net assets acquired.

Example 7.3

Acquisition of Wholly Owned Subsidiary During a Year

H Company acquired 100% of the issued share capital of S Company on 30 September 19X1, at a cost of $1,000. At that time the accounts of S Company included the following:

¶705

INTRA-GROUP INVESTMENTS

Accounts for the nine months to 30.9.19X1

	$
Issued capital	200
Reserves	200
Retained earnings	400
	800
Operating profit before tax	300
Income tax expense	120
	180
Retained earnings brought forward	220
Retained earnings	400

The accounts of H Company and S Company as at 31 December 19X1 disclosed the following:

Accounts as at 31.12.X1

	H Co. $	S Co. $	Debit $	Credit $	Group $
Issued capital	100	200			
Reserves	200	200			
Retained earnings	200	600			
	500	1,000			
Investment in S Co.	1,000	—			
Other assets (liabilities)	(500)	1,000			
	500	1,000			
Operating profit	300	600			
Income tax expense	150	220			
	150	380			
Retained earnings brought forward	50	220			
Retained earnings	200	600			

Suggested Solution to Example 7.3

Elimination Journal Entry

	$	$
Dr Issued capital of S Co.	200	
Dr Reserves of S Co.	200	
Dr Operating profit before tax of S Co.	300	
Cr Income tax expense of S Co.		120
Dr Retained earnings brought forward of S Co.	220	
Cr Investments in S Co.		1,000
Dr Goodwill	200	

Elimination of investment in H Company at 30 September 19X1

¶705

Accounts as at 31.12.X1

	H Co. $	S Co. $	Debit $	Credit $	Group $
Issued capital	100	200	200	—	100
Reserves	200	200	200	—	200
Retained earnings	200	600	520	120	400
	500	1,000	920	120	700
Investment in S Co.	1,000	—	—	1,000	—
Goodwill	—	—	200	—	200
Other Assets (liabilities)	(500)	1,000	—	—	500
	500	1,000	200	1,000	700
Total of eliminations			1,120	1,120	
Operating profit	300	600	300	—	600
Income tax expense	150	220	—	120	250
	150	380	300	120	350
Retained earnings brought forward	50	220	220	—	50
Retained earnings	200	600	520	120	400

Profit and loss account

The profit and loss accounts included in the elimination entry were the balances in those accounts at acquisition date, i.e. 30 September 19X1.

Consider the profit of the group for the year ended 31 December 19X1. This profit will consist of that earned by H Company for the full year, plus that earned by S Company during the time it was controlled by H Company, i.e. the three months from 1 October 19X1 to 31 December 19X1. These profits can be summarised as follows:

	(A) S Co. 9 months to 30.9.X1 $	(B) S Co. Year to 31.12.X1 $	(C=(B−A)) S Co. 3 months to 31.12.X1 $	(D) H Co. Year to 31.12.X1 $	(E=(C+D)) Group Year to 31.12.X1 $
Operating profit before tax	300	600	300	300	600
Income tax expense	120	220	100	150	250
	180	380	200	150	350

Compare the group profit shown in the above table with the group profit shown on the consolidation worksheet.

¶705

Goodwill

The goodwill calculation should be checked, as follows:

	$
Cost of investment	1,000
Less: Net assets of S Co. at date of acquisition, 30.9.X1	800
Goodwill	200

¶706 Share issue for acquisition

The examples considered in ¶705 above assumed that the shares in the subsidiary company were acquired for cash. Let us now consider a situation where the consideration given to acquire the shares in the subsidiary company was shares of the holding company. This is a common occurrence. A holding company can obtain the funds necessary for an acquisition in many ways, e.g. from existing cash reserves, by borrowing, by issuing shares and using the cash generated, and by issuing the shares directly to the vendor of the subsidiary company shares.

Whilst the accounting treatment to be adopted in respect of such a transaction is often considered to be a "consolidation problem", it is in fact a problem for the holding company only.

At what value does the holding company record its investment? Financial statements should present fairly the transactions entered into by the holding company. As financial statements are generally prepared in accordance with the historical cost convention, the investment should be recorded at cost. How "cost" is determined when the consideration is shares of the acquiring company is a matter of judgement.

In Australia, Approved Accounting Standard ASRB 1015: 'Accounting for the Acquisition of Assets and Statement of Accounting Standards AAS 21, "Accounting for the Acquisition of Assets (including Business Entities)" specify that such investments should be recorded at cost. Cost is to be considered in relation to the fair value of consideration offered, i.e. of the shares issued.

The following factors may be considered to provide information as to the fair value of the consideration offered.

Market value of shares offered

If the shares of the acquiring company are listed on a stock exchange, the market value of those shares prior to the acquisition may be considered an indication of the cost of the acquisition. This assumes that the previous owners of the subsidiary company could have acquired those holding company shares for cash in the market, rather than acquiring them by giving up shares in the subsidiary company. The value of the subsidiary company shares may be considered to be equal to the amount of cash which would have had to be paid in the market to acquire the holding company shares.

Market value of subsidiary company shares

If the shares of the subsidiary company are listed on a stock exchange, the holding company may have been able to buy the shares in the market for cash. As shares in H Company were issued as an alternative to paying cash, the value of those shares issued may be considered to be equal to the amount of cash H Company would have had to pay in the market.

Fair value of assets of S Company

The number of holding company shares needed to be given in the transaction may have been determined having regard to the values of the net assets of the subsidiary company. If so, this value may be considered to be the appropriate value to be attributed to the acquisition.

As can be seen from the above alternatives, the value attributed to the shares issued can only be decided with knowledge of how the consideration was determined.

Companies legislation in Australia (sec. 119(1) of the Companies Code) requires any premium received on issue of shares to be included in a share premium account.

The journal entry raised in the holding company accounts will usually include recognition of some share premium; it is rare for the value attributed to the shares issued to be equal to their "par" value. The usual journal entry in the holding company accounts would be:

	$	$
Dr investment	y	
Cr Issued capital — at par		x
Cr Share premium account		y−x

Once this entry is made in the holding company's accounts, on consideration the investment in the subsidiary company will be eliminated in the same manner as if the investment had been acquired for cash.

¶707 Asset values at date of acquisition

Should the investee company consider that any of the assets or liabilities of a subsidiary company are understated or overstated as at the time of acquisition, these factors should be taken into account in determining the difference on consolidation.

Approved Accounting Standard ASRB 1013: Accounting for Goodwill and Statement of Accounting Standards AAS 18 of the same title both specify that goodwill should be determined having regard to the fair value of assets acquired. Fair value is defined in AAS 18 as "the amount for which an asset could be exchanged between a knowledgeable, willing buyer and a knowledgeable, willing seller in an arm's length transaction".

INTRA-GROUP INVESTMENTS

Recognition of fair values of assets shown in the accounts of a subsidiary acquired can be presented in two ways:

(1) adjust the accounts of the subsidiary, or

(2) adjust on consolidation only.

Any such adjustments would need to be made at acquisition date. The preferred approach is to adjust the accounts of the subsidiary concerned to show assets at their fair values. This may involve the raising of an asset revaluation reserve in the subsidiary.

Consolidation accounting is meant to be simply an aggregation process and the elimination of double counting. Adjusting asset values on consolidation is not in accordance with this philosophy. It results in assets being shown at one value in the subsidiary company accounts and at a different value on consolidation — hardly a consistent approach.

However, the application of Approved Accounting Standard ASRB 1010: Accounting for the Revaluation of Non-Current Assets and Statement of Accounting Standards AAS 10 of the same title may render adjustment on consolidation a more favoured option in some circumstances. These standards require that any profit on sale of a revalued asset should be calculated with reference to the revalued amount, e.g. if an asset cost $100, was revalued to $150 and sold for $175, the profit on sale would be $25. The standards note that "credit" is taken for the increase in value of the asset, and therefore in the net assets of the entity, at the time of revaluation.

In certain circumstances the directors of the holding company and of the subsidiary company may wish to show the profit on sale in the profit and loss account of the subsidiary company at the time of eventual sale, rather than as an immediate increase in the asset revaluation reserve of the subsidiary.

Such an alternative is not available on consolidation. Goodwill must be determined having regard to the fair value of assets acquired. This is illustrated in the following example:

Example 7.4

H Company acquired 100% of the issued share capital of S Company on 31 December 19X1 at a cost of $500. The balance sheet of S Company at that date disclosed:

Balance sheet of S Company — 31.12.X1

	$
Issued capital	100
General reserve	100
Retained earnings	100
	300
Land	300

An independent valuation of the land as at 31.12.X1 considered the market value of the land to be $450.

¶707

The journal entries to recognise the fair value of the asset acquired, and to eliminate the investment in S Company, could be prepared in two ways:

(1) *Adjustment of the accounts of the subsidiary*

In S Company's books

	$	$
Dr Land	150	
Cr Asset revaluation reserve		150

Revaluation of land

On consolidation

	$	$
Dr Issued capital	100	
Dr Reserves	100	
Dr Retained earnings	100	
Dr Asset revaluation reserve	150	
Cr Investment		500
Dr Goodwill	50	

Elimination of investment in S Company

---

(2) *Adjustment on consolidation*

In S Company's books

No entry required

On consolidation

	$	$
Dr Land	150	
Cr Asset revaluation reserve		150

Revalue land in S Company to fair value at acquisition date

	$	$
Dr Issued capital	100	
Dr Reserves	100	
Dr Retained earnings	100	
Dr Asset revaluation reserve	150	
Cr Investment		500
Dr Goodwill	50	

Elimination of investment in S Company

As can be seen, the group accounts show the same information irrespective of which method is adopted.

¶708 Non-corporate entities

Consolidation of groups of entities provides information about the group of entities which cannot easily be obtained from individual entity financial statements. This applies equally where the entities involved are not companies. The example below illustrates the consolidation of a company and a trust, and shows that the principles of consolidation apply irrespective of the form of the entities involved.

¶708

INTRA-GROUP INVESTMENTS

Example 7.5

Group with Subsidiary Trust

H Company owns 80% of the units issued by S Trust. The investment by H Company was made 10 years ago, when the trust was formed.

P.T. is the trustee of S Trust. Balance sheets and profit and loss accounts for each entity are set out below.

	H Co. $	S Trust $	Debit $	Credit $	Group $
Issued capital	100	—			
Reserves	100	—			
Retained earnings	400	—			
Unitholders' funds	—	5,000			
	600	5,000			
Investment in trust	4,000	—			
Other assets	(3,400)	5,000			
	600	5,000			
Operating profit	800	1,000			
Income tax expense	300	—			
	500	1,000			
	500	1,000			
Retained earnings brought forward	100	—			
	600	1,000			
Dividends paid	200	—			
Trust distribution	—	1,000			
Retained earnings	400	—			

Assuming that H Company controls S Trust, prepare consolidation journal entries and consolidation worksheet.

Suggested Solution to Example 7.5

Consolidation Entries

		$	$
(a)	Dr Unitholders' funds	4,000	
	Cr Investment in trust		4,000
	Elimination of investment by parent		
(b)	Dr Unitholders' funds	1,000	
	Dr Minority interest (P/L)	200	
	Cr Minority interest (B/S)		1,200
	Allocation of minority interest		

¶708

(c) Dr Minority interest (B/S)   200
    Dr Operating profit — H Co.   800
       Cr S Trust distribution — subsidiary   1,000
    Elimination of intra-group payment

Consolidation Worksheet

	H Co.	S Trust	Debit	Credit	Group
	$	$	$	$	$
Issued capital	100	—	—	—	100
Reserves	100	—	—	—	100
Retained earnings	400	—	1,000	1,000	400
Unitholders' funds	—	5,000	^{a}4,000 ^{b}1,000	—	—
Minority interest	—	—	^{c}200	^{b}1,200	1,000
	600	5,000	6,200	2,200	1,600
TOTAL EQUITY					
Investment in trust	4,000	—	—	^{a}4,000	—
Other assets	(3,400)	5,000	—	—	1,600
NET ASSETS	600	5,000	—	4,000	1,600
Operating profit	800	1,000	^{c}800	—	1,000
Income tax expense	300	—	—	—	300
	500	1,000	800	—	700
Minority interest	—	—	^{b}200	—	200
	500	1,000	1,000	—	500
Retained earnings brought forward	100	—	—	—	100
	600	1,000	1,000	—	600
Dividends paid	(200)	—	—	—	(200)
Trust distribution	—	1,000	—	^{c}1,000	—
Retained earnings	400	—	1,000	1,000	400

¶708

8
Equity accounting

General	¶801
Different methods of equity accounting	¶802
Discontinuation	¶803
Carrying value of investment and goodwill	¶804
Realisation argument	¶805
Unrealised profits	¶806

¶801 General

Situations may arise where it is not considered appropriate to include in group accounts the assets and liabilities of all member entities. This may be the case where the subsidiary entity was purchased with intent to sell soon after balance date.

A form of reporting often practised for such investments in subsidiary companies is "equity accounting".

Equity accounting is most often used in respect of investments in companies which do not meet the "control" or "ownership" criteria required for a subsidiary relationship to exist, and in which the investor's shareholding places the investor in a position to participate in the management of the investee, although not to control that management.

At present in Australia Approved Accounting Standard ASRB 1016: Disclosure of Information About Investments in Associated Companies, and Statement of Accounting Standards AAS 14, "Equity Method of Accounting", govern the application of the equity method of accounting. These accounting standards define an equity situation as being in place where the investor is able to exert "significant influence" over the management and affairs of the investee, or "associated", entity. ASRB 1016.10 defines significant influence as follows:

> "'Significant influence' means the capacity of an investor to affect substantially either, or both, of the financial and operating policies of an investee."

The existence of significant influence is based not on objective facts, but on subjective indicators. Factors which may indicate the existence of significant influence as noted in AAS 14(8) and ASRB 1016(vi) are:

- the investor's voting power in the investee
- representation on the investee's board of directors
- participation in decisions on the distribution or retention of the investee's profits
- participation, in other ways, in policy-making decisions of the investee
- material inter-company transactions between investor and investee
- interchange of managerial personnel
- dependence on technical information.

The individual assets and liabilities of the associated company are not brought into the group accounts. The share of increases in net assets of the associated company are recorded in the group accounts as increases in the value of the investment in the associated company. Any subsequent distribution of those net assets is recorded in the group accounts as a reduction in the investment.

The "usual" journal entry to equity account for a share of profits of an associated company is as follows:

	$	$
Dr Investment in A Co.	x	
Cr Share of profit of A Co.		y
Dr Share of income tax expense of A Co.	y-x	

On receipt of a dividend the group accounts would show:

Dr Cash	x	
Cr Investment in A Co.		x

Equity accounting is based upon an assumption that the investor can influence the dividend or other distribution policies of the associated entity. Equity accounting involves the recognition in the group accounts of the investor's share of the increases in shareholders' funds of the associated company as those increases occur, irrespective of whether they are distributed.

¶801

EQUITY ACCOUNTING

¶802 Different methods of equity accounting

Three alternative forms of accounting for investments in associated companies may be adopted:

(1) cost method;

(2) cost based equity method;

(3) pure equity method.

The application of each of these three methods is illustrated below:

Example 8.1

Equity Accounting — Example of Three Different Approaches

A acquired 20% of B on 30.6.X8 at a cost of $1,500

		$
30.6.X8	B had:	
	Share capital	1,000
	Asset revaluation reserve	2,500
	Retained earnings	3,000
		6,500
30.6.X9	Profit and loss account for the year to 30.6.X9 disclosed:	
	Operating profit	1,600
	Income tax expense	800
		800
	Retained earnings at 1.7.X8	3,000
		3,800
	Dividend paid	500
	Retained earnings at 30.6.X9	3,300

	Cost method (i.e. no equity accounting)		Cost based equity		Pure equity	
	$	$	$	$	$	$
1. Purchase of shares—						
Dr Investment	1,500		1,500		1,500	
Cr Bank		1,500		1,500		1,500
2. Recognise goodwill on purchase—						
Dr Goodwill					200	
Cr Investment						200
3. Share of associated company profits—						
Dr Investment			160		160	
Cr Share of operating profit before tax (i.e. $1,600 × 20%)				320		320

¶802

Dr Share of income tax expense (i.e. $800 × 20%)	160	160
4. Dr Dividends received	100	100
Cr Investment	100	100
Being 20% × $500 dividend from post-acquisition profits		

* Assume that the books of A will have recorded the receipt of the dividend as follows:

Dr Bank
    Cr Dividends received

Therefore we now have:

(1) *Cost method*

Investment
| 1,500 |

(2) *Cost based equity*

Investment
1,500	100
160	
1,560	

(3) *Pure equity*

Investment
1,500	200
160	100
1,360	

Goodwill
| 200 | |

Proof of pure equity method, which is the recognition of the investment value at an amount equal to the share of the net assets of the associated company:

		$
Net assets of B at 30.6.X9	Share capital	1,000
	Asset revaluation reserve	2,500
	Retained earnings	3,300
		6,800
	A's share of share capital 20%	
	A's share of net assets	1,360

(which is equal to the value of the investment in B as per A's a/cs under pure equity, as shown above).

In Australia both Approved Accounting Standard ASRB 1016: *Disclosure of Information About Investments in Associated Companies* and Statement of Accounting Standards AAS 14, "Equity Method of Accounting" require the application of the cost based equity method.

¶802

¶803 Discontinuation

The application of the equity method should be discontinued where:

- an investee ceases to be an associated company; and
- the carrying amount of an investment is reduced below zero, except where the investor has undertaken to support the investee financially.

¶804 Carrying value of investment and goodwill

The initial carrying value of an investment should be the value at which the investor as a separate legal entity records the investment in its books, i.e. usually at cost.

Any goodwill or negative goodwill *should not* be separately disclosed in the financial statements. This represents a difference from the treatment required using the "pure equity" method.

However, the goodwill (or negative goodwill) element should be identified and the amount of amortisation adjusted against the share of post-acquisition profits of the investee taken up by the investor and against the investment.

The initial carrying amount should be adjusted for dividends received or receivable from pre-acquisition profits and reserves. Subsequent adjustment should be made for:

- the investor's share of the profit (loss) of the investee for the period;
- dividends received or receivable by the investor;
- post-application movements in total reserves of associated companies not recognised previously in the investee's profit and loss account, except revaluations already reflected in the cost of acquisition; and
- changes in investor's ownership.

¶805 Realisation argument

Opponents of the use of equity accounting argue that profits of associated companies should only be recorded in group accounts when actually realised, and that the recording of interests in possible distributions is not appropriate.

Proponents of equity accounting counter this by arguing that equity accounting is only appropriate where the investor's influence over the associated entity is such that it can control the distribution policies of the associated entity and therefore if the investor wishes to realise its equity share of undistributed profits it can do so.

¶806 Unrealised profits

In recognising an equity interest in an associated entity, the effect of transactions between the investor and the associated company needs to be considered.

Equity accounting may be considered to be an extension of the group entity, comprising holding and subsidiary entities, to include associated companies. Accordingly the effects of transactions between an investor and an associated company should be eliminated in the same way as if the transactions were between two members of a group.

Example 8.2

Illustration of Equity Accounting

1. A is a holding company with a wholly owned subsidiary S.
2. A acquires 40% of an associated company B on 1 October 19X7 for $1,000.
3. At 1 October 19X7 the balance sheet of B is (under the accounting rules of B):

	$		$	
Capital	1,000	Stock		3,000
Retained profits	1,400	Depreciable assets		
	2,400	Cost	2,400	
Total liabilities	6,600	Depreciation	(400)	2,000
		Other assets		4,000
	9,000			9,000

4. In assessing the purchase consideration of B, A placed different values on the following assets:

   Plant $400 increased value
   Stock $600 decreased value.

5. After the acquisition A sold stock to B at a profit of $100. This stock was still on hand at 30 June 19X8 in the books of B.
6. A and B both use 12% straight-line depreciation on all fixed assets.
7. B's stock turnover rate is 3 times per year on all stock lines.
8. Company A considers appropriate the amortisation of notional goodwill in respect of its investment in B over 4 years.
9. The dividend paid by B was out of profits earned during 19X8.
10. The balance sheets and profit and loss accounts of "A Group" and B at 30 June 19X8 (before any equity accounting considerations) were:

¶806

EQUITY ACCOUNTING

Balance sheets

				A Group $		B $
Issued capital				5,000		1,000
Retained profits				3,000		1,400
				8,000		2,400
Liabilities				29,000		5,884
				37,000		8,284
Investment in B				1,000		
Inventory				12,000		2,500
	Cost	2,500		Cost	2,400	
Depreciable assets	Depn	(1,600)	9,000	Depn	(616)	1,784
Other assets				15,000		4,000
				37,000		8,284

Profit and loss accounts

	A Group $	B $
Operating profit	4,080	2,400
Income tax expense	(1,880)	(1,200)
	2,200	1,200
Retained profits 1/7/X7	800	1,000
	3,000	2,200
Dividend paid	—	800
Retained profits 30/6/X8	3,000	1,400

Required

(1) Prepare the following at 30 June 19X8:

　(i) Journal entries for the equity portion of the consolidation.

　(ii) Consolidated profit and loss account including cost based equity accounting.

　(iii) Consolidated balance sheet including cost based equity accounting.

(2) Ignore any tax effects.

Suggested Solution to Example 8.2:

Journal Entries

	$	$
(1) Dr Investment in B	320	
Cr Share of profit of associated company		320

A's share of recorded profits for 9 months since acquisition.

¶806

Retained earnings at 1.10.X7	1,400	
Retained earnings at 30.6.X8 (before dividend)	2,200	
Profit for 9 months	800	
A's share at 40%	320	
(2) Dr Investment in B	240	
Cr Share of profit of associated company		240

Benefit from stock write-down, stock having been sold (40% of $600)

(3) Dr Share of profit of associated company	14	
Cr investment in B		14

Depreciation on increased plant valuation
40% × ¾ of a year × 12% depreciation rate × $400

(4) Dr Profit — A	40	
Cr Investment in B		40

Elimination of inter-company profit on stock

(5) Dr Dividend received by A	320	
Cr Investment in B		320

Adjustment for dividend received (40% of $800 paid by B)

(6) Dr Share of profits of associated company	30	
Cr Investment in B		30

To write off goodwill in accordance with A group policy
Goodwill is calculated as follows:

Net assets	2,400
Plant undervaluation	400
Stock overvaluation	(600)
	2,200
40%	880
Consideration	1,000
Goodwill — B	120

¶806

EQUITY ACCOUNTING

Summary

Profit of B recognised by A is:

Journal entry No.	Dr $	Cr $
(1) Profit share		320
(2) Stock benefit		240
(3) Depreciable assets	14	
(6) Goodwill amortisation	30	
	44	560
		(44)
Share of profit of associated company		516

Summarised Profit and Loss Account

	$	
Operating profit	3,720	(see note 1)
Income tax expense	(1,880)	
	1,840	
Share of profit of associated company	516	
Net profit	2,356	
Retained profits 1.7.X7	800	
Retained profits 30.6.X8	3,156	

Note 1: after eliminations—
| dividend (journal entry (5) above) | 320 |
| stock profit (journal entry (4) above) | 40 |

Summarised Balance Sheet

	$
Issued capital	5,000
Retained profits	3,156
	8,156
Liabilities	(29,000)
Investment in B (see note 2)	1,156
Inventory	12,000
Depreciable assets	9,000
Other assets	15,000
	8,156

Note 2

Cost of investment	1,000
Associated company profit	516
Inter-company stock adjustment	(40)
Dividend received	(320)
	1,156

¶806

Worksheet as at 30.6.X8

	A Group	B Co.	Debit	Credit	Equity Accounted
	$	$	$	$	$
Issued capital	5,000	1,000			5,000
Retained profits	3,000	1,400	404	560	3,156
	8,000	2,400	404	560	8,156
Investment in B	1,000		[1]320	[3]14	1,156
			[2]240	[4]40	
				[5]320	
				[6]30	
Inventory	12,000	2,500			12,000
Depreciable assets					
Cost	25,000	2,400			
Depreciation	(16,000)	(616)			
	9,000	1,784			9,000
Other assets	15,000	4,000			15,000
	37,000	8,284	560	404	37,156
Liabilities	29,000	5,884			29,000
	8,000	2,400	560	404	8,156
Operating profit	4,080	2,400	[4]40		3,720
			[5]320		
Income tax expense	(1,880)	(1,200)			(1,880)
	2,200	1,200	360		1,840
Share of profit of associated company			[3]14	[1]320	516
			[6]30	[2]240	
	2,200	1,200	404	560	2,356
Retained profits 1.7.X7	800	1,000			800
	3,000	2,200	404	560	3,156
Dividend paid	—	800			—
Retained profits 30.6.X8	3,000	1,400	404	560	3,156

¶806

9

Minority interest

What is a minority interest? ¶901
Disclosure of minority interest ¶902
Transactions involving minority interest have not been realised ¶903
Direct and indirect minority interest ¶904
When the minority owns the majority ¶905
"Second" journal entry ¶906
Acquisition date not relevant to minority ¶907
Acquisition of a non-wholly owned subsidiary ¶908
Minority interest allocation not to be combined with investment elimination ¶909
Disclosure ¶910

¶901 What is a minority interest?

One of the more difficult concepts for consolidation accountants to comprehend is that of minority interests. The term "minority interest" appears to be one of the least understood, and the most misunderstood, terms used in the accounting profession.

The shares and other equity in subsidiary entities are held, directly or indirectly, either by the holding company or by others. Where shares in

¶901

subsidiaries are held by unrelated entities we refer to such holdings as being held by "minority interests". For example:

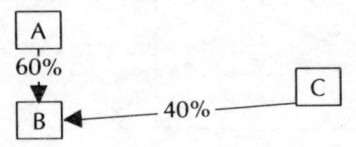

```
        A
        |
       60%
        ▼
        B ◄──── 40% ──── C
```

If "A" holds 60% of the issued shares of B, and C holds 40%, when group accounts are prepared for the A group, comprising A and B, the interests of C in the A group are referred to as minority interests.

There are a number of aspects of minority interest which need to be dealt with:

(1) Minority interest is not a liability (see below).
(2) Minority interest is part of the group (see below).
(3) Minority interest is not eliminated, it is allocated (see ¶902).
(4) Transactions involving minority interest have not been realised to any extent (see ¶903).

Minority interest is not a liability

A common fallacy propounded within the accounting world is that minority interest is, or at the very least should be thought of as, a liability. This is not the case, and the rejection of this concept is central to a true understanding of consolidation.

A liability is, to use a practical definition, an obligation to "pay" something to someone at or within a certain time. In the case of an unrelated entity owning shares in a group member, who may be said to have such an obligation? Certainly not the holding company, which has an investment in the subsidiary company and has no duty to any other shareholders in the subsidiary other than as co-owners. Certainly not the unrelated entity shareholders.

Minority interest is part of the group

The group for which consolidated accounts are prepared includes the holding company of the group and all subsidiary companies. Under the economic entity concept, which is the method which has been in use in Australia for many years, the group accounts will include all assets and liabilities of all companies within the group.

¶901

MINORITY INTEREST 69

Consider the example shown above.

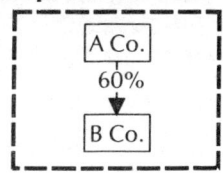

```
┌─────────────┐
│   ┌─────┐   │
│   │A Co.│   │
│   └──┬──┘   │
│    60%      │
│     ▼       │
│   ┌─────┐   │
│   │B Co.│   │
│   └─────┘   │
└─────────────┘
```

The dotted line represents the group. To assist in understanding the concept of minority interest, consider who owns shares in the group shown above.

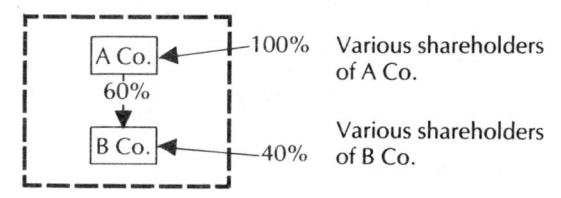

```
┌─────────────┐
│   ┌─────┐   │◄──100%   Various shareholders
│   │A Co.│   │          of A Co.
│   └──┬──┘   │
│    60%      │
│     ▼       │
│   ┌─────┐   │◄──40%    Various shareholders
│   │B Co.│   │          of B Co.
│   └─────┘   │
└─────────────┘
```

As can be seen from this diagram, persons holding shares in a group can be categorised into two sets:

(a) shareholders of the holding company, and

(b) shareholders of subsidiary companies, or "minority interests".

If it is understood that minority interests are simply a subset of "total external shareholders", the disclosure and treatment of minority interests can be readily dealt with.

The equity portion of the balance sheet will show, for disclosure purposes only, the relative equities held in the group by holding company shareholders and by minority interests. This is commonly shown in the "equity" section of the group balance sheet (also referred to as the "proprietorship funds" or "share capital and reserves" section).

¶902 Disclosure of minority interest

There are a number of different ways to disclose minority interest in the balance sheet. The disclosure required by Australian companies legislation (Schedule 7 of the Companies Regulations) — and which was also almost universally used prior to its incorporation into legislation — is set out below as Disclosure I.

¶902

Disclosure I

	Group $000
SHAREHOLDERS' EQUITY	
Share capital	10
Reserves	20
Retained profits	30
Shareholders' equity attributable to members of the holding company	60
Minority shareholders' interest in subsidiaries	30
TOTAL SHAREHOLDERS' EQUITY	90

Disclosure II

SHAREHOLDERS' EQUITY	
Shareholders' equity attributable to members of the holding company	
Share capital	10
Reserves	20
Retained profits	30
	60
Shareholders' equity of subsidiaries attributable to minority shareholders	
Share capital	10
Reserves	10
Retained profits	10
	30
TOTAL SHAREHOLDERS' EQUITY	90

Disclosure III

SHAREHOLDERS' EQUITY	
Share capital	20
Reserves	30
Retained profits	40
TOTAL SHAREHOLDERS' EQUITY	90

Consider the three possible disclosures shown above. It is clear that the disclosures of minority are different only in presentation, and this is the key to understanding the consolidation aspects of minority interest.

Minority interest disclosed in group accounts is a reallocation of shareholders' equity, to show effectively details of the holding company's share of the group's shareholders' equity, and to show the minority shareholders' interest in the group shareholders' equity. This minority interest can be disclosed on a single line (Disclosure I), or showing its various components (Disclosure II), or not disclosing separately the interests of the holding company and minority shareholders (Disclosure III).

Minority interest is not eliminated, it is allocated

Nothing in relation to these three alternative disclosure formats affects assets and liabilities. Minority interest is arrived at by simply reallocating the disclosure within the proprietorship section of the balance sheet.

¶902

¶903 Transactions involving minority interest have not been realised

Transactions between members of the group are reported in the individual accounts of each of the members involved in the transaction. However, from a group point of view such transactions should not be reported upon, given that the aim of consolidated financial statements is to report on transactions between the group and "outsiders". Accordingly such transactions need to be eliminated at the consolidation level prior to finalising the group accounts.

Group accounts prepared using the "economic entity" concept show all assets and liabilities of all the members of the group. The economic entity concept is adopted in Australia, the U.K. and the U.S.A. Other possible consolidation concepts noted in accounting literature are:

(1) the proprietary concept, whereby only ownership interests in subsidiary company assets and liabilities are consolidated (e.g. 60% of the value of land in a subsidiary's accounts is included in the group accounts);

(2) the parent entity concept, which is similar to the economic entity concept except that minority interest is considered a liability.

In relation to transactions between members of the group where part of the equity of one of those members is owned, directly or indirectly, by minority interest, an approach often promulgated is that part of the transaction should be reported upon by the group, since from the minority interest point of view the transaction has in fact occurred. This approach ignores the aim of preparation of the accounts of a group from a group point of view, and confuses this with the right of minority shareholders to see the transaction reflected in financial statements. The transaction would certainly be recorded in the accounts of the subsidiary in which the minority shareholders have an interest; should minority shareholders wish to see the results of a transaction it is to the accounts of that subsidiary that they should look.

The group accounts show transactions between members of the group and outsiders. If a subsidiary is a member of the group, transactions between that member and other members of the group should be eliminated. There is no scope to argue that part of a transaction between two group members should be reported on by the group.

To illustrate the effect of eliminating only part of a transaction between two member companies, consider the following.

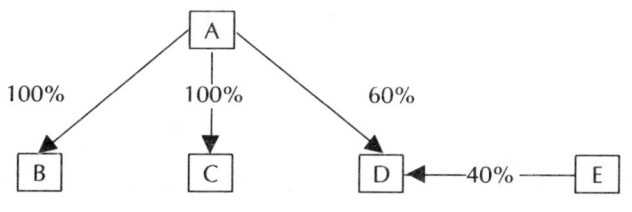

Company A owns 100% of the issued share capital of Companies B and C, and 60% of the issued share capital of Company D. Company E owns the remaining 40% of the issued share capital of Company D.

During the year Company D sold an item of inventory to Company C. This item had cost Company D $100 and it was sold to Company C for $120, resulting in a profit of $20 to Company D.

We need to consider what the group has done. The group has simply moved an item from one member to another; overall the group still owns that item. Under the historical cost concept, the item should be shown at the cost paid by the group for that item, i.e. $100.

The group should not be shown as having made a profit from itself. Were this possible, assets could be sold back and forth within a group simply to generate "profits" — obviously not transactions which should be reported on. Thus the profit of $20 should be eliminated, and the group cost of the inventory item should be reduced by $20, from the $120 cost shown by Company C.

Had we taken the approach that the part of the transaction "involving" the minority interest should be disclosed, 40% of the profit, i.e. $8 would have been considered to be earned by the group, and the "cost" of the item in the group accounts would have been shown as $108. Clearly, the group did not pay $108 to acquire the item — $100 was the amount paid by the group member, Company D, to outsiders. No profit should be reported by the group, since the transaction took place between members of the group, i.e. Company C and Company D. The adoption of the "partial realisation" approach would result in overstatement of both the cost of the item involved and the profit earned by the group.

¶904 Direct and indirect minority interest

Direct minority interests are those shareholdings held in subsidiary companies by shareholders other than the holding companies of those subsidiaries. For example:

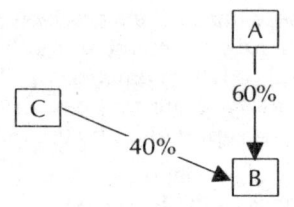

```
                      A
                      |
                     60%
          C           |
           \          ▼
            40% ─────▶ B
```

Here, C is said to be a direct minority shareholder.

MINORITY INTEREST

An *indirect* minority interest arises where a minority shareholder has an interest in a company by way of that shareholder's interest in another company. For example:

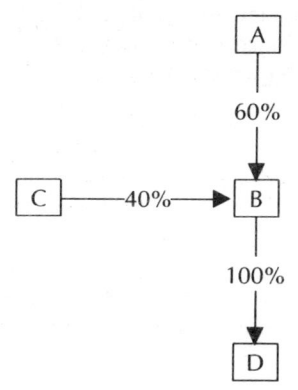

```
            A
            |
           60%
            ↓
   C --40%→ B
            |
           100%
            ↓
            D
```

In the above example, C is said to have an indirect minority interest in D. A detailed discussion of the particular problems posed for consolidation accountants by indirect interests is included in Chapter 19.

¶905 When the minority owns the majority

Under traditional accounting methods, the holding company will usually hold an ownership interest greater than 50% of its subsidiary companies. However, situations can and do occur where a holding company does not own more than 50% of a subsidiary.

Under Australian companies legislation (Companies Code sec. 7(1)), if a company "controls the composition of the board of directors" of another company, that first-mentioned company is said to be the holding company of that other company, which is in turn defined as being a subsidiary of that holding company. The group accounts of the holding company would include the accounts of that subsidiary.

The ownership entitlement of the holding company is not necessarily considered in determining which entities are to be consolidated. It is possible that the holding company may, for example, own only 10% of the issued capital of that subsidiary. Also, the determination of the holding/subsidiary relationship may rely upon "control" aspects.

Current international and U.S. accounting standards require the existence of the holding/subsidiary relationship to be determined by "control". This concept requires consideration to be given to ownership only as a factor which may indicate control. In such situations, the method of determining amounts to be disclosed as relating to minority interest needs to be considered. The two possible alternatives are:

(a) ownership, or
(b) control.

¶905

Notwithstanding that the definition of holding/subsidiary may be based on either ownership or control, separate consideration needs to be given to the question of what we are attempting to achieve in disclosing separately minority interests in the group shareholders' funds. The alternatives are therefore the same as those noted above, i.e. such disclosure should be based on either ownership or control.

Disclosure of minority interest on the basis of ownership would result in the minority interest disclosed being equal to the amount expected to be "realised" by the minority interest on a distribution of the shareholders' funds of the subsidiary from a group point of view.

It must be recognised that consolidated accounts are not prepared for use by minority shareholders, but for the use of shareholders of the group's holding company. To determine the preferred approach to disclosure of the interests of those holding company shareholders, consider the group shown below:

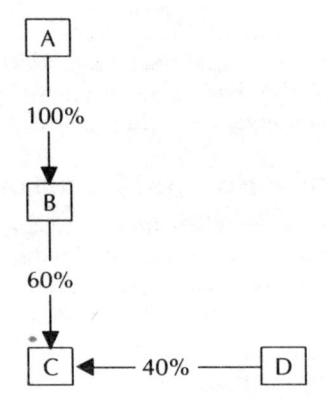

```
         ┌───┐
         │ A │
         └───┘
           │
          100%
           │
           ▼
         ┌───┐
         │ B │
         └───┘
           │
          60%
           │
           ▼
         ┌───┐              ┌───┐
         │ C │◄──── 40% ────│ D │
         └───┘              └───┘
```

If Company C sells an asset to Company B and records a profit of $10, Company C can then pay a dividend of $6 to Company B, which can pass on this dividend to Company A which can in turn pass on the dividend of $6 to its shareholders.

The profit cannot be said to have been earned by the Company's group, comprising Companies A, B and C, as the transaction for the sale of the asset was between two group companies, Company C (seller) and Company B (buyer). From a group point of view the transaction should not be reported upon, and the profit earned by Company C on the transaction would be eliminated in preparing the consolidated accounts of Company A group. In those consolidated accounts, no profit would be shown, and therefore no dividend would be seen as being payable.

Should the group follow the dividend payment option outlined above, resulting in A paying its shareholders a $6 dividend, such a dividend would have to be financed from the reserves existing prior to the transaction. From the group point of view, the "dividend" has been financed by increasing the value of the asset shown in Company B accounts. This of course would

¶905

result in a depletion of the resources of Companies A and B, and is therefore not considered a viable option.

The separate disclosure of shareholders' funds attributable to shareholders of Company A on the ownership basis shows the amounts which those shareholders could expect to receive as dividends should a distribution of assets occur. The minority interest disclosed would therefore also be based on ownership.

Under the control concept, capacity to control, by whatever means, results in the consolidation of the assets and liabilities of a controlled entity. Separate disclosure of shareholders' funds attributable to holding company shareholders and minority shareholders on a control basis would require some subjective decision as to the degree of control held. This would seem to be at odds with the control concept which may be considered to be an absolute concept — a company either controls another or it does not; the notion of control of X% is meaningless.

Therefore it is considered that under the control concept of consolidation, only two alternative methods of disclosing holding company shareholders' and minority shareholders' interest in the group are available:

(a) disclosure based on ownership, i.e. separate disclosure of what is attributable to holding company shareholders and what to minority shareholders; or

(b) no separate disclosure of holding company shareholders'/minority shareholders' share of the consolidated shareholders' funds.

The prime purpose of financial statements is to provide information. Accordingly it is considered that alternative (a), disclosure of minority interest on the basis of ownership, is preferable, under both the ownership and the control concepts of consolidation.

¶906 "Second" journal entry

There are two common methods of preparing the consolidation journal entry to disclose minority interests:

(a) as the last consolidation journal, and

(b) as the "second" consolidation journal.

The first of these alternatives requires all consolidation entries in relation to the elimination of investments and inter-company transactions to be prepared, and then an allocation to be made to minority interest of the proportion owned of the "adjusted" net assets of the relevant subsidiaries. This requires maintenance of details as to the adjustments made notionally to the subsidiary's accounts.

The second of these two methods is preferred. Using this approach, the "first" consolidation entry is the elimination of investments in subsidiary companies (see Chapter 7). The "second" entry is to allocate to minority interests a proportion of the net assets of the subsidiary company in which the minority has an interest.

When the "third" entries are made, i.e. to eliminate intra-group transactions, the effect on the minority interest previously allocated is considered, and if necessary an adjustment is made to the minority interest previously allocated. This approach results in more journal entries being required, but does away with the requirement to track back through journal entries and keep schedules of adjustments notionally affecting particular subsidiaries.

Whenever a consolidation elimination entry is prepared, we can notionally attribute each part of the entry to a company in the group. This recognises that the accounts of a particular company include transactions which will not be reported on by the group in a particular period.

For example, assume that the only transaction within a group during the year was the earning of fee income of $100 by Company B from Company A. Company A is a 100% owned subsidiary of the group's holding company, whilst Company B is a 60% owned subsidiary of the group. The accounts of Company B will show a profit of $100 and the accounts of Company A a loss of $100.

Overall, the group has earned neither a profit nor a loss during the year, because the only transaction was within the group.

If the minority interest is allocated as the second journal entry, i.e. before the adjustment for inter-company transactions, the minority will be shown in the balance sheet as having a 40% interest in the $100 profit earned by Company B. The profit and loss account will show this allocation as a deduction from the total profit of Company B, to leave the balance of Company B's profit in the profit and loss account as relating only to the group holding company's interest. For example:

	$	$
Dr Minority interest (profit and loss account)	40	
Cr Minority interest (balance sheet)		40

The second journal entry results in the allocation to minority interest of a share of all net assets of Company B. The inter-company transaction is eliminated on consolidation using the following journal entry:

	$	$
Dr Operating profit of Company B	100	
Cr Operating loss of Company A		100

This effectively negates the profit reported by Company B and reduces the net assets of Company B. However, we have already allocated part of that "non-profit" to minority interest; this must be reversed, as follows:

	$	$
Dr Minority interest (balance sheet)	40	
Cr Minority interest (profit and loss account)		40

¶906

MINORITY INTEREST

In this simple example the approach suggested appears "long-winded". However, its benefits will be readily apparent as the issues become more complex.

¶907 Acquisition date not relevant to minority

The amount allocated to the minority represents a proportion of the net assets of the subsidiary in which the minority has an interest as at balance date.

The date that the holding company acquired its interest in the subsidiary is not relevant to the minority. The acquisition date is important to the holding company group as it is used to determine pre-acquisition reserves. As far as the minority is concerned, its share of the net assets at balance date includes *all* net assets at that date, irrespective of their source.

¶908 Acquisition of a non-wholly owned subsidiary

In order to illustrate the allocation of minority interest consider the following example:

Example 9.1
Acquisition of Part of a Subsidiary

H Company acquired 80% of the issued shares of S Company on 31.12.X5 at a cost of $500. Net assets of S Company at that date were:

	$
Issued capital	100
Reserves	100
Retained earnings	200
	400

Set out below are abbreviated balance sheets and profit and loss statements for H Company and S Company as at 31 December 19X5.

Accounts as at 31.12.X5	H Co.	S Co.	Debit	Credit	Group
	$	$	$	$	$
Issued capital	100	100			
Reserves	200	100			
Retained earnings	1,200	600			
	1,500	800			
Investment in S Co.	500	—			
Other assets	1,000	800			
	1,500	800			
Operating profit	600	400			
Income tax expense	240	200			
	360	200			
Opening retained earnings	840	400			
Retained earnings	1,200	600			

What consolidation entries are required as at 31.12.X5?

¶908

Suggested Solution to Example 9.1

Elimination entries

		$	$
(a)	Dr Issued capital of S	80	
	Dr Reserves of S	80	
	Dr Opening retained earnings of S	160	
	Cr Investment in S		500
	Dr Goodwill	180	

Elimination of investment by H Company in S Company

		$	$
(b)	Dr Issued capital of S	20	
	Dr Reserves of S	20	
	Dr Minority interest (profit and loss account)	40	
	Dr Opening retained earnings of S	80	
	Cr Minority interest (balance sheet)		160

Allocation of minority interest

Note:

Minority interest in the balance sheet represents:

Net assets of S Co. at balance date	$800
Minority interest proportion — 20%	
Minority interest disclosed in balance sheet (800 × 20%)	$160

Accounts as at 31.12.X5

	H Co.	S Co.	Debit	Credit	Group
	$	$	$	$	$
Issued capital	100	100	ª80 ᵇ20		100
Reserves	200	100	ª80 ᵇ20		200
Retained earnings	1,200	600	280		1,520
Minority interest				ᵇ160	160
	1,500	800	480	160	1,980
Goodwill	—	—	ª180		180
Investment in S Co.	500	—		ª500	
Other assets	1,000	800			1,800
	1,500	800	180	500	1,980
Operating profit	600	400			1,000
Income tax expense	240	200			440
	360	200			560
Minority interest	—	—	ᵇ40		40
Opening retained earnings	840	400	ª160 ᵇ80	—	1,000
Retained earnings	1,200	600	280	—	1,520

¶908

The "proof" of the minority interest should always be prepared to ensure that the minority interest has been correctly allocated. This proof should be prepared immediately following the second journal entry.

Some authorities suggest that minority interest should be allocated a share of pre-acquisition net assets and a share of post-acquisition net assets. This will result in the correct allocation to minority interest; however, it brings to the allocation unnecessary complications. Allocation of minority interest should be done at balance date.

¶909 Minority interest allocation not to be combined with investment elimination

A tendency often observed is to net the "first" (¶702) and "second" (¶906) journal entries at acquisition date, i.e. to eliminate all pre-acquisition shareholders' funds, with part against the investment and part to minority interest. This also brings in unnecessary complications, and requires supporting information to be maintained as to how the allocation has been done, and also a further entry to allocate to minority interest a share of post-acquisition shareholders' funds.

¶910 Disclosure

Balance sheet

Minority interest is allocated a share of net assets of relevant subsidiary companies as at balance date. This entry we refer to as the "second entry".

Profit and loss account

Having prepared the second journal entry, whenever a consolidation entry is prepared which adjusts the profit of a group company, if that group company has a minority shareholder, an adjustment needs to be made to the profit allocated to minority interest in that second journal entry.

10
Dividends

Dividends from profits —— ¶1001
Dividends from other reserves —— ¶1002
All subsidiary dividends to
 be eliminated —— ¶1003
Dividends paid from
 pre-acquisition profits —— ¶1004
Dividends paid from
 post-acquisition profits —— ¶1005
Dividends proposed: pre- and
 post-acquisition —— ¶1006
Dividend proposed by
 subsidiary, not recognised by
 holding company —— ¶1007

¶1001 Dividends from profits

For the purposes of consolidation accounting, four types of dividends need to be considered:

(1) paid pre-acquisition (¶1004);

(2) paid post-acquisition (¶1005);

(3) proposed pre-acquisition (¶1006);

(4) proposed post-acquisition (¶1006).

Dividends are simply distributions of profits. Payment of dividends from retained earnings is shown in the profit and loss account.

¶1002 Dividends from other reserves

Payment of dividends from other reserves is shown only in notes to the accounts disclosing movements in reserves. From a consolidation point of view, the dividend is treated in the same way as it was treated before it was paid, e.g. if a dividend is paid out of pre-acquisition profits, and those pre-acquisition profits were included in the determination of goodwill on consolidation, then the dividend should also be included in the goodwill calculation.

¶1003 All subsidiary dividends to be eliminated

The consolidation treatment of dividends results in the consolidated profit and loss account's showing nothing with respect to dividends paid/proposed by subsidiary companies. All such dividends are eliminated because they are paid from one group member to another, i.e. they are an intra-group transaction.

In order to give full disclosure it is recommended that a note be included in consolidated financial statements to show the amount of dividends paid/proposed by subsidiaries.

The group accounts will show only dividends paid by the group holding company to its shareholders. Subsidiary company dividends are either paid or payable to:

(a) other group companies, or

(b) minority shareholders.

Dividends to other group companies are eliminated against dividends received by those group companies.

Dividends to minority shareholders effectively reduce the minority's interest in the group. A minority shareholder cannot have a dividend in its bank account and also recognise an interest in the profit from which the dividend was paid. The interest in those profits has been realised.

¶1004 Dividends paid from pre-acquisition profits

Consider the effect on the holding company's accounts of dividends paid by a subsidiary company from pre-acquisition profits. Profits earned by subsidiary companies prior to their acquisition by the holding company should not be shown as profits available for distribution by the holding company.

When a holding company makes an investment in a subsidiary company, the holding company effectively "buys" the retained profits as at that date. Should the subsidiary company distribute any of those retained profits, it is a return *of* the investment, rather than a return *on* the investment. The holding company must record the receipt of the dividend from pre-acquisition profits as a reduction of the investment, and not as income. In many cases this will not have been done in the holding company's accounts, and an adjustment will need to be made to those holding company accounts.

For example, where a holding company received a dividend of $100 from pre-acquisition profits of a subsidiary company, this dividend was credited to income by the holding company. The following adjustment was required:

Dr Income	$100
Cr Investment	$100

Any dividend paid by a subsidiary from such profits is regarded by the holding company as a "capital" receipt and is used to write down the purchase price of the shares. Thus the value at which the asset "investment in subsidiaries" will appear in the holding company's books is its cost less any amount subsequently received as a dividend out of pre-acquisition profits or reserves.

Effective goodwill

The receipt of dividends paid from pre-acquisition profits of the subsidiary does not affect the goodwill or surplus on consolidation. The payment of a dividend from pre-acquisition profits is simply the realisation of the profits purchased by the holding company.

Example 10.1

Dividends Paid — Pre-acquisition

H Company acquired 80% of the shares in S Company on 30 June 19X3 at a cost of $750. Set out below are abbreviated balance sheets of H Company and S Company at 30 June 19X4.

Accounts as at 30.6.X4

	H. Co.	S. Co.	Eliminations Debit	Eliminations Credit	Group
	$	$	$	$	$
Issued capital	1,000	500			
Retained earnings	1,000	350			
	2,000	850			
Investment in S Co.	750				
Other assets	1,300	950			
Other liabilities	(500)	(100)			
	2,000	850			
Operating profit after tax	160	100			
Dividend received	40				
	200	100			
Retained earnings 1.7.X3	800	300			
Dividends paid from 19X3 profits		(50)			
Retained earnings 30.6.X4	1,000	350			

Prepare consolidated accounts as at 30 June 19X4.

¶1004

DIVIDENDS

Suggested Solution to Example 10.1
Journal Entries

		$	$
Holding company's books			
(a) Dr Dividends received by H Co.		40	
Cr Investment in S Co.			40

Correction to reflect that the dividend received is a refund of the investment

On consolidation
(b) Dr Issued capital (80% of $500) — 400
    Dr Retained earnings 1.7.X3 (80% of $300) — 240
    Cr Dividends paid — 40
    Cr Investment in S Co. — 710
    Dr Goodwill — 110

Elimination of investment in S Company

(c) Dr Issued capital (20% of $500) — 100
    Dr Retained earnings 1.7.X3 (20% of $300) — 60
    Dr Minority interest (P/L) (20% of $100) — 20
    Cr Dividends paid (P/L) — 10
    Cr Minority interest (B/S) — 170

Allocation of minority interest

Consolidation Worksheet at 30.6.X4

	H. Co.	S. Co.	Eliminations Debit	Eliminations Credit	Group
	$	$	$	$	$
Issued capital	1,000	500	ᵇ400		1,000
			ᶜ100		
Retained earnings	1,000	350	360	50	1,040
Minority interest				ᶜ170	170
	2,000	850	860	220	2,210
Investment in S Co.	750			ᵃ40	
				ᵇ710	
Other assets	1,300	950			2,250
Other liabilities	(50)	(100)			(150)
Goodwill			ᵇ110		110
	2,000	850	110	750	2,210
Operating profit after tax	160	100			260
Dividend received	40		ᵃ40		
Minority interest	—	—	ᶜ20		(20)
	200	100	60		240
Retained earnings 1.7.X3	800	300	ᵇ240		800
			ᶜ60		
Dividends paid from 19X3 profits		(50)		ᶜ10	
				ᵇ40	
Retained earnings 30.6.X4	1,000	350	360	50	1,040

¶1004

An alternative approach is to ignore inter-company dividends when preparing the first and second consolidation entries, then prepare a separate entry to eliminate the inter-company dividend.

A benefit of this approach is that the initial elimination entry does not alter from that of the period prior to payment of the pre-acquisition dividend. However, the dividend elimination will become in itself a "perpetual" entry. Another benefit of this approach is that it makes the adjusting entry required for a pre-acquisition dividend similar to that for a post-acquisition dividend.

Had the alternative approach been adopted, the elimination entry would have been as follows:

		$	$
(a)	Dr Issued capital	400	
	Dr Retained earnings 1.7.X3	240	
	Cr Investment in S Co.		750
	Dr Goodwill	110	
	Elimination of investment in S Company		
(b)	Dr Issued capital	100	
	Dr Retained earnings 1.7.X3	60	
	Dr Minority interest (P/L)	20	
	Cr Minority interest (B/S)		180
	Allocation of minority interest		
(c)	Dr Investment	40	
	Dr Minority interest (B/S)	10	
	Cr Dividend paid (P/L)		50
	Elimination of dividend paid by S Company		

¶1005 Dividends paid from post-acquisition profits

Dividends received or receivable by a holding company from profits earned by subsidiaries subsequent to acquisition and which have been credited to the holding company's profit and loss account should be eliminated against the amount of dividends paid/payable by the subsidiaries.

Such dividends are simply a transfer of funds from one member of the group to another. The usual entry to eliminate dividends which were paid from post-acquisition profits is as follows:

Dr Dividend received — H Co. (P/L)	X	
Dr Minority interest (B/S)	Y	
Cr Dividends paid S Co. (P/L)		X + Y

Elimination of the dividend received by the holding company against the dividend paid by the subsidiary company is simply a reversal of the transaction between two group members.

¶1005

DIVIDENDS

The minority interest adjustment is made because of the approach taken in allocating minority interest (see Chapter 9). In the second consolidation entry, minority interest is allocated a share of issued capital, reserves, retained earnings brought forward and current year profits. The balance sheet will then disclose that the minority has an interest in the group equal to, inter alia, their share of those items.

Now if some or all of current year profits have been paid to the shareholders of the subsidiary, including of course the shareholders referred to as the minority, those minority shareholders will no longer have an interest in those profits. The profits may be said to be held by the minority, having been paid to them, and therefore they no longer have an interest in those profits as far as the group accounts are concerned.

Therefore, after payment of a dividend from post-acquisition profits the "second" journal entry (¶906) needs to be "corrected", by reducing the minority interest in the group shareholders' funds: in the second journal entry the minority interest in the balance sheet was credited with a share of current year profits; the adjustment noted above debits minority interest in the balance sheet to reverse part of that "second" entry.

Example 10.2

Dividends Paid — Post-acquisition

H Company acquired 80% of the shares in S Company on 30 June 19X3 at a cost of $750. Assuming the same information as in ¶1004, Example 10.1, except that dividends are paid out of post-acquisition profits, prepare consolidated accounts as at 30 June 19X4.

Suggested Solution to Example 10.2

Journal Entries

		$	$
(a)	Dr Issued capital (80% of $500)	400	
	Dr Retained earnings 1.7.X3 (80% of $300)	240	
	Cr Investment in S Co.		750
	Dr Goodwill	110	
	Elimination of investment in subsidiary company		
(b)	Dr Issued capital (20% of $500)	100	
	Dr Retained earnings 1.7.X3 (20% of $300)	60	
	Dr Minority interest (P/L) (20% of $100)	20	
	Cr Minority interest (B/S)		180
	Recognition of minority interest		
(c)	Dr Minority interest (B/S)	10	
	Dr Dividends received (by H Co.)	40	
	Cr Dividends paid (by S Co.)		50
	Elimination of dividend paid		

This is the correct method of treatment of any post-acquisition dividends paid, and has the result that the group profit and loss account shows only dividends

¶1005

paid by the holding company, with all dividends paid by subsidiary companies being eliminated.

An alternative promulgated by some accountants is to use in place of journal (c) above the following entry on consolidation:

Dr Dividends received (by H Co.)	40	
Cr Dividends paid (by S Co.)		40

This will leave the group profit and loss account showing a dividend paid to minority shareholders, and as noted above this is not the method followed in current practice.

This method also has the disadvantage of overstating minority shareholders' interest in the group. Group accounts under this method will show minority shareholders in the balance sheet as having a full interest in current year profits when in fact the minority shareholders have realised part of their interest in current year profits by virtue of the payment of the dividend by the subsidiary company.

Consolidation Worksheet at 30.6.X4

	H Co. $	S Co. $	Eliminations Debit $	Eliminations Credit $	Group $
Issued capital	1,000	500	^{a}400 ^{b}100		1,000
Retained earnings	1,000	350	360 ^{c}10	50 ^{b}180	1,040
Minority interest					170
	2,000	850	870	230	2,210
Investment in S Co.	750			^{a}750	
Other assets	1,300	950			2,250
Other liabilities	(50)	(100)			(150)
Goodwill			^{a}110		110
	2,000	850	110	750	2,210
Operating profit after tax	160	100			260
Dividends received	40		^{c}40		
Minority interest	—	—	^{b}20		20
	200	100	60		240
Retained earnings 1.7.X3	800	300	^{a}240 ^{b}60		800
Dividends paid from 19X3 profits		(50)		^{c}50	
Retained earnings 30.6.X4	1,000	350	360	50	1,040

¶1005

DIVIDENDS

¶1006 Dividends proposed: pre- and post-acquisition

The only difference between a dividend paid and a dividend proposed is that a dividend paid reduces an asset (e.g. cash) and a dividend proposed increases a liability (e.g. inter-company amount payable).

The journal entries to eliminate the dividend proposed from the profit and loss account are identical to those for a dividend paid.

An additional entry is required to eliminate the inter-company amounts receivable and payable.

Example 10.3

Dividends proposed — Post-acquisition

H Company acquired 80% of the shares in S Company on 30 June 19X3 at a cost of $750.

Accounts as at 30.6.X4

	H Co.	S Co.	Eliminations Debit	Eliminations Credit	Group
	$	$	$	$	$
Issued capital	1,000	500			
Retained earnings	960	350			
	1,960	850			
Investment in S Co.	750				
Other assets	1,220	1,000			
Other liabilities	(50)	(110)			
Owing to H Co.		(40)			
Receivable from S Co.	40				
	1,960	850			
Operating profit after tax	160	100			
Retained earnings 1.7.X3	800	300			
Dividends proposed from 19X3 profits		(50)			
Retained earnings 30.6.X4	960	350			

You are required to prepare consolidated accounts as at 30 June 19X4.

Suggested Solution to Example 10.3

Journal Entries

		$	$
(a)	Dr Issued capital (80% of $500)	400	
	Dr Retained earnings 1.7.X3 (80% of $300)	240	
	Cr Investments		750
	Dr Goodwill	110	

Elimination of investment in subsidiary company

¶1006

ACCOUNTING FOR BUSINESS CONSOLIDATIONS

(b) Dr Issued capital (20% of $500)   100
     Dr Retained earnings 1.7.X3 (20% of $300)   60
     Dr Minority interest (P/L) (20% of $100)   20
       Cr Minority interest (B/S)   180
     Recognition of minority interest

(c) Dr Dividend receivable — H Co. (P/L)   40
     Dr Minority interest (B/S)   10
       Cr Dividends proposed — S Co. (P/L)   50
     Elimination of dividend proposed by subsidiary

(d) Dr Payable by S Co.   40
       Cr Receivable by H Co.   40
     Elimination of inter-company debt

As can be seen, the only difference between the entries required for a dividend paid and a dividend proposed (if both are post-acquisition) is the debit to dividend receivable rather than to dividends received by the holding company.

The only difference between the two is that one is a cash transaction and the other is a credit transaction.

Consolidation Worksheet at 30.6.X4

	H Co.	S Co.	Eliminations Debit	Eliminations Credit	Group
	$	$	$	$	$
Issued capital	1,000	500	ᵃ400 ᵇ100		1,000
Retained earnings	960	350	360	50	1,000
Minority interest			ᶜ10	ᵇ180	170
	1,960	850	870	230	2,170
Investment in S Co.	750			ᵃ750	
Other assets	1,220	1,000			2,220
Other liabilities	(50)	(110)			(160)
Goodwill			ᵃ110		110
Owing to H Co.		(40)	ᵈ40		
Receivable from S Co.	40			ᵈ40	
	1,960	850	150	790	2,170
Total of eliminations			1,020	1,020	
Operating profit after tax	160	100	ᶜ40		220
Minority interest	—	—	ᵇ20		20
	160	100	60	—	200
Retained earnings 1.7.X3	800	300	ᵃ240 ᵇ60		800
Dividends proposed from 19X3 profits		(50)		ᶜ50	
Retained earnings 30.6.X4	960	350	360	50	1,000

¶1006

¶1007 Dividend proposed by subsidiary, not recognised by holding company

In very rare circumstances a subsidiary company may propose a dividend, and the holding company may not record the dividend receivable. Such a circumstance is probably only encountered in exam questions for accounting students, rather than in practice.

For such an event to occur, the board of directors of the holding company would normally instruct the directors of the subsidiary company to propose a dividend, and then the holding company directors would not account for the dividend receivable at the holding company level. This would obviously require inconsistent behaviour.

Also, the subsidiary company is required by companies legislation (Schedule 7 of the Companies Regulations and Approved Accounting Standard ASRB 1017: Related Party Disclosures) to disclose separately amounts owing to related corporations. The portion of the dividend proposed by the subsidiary company which is to be paid to the holding company will therefore have to be disclosed separately.

An auditor of such a subsidiary would have difficulty in obtaining the usual confirmation of inter-company payables if the holding company had not recorded the dividend receivable.

11

Intra-group inventory movements

Cost of inventory	¶1101
Profit effect	¶1102
Minority interest	¶1103
Subsequent sale outside the group	¶1104
Entry in subsequent year if not sold outside the group	¶1105
Inventory write-downs	¶1106
Intra-group sales at arm's length prices	¶1107

¶1101 Cost of inventory

Inventory should be stated at the cost to the group. Adjustments need to be made on consolidation whenever any inventory included in the accounts of a group company is at a value higher than that cost. This usually occurs when inventory is sold by one group company to another at a profit, and the inventory remains within the group at year end.

Should the inventory be sold outside the group after first being sold within the group, no adjustment needs to be made on consolidation. The overall transaction from the group point of view is the sale by the original holder of the inventory to a party outside the group. This transaction has been recorded in the accounts of two companies in the group, the original holder recording its sale to the intermediate holder (a group member) and that intermediate holder recording its sale to the outside party.

¶1102 Profit effect

If inventory has not yet been sold outside the group, any profit disclosed by a group member which has been earned from a sale within the group should not be reported in the group accounts. The group overall has done nothing but move the ownership of the inventory.

¶1103 Minority interest

When one of the companies involved in a transaction for the sale of inventory within a group has a minority owner, the allocation of minority interest within the group needs to be considered.

Journals required with minority interest in subsidiary

Current texts show three alternative methods of adjusting for the unrealised profit which exists within group companies as a result of inter-company inventory movements:

Example 11.1

Company A owns 75% of Company B.

B sells to A inventory with a total invoice value of $16,000. B's mark up is $33 1/3 \%$. Profit to B is therefore $4,000.

	Alternative 1 Dr(Cr)	Alternative 2 Dr(Cr)	Alternative 3 Dr(Cr)
Subsidiary company profit	4,000	3,000	4,000
Minority interest (P/L)			(1,000)
Inventory	(4,000)	(3,000)	(4,000)
Minority interest (B/S)			1,000

Alternative 1

Eliminate all unrealised profit, and reduce inventory value by the amount of unrealised profit. Thus inventory is stated at cost to the group. This approach asserts that the minority should not have part of their profit eliminated.

Alternative 2

Eliminate only that portion of the unrealised profit which may be said to relate to the holding company. This approach asserts that part of the profit, the minority's share, has been realised and therefore should be recorded as such. Inventory is considered to have increased in value.

Alternative 3

As for Alternative 1, but allocate part of the "profit reversal" to minority interests, on the basis that minority interest is part of the group. Also, as the transaction is between group members, from a group point of view nothing has happened to the value of inventory.

Alternative 3 is the preferred method. Alternative 1 ignores the fact that minority interest is part of the group and that in the second journal entry minority interests have been given a share of all profits of Company B. If we now say that from a group point of view those profits do not exist, it follows that the minority interest cannot be shown as having an interest in those profits. Alternative 2 also shows inventory at a value higher than cost to the group.

Minorities could be involved in three situations:

(1) sale from wholly owned member to member with some minority ownership;
(2) sale from a member with some minority ownership to a wholly owned member;
(3) sale from a member with some minority ownership to another member which has some minority ownership.

For ease of reference, assume Company A is wholly owned, and Companies B and C have some minority ownership, for example:

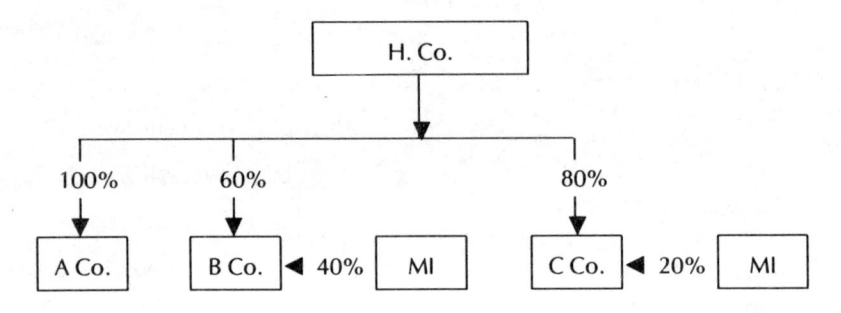

```
                      H. Co.
         ┌──────────────┼──────────────┐
        100%           60%            80%
         ↓              ↓              ↓
       A Co.          B Co. ◄ 40% MI   C Co. ◄ 20% MI
```

Wholly owned subsidiary to a partly owned subsidiary
A sells to B

In this situation the unrealised profit sits in the accounts of Company A and it is this profit which is not to be reported by the group. In our second journal entry to allocate minority, no allocation to the minority was made in respect of Company A's profits, as there is no minority interest in that profit. Therefore there is no requirement to adjust any allocation of profit to minority interest.

40% of the profit reported by Company B will have been allocated to minority interest. Company B will have recorded no profit on purchase of the inventory, and accordingly, none of Company B's profit is considered unrealised from a group point of view; there is no requirement to adjust the amount allocated to minority interest in the second journal entry.

The minority allocation is only of a share of shareholders' funds; hence, the elimination of the over cost portion of the inventory held by Company B has no relevance to the minority interest disclosed.

¶1103

Sale from partly owned subsidiary to wholly owned subsidiary
B sells to A

The second consolidation journal entry allocated to minority interest 40% of the reported profit of Company B. We now recognise that part of Company B's profit is unrealised from a group point of view and needs to be eliminated. As the minority interest has been allocated a share of this "non-profit" we must reverse the amount allocated in respect of the non-profit.

The amount allocated to minority interest was a share of the after tax profit of Company B; accordingly an amount equal to 40% of the after tax unrealised profit should be reversed.

Sale from partly owned subsidiary to partly owned subsidiary
B sells to C

The minority share of Company B's profit needs to be adjusted as for the situation where A sells to B, above.

In our second journal entry, the minority would have been allocated 20% of the reported profit of Company C. As none of Company C's profits are considered to be unrealised, no adjustment should be made to the minority interest already allocated in respect of Company C.

Sale from partly owned subsidiary to holding company

Example 11.2

A subsidiary company has sold inventory to a holding company and made $3,000 profit on the sale. At the end of Year 1, the holding company had all inventory purchased from the subsidiary still on hand.

The holding company owns 80% of the subsidiary. Assume an income tax rate of 39%.

Prepare journal entries at end of Year 1.

Suggested Solution to Example 11.2

At end Year 1

To eliminate unrealised profit in closing inventory:

	$	$
Dr Operating profit (closing inventory)	3,000	
Cr Inventory		3,000
Cr Income tax expense		1,170
Dr Future income tax benefit	1,170	
Dr Minority interest (B/S)	360	
Cr Minority interest (P/L)		360

This will result in the group's showing reduced retained earnings (i.e. group retained earnings will be reduced by $3,000 (operating profit) less $1,170 (income tax expense) less $360 (minority interest)) = $1,470.

The example brings in for the first time the tax consequences of consolidation entries. Let us consider each component of the above journal entry.

¶1103

(1) *Dr Operating profit*

The profit recorded by the subsidiary company on the inter-company transaction was $3,000. From a group point of view this transaction has not occurred, and accordingly the profit is eliminated.

(2) *Cr Inventory*

Inventory must be shown at cost. From a group point of view this is the cost paid to an outside party by a group member, i.e. the cost shown before the inter-company sale. Inventory is shown in the accounts of the holding company at the cost paid by the holding company; therefore an adjustment is required.

(3) *Cr Income tax expense*

Income tax expense is directly related to operating profit. Any adjustment to operating profit will therefore necessitate adjustment to income tax expense. An increase in profit results in an increase in income tax expense, and vice versa.

The exception to this rule is when the adjustment to profit represents a "permanent difference" for income tax purposes, in which case the income tax expense related to that operating profit is $nil. However, the elimination of unrealised profit is a "timing" difference. We must assume that the profit will eventually be realised by the group when the inventory is sold outside the group.

(4) *Dr Future income tax benefit*

The subsidiary company that has recorded the inter-company profit will have to include that profit as income in its income tax return. Income tax returns are prepared on an individual entity basis and the group point of view has no relevance to those returns. The subsidiary will therefore pay tax on the profit at the time of the inter-company sale.

From a group point of view, that tax payment by the subsidiary relates to profit not yet recognised by the group, and therefore a timing difference exists. This timing difference is disclosed as a future income tax benefit.

(5) *Dr Minority interest (B/S)*

(6) *Cr Minority interest (P/L)*

In the second journal entry the minority would have been allocated a share of all recorded current year after tax profits of the subsidiary company. Because part of those profits, the portion unrealised from a group point of view, has now been eliminated from the group accounts, the minority cannot be shown as having an interest in that part.

Accordingly, the allocation of a share of those profits to the minority interest in the second journal entry is reversed.

Note that, had the inventory profit been made by the holding company, minority interest allocation would not be affected and parts (5) and (6) of the above elimination entry would not be required.

¶1104 Subsequent sale outside the group

When the inventory referred to in ¶1103 Example 11.2 above is finally sold outside the group by the holding company, the holding company will recover profit equal to the difference between the amount paid by the holding company to the subsidiary company and the outside sale proceeds.

However, from a group point of view the profit on sale outside the group is the difference between the original cost to the group and the proceeds of the outside sale. Therefore, the profit made by the subsidiary, previously considered unrealised from a group point of view, has now been realised.

Let us consider Example 11.2, and assume that in Year 2 the inventory is sold outside the group.

At end Year 2

To eliminate unrealised profit in *opening inventory*:

	$	$
Cr Operating profit		3,000
Dr Income tax expense	1,170	
Dr Minority interest (P/L)	360	
Dr Retained earnings brought forward	1,470	

Each component of the journal entry can be explained as follows:

(1) *Cr Operating profit*

To record in the group accounts the profit previously considered unrealised.

(2) *Dr Income tax expense*

The income tax expense related to (1) above at 39%.

(3) *Dr Minority interest (profit and loss)*

Whenever operating profit is adjusted in respect of a subsidiary which has a minority shareholder, the minority interest in the current year's profit must be adjusted.

(4) *Retained earnings brought forward*

The individual accounts of the subsidiary company disclosed in Year 1 the inter-company profit. The accounts of the subsidiary company for Year 2 will disclose those profits, net of income tax expense, as part of retained earnings brought forward. On consolidation at the end of Year 1 these profits were eliminated from the group accounts. As these profits are now on the retained earnings brought forward line of the subsidiary company accounts, the prior year's profit adjustment at consolidation level must be repeated. This will make retained earnings brought forward in Year 2 the same as closing retained earnings at the end of Year 1. Also on consolidation in Year 1 the minority share of those profits was adjusted in the profit and loss account.

Note that each component of this journal entry is a profit and loss account item. There is no requirement to adjust balance sheet accounts.

Inventory in the group accounts will be correct, as the inventory in question has been sold outside the group and will therefore not be shown in either individual accounts of any member of the group or the group accounts.

¶1104

The future income tax benefit raised in Year 1 no longer exists at the end of Year 2 and it is not included in the accounts of the individual group companies which form the basis of Year 2. Therefore it will not be shown on the consolidation worksheet and will not require to be eliminated.

What is the objective of dealing with ultimate realisation of unrealised profit?

Profit that was recognised in Year 1 in the subsidiary company accounts is, from a group point of view, to be recognised in Year 2. As the individual subsidiary company's accounts for Year 2 show the Year 1 profit as part of retained earnings brought forward, we must transfer that profit from retained earnings brought forward to current year profit.

¶1105   Entry in subsequent year if not sold outside the group

Consider the situation where a partly owned subsidiary sells inventory to its holding company during Year 1, and at the end of Year 2 the inventory is still held by the holding company. Using the information from Example 11.2 in ¶1103, what elimination entry is required at the end of Year 2?

(1) As the inventory is still on hand, it will need to be adjusted to reduce its cost as shown in the holding company's accounts to cost to the group.

(2) The unrealised profit will need to be eliminated. This unrealised profit from Year 1 now sits in retained earnings brought forward. The journal entry to eliminate the unrealised profit will therefore be against retained earnings brought forward.

(3) Minority interest will have been allocated a share of the unrealised profit in the second journal entry as this will need to be revised.

(4) A timing difference still exists between recognition of profit for tax purposes (i.e. Year 1 in the subsidiary company's tax return) and for group accounts purposes — the profit is still unrealised from a group point of view.

The journal entry required is as follows:

	$	$
Dr Retained earnings brought forward	1,470	
Cr Inventory		3,000
Dr Future income tax benefit	1,170	
Dr Minority interest (B/S)	360	

The components of the entry to retained earnings brought forward are taken from the journal entry at the end of Year 1 as shown in Example 11.2 in ¶1103.

	$
Operating profit	3,000
Income tax expense	(1,170)
Minority interest (P/L)	(360)
	1,470

¶1105

INTRA-GROUP INVENTORY MOVEMENTS

Note that there is no requirement at the end of Year 2 to adjust the minority's share of current year profit, as all current year profit of the subsidiary has been realised.

An adjustment has been made to the minority's share ($360) of retained earnings brought forward.

Example 11.3

Combination of Adjustments to Opening and Closing Inventory

Company A owns 80% of Company B.
Company B sells stock to Company A at a mark up of 25%.
At 31 December 19X2 A Company had on hand $50,000 of stock purchased from B Company, and at 31 December 19X3 it had on hand stock purchased from B which had a cost to B of $20,000.
Prepare elimination journal entries at 31 December 19X3 to account for inter-company stock. Assume an income tax rate of 39%.

Suggested Solution to Example 11.3

Journal Entries

Opening stock (31.12.X2)

	$	$
Dr Retained earnings brought forward	4,880	
Cr Operating profit before tax		10,000
Dr Income tax expense ($10,000 × 39%)	3,900	
Dr Minority interest (P/L) (($10,000 − $3,900) × 20%)	1,220	

(Assume that minority interest (B/S) has already been given a share of B's retained earnings brought forward and current year profit in the "second" journal entry)

Note:
Stock on hand at 31 December 19X2

(a) Amount of unrealised profit—

	$
Book value in hands of purchaser	50,000
Profit mark up 25%	
Therefore the cost before mark up ($50,000 ÷ 125% × 100)	40,000
Profit ($50,000 − $40,000)	10,000

(b) Adjustment to retained earnings brought forward—

At the end of 19X2, an adjustment would have been made on consolidation to eliminate the unrealised profit in inventory on hand at that time.

The profit and loss account components of that adjustment would have been as follows:

	$
1. Eliminate unrealised profit	10,000
2. Tax effect at 39%	(3,900)
3. Amount allocated to minority interest now reversed (20% of after tax unrealised profit)	(1,220)
	4,880

¶1105

When the accounts of Company B are entered on to the 19X3 consolidation worksheet, the after tax, after minority unrealised profit of $4,880 will be shown as part of the "retained earnings brought forward" of Company B. As this amount had been eliminated from the 19X2 group accounts, and therefore was not included in 19X2 group closing retained earnings, it cannot be included in 19X3 group opening retained earnings.

Closing stock (31.12.X3)

	$	$
Dr Operating profit before tax	5,000	
Cr Income tax expense ($5,000 × 39%)		1,950
Cr Stock		5,000
Dr Future income tax benefit	1,950	
Dr Minority interest (B/S) (20% × ($5,000 − $1,950))	610	
Cr Minority interest (P/L)		610

Note:
Stock on hand at 31 December 19X2

Amount of unrealised profit—

	$
Cost to B	20,000
Mark up 25%	
Profit	5,000

¶1106 Inventory write-downs

What is required when the inventory purchased by one group member from another is written down to:
- an amount equal to or above cost to the group?
- an amount less than cost to the group?

Equal to or above cost

If inventory is sold to a wholly owned subsidiary which then values the inventory at a net realisable value equal to or above the cost to the group, what has happened from a group point of view?

Overall inventory has been increased in value, then decreased. Both of these transactions should effectively be reversed; the write-down was only necessary to correct an overvaluation.

Can a "net" adjustment be made? It is considered that a proper determination of contributions to group profit necessitates a reversal of each transaction. This is especially necessary when one of the group members involved has a minority ownership. The proper allocation of profit to the minority can only be made if the true "group profit" of each separate subsidiary is known. The making of net journal entries would severely complicate the allocation of minority interest.

Below cost

The write-down below cost should be kept in the company in which the inventory resides. It is that company which made the decision to write down the inventory; accordingly when considering contributions by each group member to total group profits the write-down should affect the contribution by the company making the write-down.

¶1107 Intra-group sales at arm's length prices

A question often arises as to whether profit made on an inter-company sale at an arm's length price can be considered, on consolidation, to have been realised.

This argument is often put forward where one company in the group is a manufacturer and another company a distributor. Proponents of this approach argue that had the distributor bought the asset from an outsider, it would have had to pay the same price as it paid to the related company, and therefore the assets should not be said to be overvalued. This argument is also often put forward by construction and development companies, in situations where a subsidiary which is a developer seeks tenders for construction work, and a related party submits an arm's length tender and wins the work.

However, this argument does not consider what has happened from a group point of view. The only transaction carried out during the year between the group and an outside partner was the manufacture of the inventory, through the purchase of raw materials and the payment of labour.

Had the manufacturing company not sold the inventory to the related party, it would not have considered revaluation of the inventory to market selling price. Such an action would be in contravention of the principles of historical cost accounting, and in direct non-compliance with Australian Accounting Standard AAS 2, "Measurement and Presentation of Inventories in the Context of the Historical Cost System" which specifies that inventory must be valued at the lower of cost and net realisable value.

To argue on the basis of what would have been the situation if the inventory had been purchased by the distribution company from an outsider is inappropriate. Financial statements are prepared on the basis of what has happened, not what might have happened.

From a group point of view the asset must be shown at cost to the group, which is also cost to the manufacturer, and to the construction company, in the examples noted in this chapter.

12

Intra-group fixed asset movements

Fixed asset movements	¶1201
Sale of fixed assets — holding company to subsidiary company	¶1202
Sale from subsidiary company to holding company	¶1203
Sale from subsidiary company to another subsidiary company	¶1204
Summary	¶1205

¶1201 Fixed asset movements

Fixed asset movements within a group may give rise to unrealised profits or losses on sale in the same manner as for inventory sales. In addition, ongoing depreciation charges need to be considered.

The accounting treatment to eliminate unrealised profit on the sale of fixed assets is similar to the adjustment necessary for unrealised profits on the sale of inventory, i.e. where a related company makes a profit on the transaction this is eliminated by crediting the asset account and debiting the operating profit.

However, there is a difference in the manner in which the unrealised profit on a fixed asset sale is eventually realised. Rather than by sale to an outsider, the depreciable amount (assuming this to be the cost) of an asset is allocated over time by depreciation charges. The group member acquiring the fixed asset from another group member will base its depreciation charge

INTRA-GROUP FIXED ASSET MOVEMENTS

on the actual purchase price it pays to that other group member. However, there may be an unrealised profit (or loss) as far as the group is concerned. Thus the amortisation of the actual purchase price will result in larger (or smaller) depreciation charges for the purchaser — and therefore for the group — than would have been made by the original owner of the fixed asset. There are three aspects to be considered;

(1) cost of asset;
(2) profit effect;
(3) depreciation charge.

Cost of asset

The cost of the asset shown in the group accounts should remain at the original cost to the group.

Profit effect

As with inventories, the whole of any unrealised profit on the sale of fixed assets should be eliminated. If the profit is earned by a non-wholly owned subsidiary, a portion of the unrealised profit will "relate" to minority shareholders and accordingly an adjustment to minority interest will be required. This is necessary because the second consolidation entry allocated to minority interests a share of the profit which we now know to be unrealised from a group point of view.

If the sale is from the holding company, again as for inventories no minority interest adjustment is required.

Depreciation charge

The only depreciation charge which should be made in the consolidated accounts is to allocate the cost to the group of an asset over its estimated useful life. If a different value is being depreciated, consolidation adjustment is required.

The total amount to be depreciated in respect of an asset is its "depreciable amount", i.e. the difference between cost and expected realisable value. In this discussion it will be assumed that the whole cost of the asset is depreciable, i.e. that there will be no proceeds from sale of the asset at the end of its useful life.

As with unrealised profit, if the asset is owned by the holding company no minority interest adjustment is required.

If the asset is owned by a partly owned subsidiary company, the excess depreciation charged will have to be eliminated, and the allocation to minority interest also adjusted.

¶1201

In the second (minority interest) consolidation entry, the minority interest is given a share of the current year profits of the subsidiary. The current year profit of the subsidiary has been reduced by the "excess" depreciation charged. On consolidation that extra charge to profit is eliminated, and the profit of the subsidiary company in the group accounts is higher than that in the subsidiary's own accounts. The minority shareholders must be allocated a portion of that increased profit, for the same reason as minority interest shareholders bear part of the reduced profit on adjustment for unrealised profit on sale by a partly owned subsidiary. The converse applies if depreciation charged is decreased as a result of the inter-company sale.

Depreciation charges continue for the life of the asset; an adjustment for depreciation is required each year for over-depreciation or under-depreciation in prior years. This adjustment will be against opening retained earnings. The amount to be adjusted against opening retained earnings will be the net profit and loss effect of all previous depreciation adjustment entries, i.e. net of income tax expense and any minority interest allocation.

Having discussed the concept of consolidation adjustments required when fixed assets are moved from one group entity to another, we can now consider the application of these concepts in practice.

The relationship between the entities involved affects the adjustments required. Such effects are illustrated in the following examples of inter-entity sales involving various relationships.

¶1202 Sale of fixed assets — holding company to subsidiary company

A sale from a holding company to a subsidiary company is the first example to consider.

Example 12.1

Sale of Fixed Assets — Holding Company to Subsidiary Company

H Company acquired 80% of the shares in S Company on 30 June 19X3 at a cost of $750, at which time S Company had retained earnings of $100.

On 1 July 19X5 H Company sold a fixed asset to S Company for $550. This asset had cost H Company $600. H Company's accounts as at 30 June 19X6 show a profit on sale of fixed assets with respect to sales to S Company of $130. Both companies use 10% straight-line depreciation for this asset.

Assume an income tax rate of 46%.

INTRA-GROUP FIXED ASSET MOVEMENTS

19X6 Accounts

	H Co.	S Co.	Debit	Credit	Group
	$	$	$	$	$
Issued capital	1,000	500			
Retained earnings	1,000	400			
	2,000	900			
Investments in S Co.	750				
Other assets	1,300	505			
Other liabilities	(50)	(100)			
Fixed assets—					
Cost	—	550			
Provision for depreciation	—	(55)			
	2,000	900			
Profit on sale of fixed assets	130	—			
Operating profit	170	150			
Income tax expense	(100)	(50)			
	200	100			
Retained earnings 1.7.X5	800	300			
Retained earnings 30.6.X6	1,000	400			

19X7 Accounts

	H Co.	S Co.	Debit	Credit	Group
	$	$	$	$	$
Issued capital	1,000	500			
Retained earnings	1,000	345			
	2,000	845			
Investment in S Co.	750				
Other assets	1,300	530.3			
Other liabilities	(50)	(125.3)			
Fixed assets—					
Cost		550			
Provision for depreciation		(110)			
	2,000	845			
Operating profit	—	(55)			
Income tax expense	—	—			
		(55)			
Retained earnings 1.7.X6	1,000	400			
Retained earnings 30.6.X7	1,000	345			

Prepare consolidated accounts as at 30 June 19X6 and as at 30 June 19X7 (assuming no 19X7 transactions apart from depreciation).

¶1202

Suggested Solution to Example 12.1

As with any consolidation problem the facts must first be determined:

(1) At 1.7.X5 before the sale to S Company, H Company had an asset with

	$
— Cost	600
— Provision for depreciation	180
Written down value	420

(2) This asset is now shown in the accounts of S Company with

— Cost	550
— Provision for depreciation	55
Written down value	495

(3) The depreciation by S Company of the asset at 10% on a straight-line basis assumes that as at 1.7.X5 the asset has 10 years' useful life remaining. Thus the total useful life of the asset is now considered to be 13 years, i.e.:

Cost to H Company	$600
Depreciation charge @ 10% p.a.	$60
Total provision for depreciation at time of sale	$180
Therefore number of years held by H ($180 ÷ $60)	3 years
Remaining life assessed by S Company	10 years
	13 years

(4) The estimated useful life of the asset has changed. In H's accounts the asset had a further useful life of 7 years at 1.7.X5, i.e. 6 years at 30.6.X6. Now in S's accounts that asset has a remaining useful life of 9 years as from 30.6.X6.

The group cost of the asset is $600 and this is what must be depreciated over the estimated useful life. Following reassessment of the useful life as at 1.7.X5, the asset had a remaining useful life of 10 years for its written down value of $420. The group therefore requires an annual depreciation charge of $42.

(An alternative situation might be that the group has *not* reassessed the useful life, and both Company S and the group have charged incorrect depreciation. This would necessitate an adjustment to the accounts of Company S, and an adjustment to the depreciation charged in the group accounts.)

¶1202

INTRA-GROUP FIXED ASSET MOVEMENTS

Journal Entries Required at 30.6.X6

		$	$
(a)	Dr Issued capital	400	
	Dr Retained earnings brought forward	80	
	Dr Goodwill	270	
	Cr Investment		750

Elimination of investment in S Co.

		$	$
(b)	Dr Issued capital	100	
	Dr Retained earnings brought forward	60	
	Dr Minority interest, (P/L)	20	
	Cr Minority interest (B/S)		180

Allocation of minority interest in S Co.

		$	$
(c)	Dr Profit on sale of fixed assets	130	
	Dr Fixed assets (cost)	50	
	Cr Provision for depreciation		180
	Dr Future income tax benefit	59.8	
	Cr Income tax expense		59.8

Elimination of profit on sale of fixed assets as shown in books of H Co.
Note: No minority interest adjustment is required here as the profit was earned by the holding company.

		$	$
(d)	Dr Provision for depreciation	13	
	Cr Operating profit (depreciation expense)		13
	Dr Income tax expense	5.98	
	Cr Future income tax benefit		5.98

To adjust depreciation charge so that this charge is based on cost to the group of the asset concerned.

		$	$
(e)	Dr Minority interest (P/L)	1.404	
	Cr Minority interest (B/S)		1.404

Minority adjustment for depreciation charge — 20% of after-tax effect of journal entry (d) above.

¶1202

19X6 Accounts

	H Co. $	S Co. $	Debit $	Credit $	Group $
Issued capital	1,000	500	ª400 ᵇ100		1,000
Retained earnings	1,000	400	297.384	72.8	1,175.416
Minority interest				ᵇ180 ᵉ1.404	181.404
	2,000	900	797.384	254.204	2,356.82
Investment in S Co.	750			ª750	—
Other assets	1,300	505	ᶜ59.8	ᵈ5.98	1,858.82
Other liabilities	(50)	(100)			(150)
Goodwill			ª270		270
Fixed assets— Cost		550	ᶜ50		600
Provision for depreciation		(55)	ᵈ13	ᶜ180	(222)
	2,000	900	392.8	935.98	2,356.82
Total of eliminations			1,190.184	1,190.184	
Profit on sale of fixed assets	130	—	ᶜ130		—
Operating profit	170	150		ᵈ13	333
Income tax expense	(100)	(50)	ᵈ5.98	ᶜ59.8	(96.18)
	200	100	135.98	72.8	236.82
Minority interest	—	—	ᵇ20 ᵉ1.404		21.404
	200	100	157.384	72.8	215.416
Retained earnings 1.7.X5	800	300	ª80 ᵇ60		960
Retained earnings 30.6.X6	1,000	400	297.384	72.8	1,175.416

¶1202

INTRA-GROUP FIXED ASSET MOVEMENTS

Journal Entries Required at 30.6.X7

		$	$
(a)	As for 19X6 journal entry (a)		
(b)	Dr Issued capital	100	
	Dr Retained earnings brought forward	80	
	Cr Minority interest (P/L)		11
	Cr Minority interest (B/S)		169

Minority share of S Co. at 30.6.X7

(c) Dr Retained earnings brought forward 70.2
    Dr Fixed assets — cost 50
      Cr Fixed assets —
        provision for depreciation   180
    Dr Future income tax benefit 59.8

Prior year's adjustment to remove the
    unrealised profit on sale of fixed assets

Note: Retained earnings brought forward
    = prior year P/L components of 19X6 entry (c)
    = Dr Profit on sale   130.0
        Cr Income tax expense   (59.8)
                                         70.2

(d) Dr Provision for depreciation 13
    Cr Retained earnings brought forward   5.616
    Cr Future income tax benefit   5.98
    Cr Minority interest (B/S)   1.404

Prior year's adjustment for group depreciation
    (ongoing effect of 19X6 entries (d) and (e))

Note: Retained earnings brought forward
    = prior year entry components of entries
      (d) and (e)
    = Cr Operating profit   13
      Dr Income tax expense   (5.98)
      Dr Minority interest (P/L)   (1.404)
                                   5.616

(e) Dr Provision for depreciation 13
    Cr Operating profit—
        Depreciation expense   13
    Dr Income tax expense 5.98
      Cr Future income tax benefit   5.98
    Dr Minority interest (P/L) 1.404
      Cr Minority interest (B/S)   1.404

Adjustment for 19X7 depreciation

Note: When operating profit is adjusted, income tax expense is to be adjusted, and if the profit being adjusted is in a minority owned subsidiary, minority share of profit needs to be adjusted.

¶1202

19X7 Accounts

	H Co.	S Co.	Debit	Credit	Group
	$	$	$	$	$
Issued capital	1,000	500	ª400 ᵇ100		1,000
Retained earnings	1,000	345	237.584	29.616	1,137.032
Minority interest				ᵇ169 ᵈ1.404 ᵉ1.404	171.808
	2,000	845	737.584	201.424	2,308.84
Investment in S Co.	750			ª750	—
Other assets	1,300	530.3	ᶜ59.8	ᵈ5.98 ᵉ5.98	1,878.14
Other liabilities	(50)	(125.3)			(175.3)
Goodwill			ª270		270
Fixed assets—					
Cost		550	ᶜ50		600
Provision for depn		(110)	ᵈ13 ᵉ13	ᶜ180	(264)
	2,000	845	405.8	941.96	2,308.84
Total of eliminations			1,143.384	1,143.384	
Operating profit	—	(55)		ᵉ13	(42)
Income tax expense	—	—	ᵉ5.98		5.98
	—	(55)	5.98	13	(47.98)
Minority interest	—	—	ᵉ1.404	ᵇ11	9.596
	—	(55)	7.384	24	(38.384)
Retained earnings 1.7.X6	1,000	400	ª80 ᵇ80 ᶜ70.2	ᵈ5.616	1,175.416
Retained earnings 30.6.X7	1,000	345	237.584	29.616	1,137.032

¶1202

INTRA-GROUP FIXED ASSET MOVEMENTS

¶1203 Sale from subsidiary company to holding company

Where fixed assets are sold from a subsidiary company to a holding company, the basic components of the journal entries required are as for a sale from a holding company to a subsidiary company.

However, the minority interest in the transaction will differ. When fixed assets are sold by a partly owned subsidiary company, a minority interest adjustment will be required in respect of the unrealised profit because the unrealised profit will be in the accounts of the subsidiary company. As discussed previously (¶1201), the minority interest is allocated a share of profit of the subsidiary, and any adjustment to that profit requires adjustment to the allocation.

Also, no minority interest adjustment will be required in respect of depreciation charges, as the asset is now owned by the holding company and depreciation charges affect the holding company's profit. The minority has no interest in the profit of the holding company.

¶1204 Sale from subsidiary company to another subsidiary company

Where a partly owned subsidiary sells fixed assets to another partly owned subsidiary, minority interest adjustments will be required in respect of both the unrealised profit on sale and any difference in depreciation charges. An adjustment to minority previously allocated will be required in respect of:

(a) unrealised profit — in proportion to the minority's interest in the seller;

(b) depreciation — in proportion to the minority's interest in the current owner.

Consider the following example:

Example 12.2

Sale of Fixed Assets Between Two Partly Owned Subsidiary Companies

H Company owns interests in the following subsidiary companies:

	A Co.	B Co.
Percentage ownership	80%	75%
Cost of investment	$450	$700
Net assets at acquisition date (30.6.X1)	$	$
Issued capital	100	200
Retained earnings	400	600
	500	800

On 30.6.X5 A Company sold a truck to B Company for a consideration of $100. This truck was shown in the accounts of A Company immediately prior to the sale as follows:

¶1204

	$
Cost	200
Provision for depreciation	120
Net book value	80

Both A Company and B Company depreciate trucks at 20% p.a. and the income tax rate is 50%.

Set out below are abbreviated profit and loss statements and balance sheets for H Co., A Co. and B Co. as at 31 December 19X5.

Accounts as at 31.12.X5

	H Co. $	A Co. $	B Co. $	Debit $	Credit $	Group $
Issued capital	500	100	200			
Reserves	1,000	—	700			
Retained earnings	500	700	700			
	2,000	800	1,600			
Truck	—	—	95			
Investment in subsidiaries	1,150	—	—			
Other assets	850	800	1,505			
	2,000	800	1,600			
Operating profit	400	500	600			
Income tax expense	200	200	100			
	200	300	500			
Retained earnings brought forward	300	400	200			
Retained earnings	500	700	700			

Prepare consolidation journals and worksheets as at 31.12.X5.

Solution to Example 12.2

Journal entries

	$	$
(1) Dr Issued capital — A Co. (80% of $100)	80	
Dr Retained earnings brought forward — A Co. (80% of $400)	320	
Cr Investment in A Co.		450
Dr Goodwill	50	

Elimination of investment by H Co. in A Co.

¶1204

INTRA-GROUP FIXED ASSET MOVEMENTS

(2) Dr Issued capital — B Co. (75% of $200) 150
    Dr Retained earnings brought forward (75% of $600) 450
        Cr Investment in B Co. 700
    Dr Goodwill 100

Elimination of investment by H Co. in B Co.

(3) Dr Issued capital — A Co. (20% of $100) 20
    Dr Retained earnings brought forward — A Co. (20% of $400) 80
    Dr Minority interest (P/L) (20% of $300) 60
        Cr Minority interest (B/S) 160

Allocation of minority interest in A Co.

(4) Dr Issued capital — B Co. (25% of $200) 50
    Dr Reserves — B Co. (25% of $700) 175
    Dr Retained earnings brought forward — B Co. (25% of $200) 50
    Dr Minority interest (P/L) (25% of $500) 125
        Cr Minority interest (B/S) 400

Allocation of minority interest in B Co.

(5) Dr Operating profit — A Co. 20
        Cr Truck — at cost — B Co. 20
    Dr Future income tax benefit 10
        Cr Income tax expense — A Co. 10
    Dr Minority interest (B/S) (20% of $20 − $10) 2
        Cr Minority interest (P/L) 2

Elimination of inter-company profit on sale of truck

(6) Dr Operating profit — B Co. 5
        Cr Provision for depreciation — B Co. 5
    Dr Future income tax benefit 2.5
        Cr Income tax expense — B Co. 2.5
    Dr Minority interest (B/S) (25% of $5 − $2.50) 0.625
        Cr Minority interest (P/L) 0.625

Additional depreciation charge

The additional depreciation charge is necessary, as for the 6 months to 31 December 19X5 B Co. charged only $5 depreciation (cost $100 × 10% for 6 months).

Had A Co. still held the asset, A Co., and therefore the group, would have charged $10 depreciation (cost $200 × 10% for 6 months).

¶1204

ACCOUNTING FOR BUSINESS CONSOLIDATIONS

Consolidation Worksheet
Accounts as at 31.12.X5

	H Co.	A Co.	B Co.	Debit	Credit	Group
	$	$	$	$	$	$
Issued capital	500	100	200	^{1}80		500
				^{2}150		
				^{3}20		
				^{4}50		
Reserves	1,000	—	700	^{4}175		1,525
Retained earnings	500	700	700	1,110	15.125	805.125
Minority interest				^{5}2	^{3}160	
				^{6}0.625	^{4}400	557.375
	2,000	800	1,600	1,587.625	575.125	3,387.5
Truck	—	—	95		^{5}20	70
					^{6}5	
Investment in subsidiaries	1,150	—	—		^{1}450	—
					^{2}700	
Goodwill	—	—	—	^{1}50		150
				^{2}100		
Other assets	850	800	1,505	^{5}10		3,167.5
				^{6}2.5		
	2,000	800	1,600	162.5	1,175	3,387.5
Total of eliminations				1,750.125	1,750.125	
Operating profit	400	500	600	^{5}20		1,475
				^{6}5		
Income tax expense	200	200	100		^{5}10	487.5
					^{6}2.5	
	200	300	500	25	12.5	987.5
Minority interest	—	—	—	^{3}60	^{5}2	182.375
				^{4}125	^{6}0.625	
	200	300	500	210	15.125	805.125
Retained earnings brought forward	300	400	200	^{1}320		—
				^{2}450		
				^{3}80		
				^{4}50		
Retained earnings	500	700	700	1,110	15.125	805.125

¶1204

¶1205 Summary

When fixed assets are sold within the group, the following procedures must be carried out:

(1) Adjust the asset cost to be the original group cost.

(2) Remove the unrealised profit on the asset sale.

(3) Adjust the depreciation charge to that which would have been charged had the asset not been transferred within the group, having regard to any reassessment of useful life.

(4) Consider minority interests — if the profit on sale or the depreciation charge of a company with a minority is being adjusted, minority interests therein also need to be adjusted.

13

Equity accounting prior to consolidation

Equity accounting procedures ―― ¶1301

¶1301 Equity accounting procedures

Equity accounting involves including in the group profits a share of the investee company's profits. Current Australian accounting standards direct that equity accounting entries be recorded on consolidation and not in the books of the investor company.

Should the investee subsequently become a subsidiary, certain profits of that subsidiary which would normally be capitalised as pre-acquisition (i.e. which would form part of that which is being acquired) have already been included in the group profits. These equity accounted profits must be subtracted from retained earnings at the date control is acquired in order to determine the amount of assets acquired, and the amount of profits eliminated as pre-acquisition.

Equity accounting prior to control has the effect of including items in group profit which would normally be included in goodwill or premium on consolidation.

Example 13.1
Equity Accounting Prior to Consolidation

H Company had an investment in S Company acquired on 30 June 19X5 at a cost of $200. This investment entitled H Company to 40% of the shares in S Company. The balance sheet of S Company at that date disclosed the following:

	$
Issued capital	100
Retained earnings	120
	220

¶1301

EQUITY ACCOUNTING PRIOR TO CONSOLIDATION

H Company equity accounted for this investment.

On 30 June 19X7 certain fixed assets owned by S Company were revalued by $100.

On 30 June 19X8 H Company acquired a further 20% interest in S Company through the purchase of existing shares at a cost of $120.

Accounts as at 30.6.X8

	H Co.	S Co.	Debit	Credit	Group
	$	$	$	$	$
Issued capital	1,000	100			
Retained earnings	1,000	400			
Asset revaluation reserve		100			
General reserve		100			
	2,000	700			
Investment in S Co.	320				
Other assets	1,730	800			
Other liabilities	(50)	(100)			
	2,000	700			
Operating profit after tax	200	100			
Retained earnings 1.7.X7	800	300			
Retained earnings 30.6.X8	1,000	400			

Prepare consolidation journal entries and consolidation worksheet as at 30 June 19X8.

Suggested Solution to Example 13.1

Journal Entries at 30.6.X8

		Note	$	$
(a)	Dr Issued capital	(i)	60	
	Dr Asset revaluation reserve	(ii)	20	
	Dr General reserve	(iii)	20	
	Dr Retained earnings brought forward	(iv)	108	
	Dr Operating profit after tax	(v)	20	
	Cr Investment	(vi)		320
	Dr Goodwill	(vii)	92	

Elimination of investment in subsidiary

Notes: (i) H Company now owns 60% of the issued capital of S Company of $100.

(ii) H Company will have taken into its group accounts 40% of the asset revaluation reserve in the year in which the revaluation was

¶1301

made. By acquiring control, the group has acquired a 60% interest in that reserve. However, part of that reserve has already been recognised as a group reserve, being a reserve "earned" by an associated company. The amount to be eliminated is therefore 60% of $100 less 40% of $100, i.e. $20. This is the amount now owned that had not previously been recorded in the group accounts.

(iii) As for asset revaluation reserve ((ii) above).

(iv) Of $300 of retained earnings brought forward, 40% of any amount earned since the date of acquisition of the 40% interest will have been taken into group profits. Therefore, the amount acquired on attainment of control will be (60% × $300) less (40% of ($300 less $120)).

(v) Control was established on the last day of the year. The operating profit for the year must be equity accounted as H Company held a 40% interest in those profits. Thus (60% of $100 less 40% of $100) must be eliminated on consolidation, i.e. $20, and 40% of $100, i.e. $40, must be equity accounted.

(vi) Note that as control was attained as at 30 June 19X3, this is the date on which the total cost of the investment is to be eliminated.

(vii) Had we used the possible (but considered incorrect) alternative of consolidation whereby goodwill was determined from two separate investments, the amount of goodwill as at 30 June 19X8 would have been identical with that determined where an investee was equity accounted prior to consolidation. This can be a useful check on the elimination entry.

		$	$
(b)	Dr Issued capital	40	
	Dr Asset revaluation reserve	40	
	Dr General reserve	40	
	Dr Retained earnings brought forward	120	
	Dr Minority interest (P/L)	40	
	Cr Minority interest (B/S)		280
	Recognition of minority interest		
(c)	Dr Operating profit after tax	40	
	Cr Interest in profit of associated company		40

To equity account the 19X8 profit of S Company

Note:

As $40 of asset revaluation reserve, $40 of general reserve, $72 of retained earnings brought forward and $40 of current year profits have already been equity accounted and included in the group accounts, these items are not acquired on attainment of control.

Had H company not equity accounted for its 40% interest in S Company, the goodwill on consolidation would have been:

¶1301

EQUITY ACCOUNTING PRIOR TO CONSOLIDATION

		$
Net tangible assets of S Company at date control acquired (i.e 30.6.X8)		700
Percentage interest acquired 60%		
Interest in net assets acquired		420
Cost of investment		320
Discount on acquisition with no prior equity accounting		100
Compare this with:		
Goodwill after equity accounting (journal (a) above)		92
Difference		192
This difference is made up of items treated as post-acquisition under equity accounting:		
Asset revaluation reserve		40
General reserve		40
Operating profit after tax		40
Retained earnings brought forward		72
		192

i.e. 40% of the movement in each reserve account from the date equity accounting commenced to the date control was acquired.

Consolidation Worksheet at 30.6.X8

	H Co.	S Co.	Debit	Credit	Total
	$	$	$	$	$
Issued capital	1,000	100	ᵃ60		
			ᵇ40		1,000
Retained earnings	1,000	400	328	40	1,112
Asset revaluation reserve		100	ᵃ20		
			ᵇ40		40
General reserve		100	ᵃ20		
			ᵇ40		40
Minority interest				ᵇ280	280
	2,000	700	548	320	2,472
Investment in S Co.	320			ᵃ320	—
Other assets	1,730	800			2,530
Other liabilities	(50)	(100)			(150)
Goodwill			ᵃ92		92
	2,000	700	92	320	2,472
Operating profit after tax	200	100	ᵃ20 ᶜ40		240
Interest in profit of associated company				ᶜ40	40
Minority interest			ᵇ40		(40)
	200	100			240
Retained earnings 1.7.X7	800	300	ᵃ108 ᵇ120		872
Retained earnings 30.6.X8	1,000	400	328	40	1,112

¶1301

14

Piecemeal or creeping acquisition

General ¶1401
Purchase of further shares from
 minority shareholders ¶1402

¶1401 General

Where a holding company acquires control of another company through a number of share purchases, this is said to be a creeping acquisition or a piecemeal acquisition.

This gives rise to a consolidation problem in the determination of what is to be included as pre-acquisition retained earnings. It is suggested by some that there are two acceptable methods of accounting for such acquisitions. These can be examined by considering the following example.

Example 14.1

Assume the following abbreviated balance sheet in respect of a subsidiary company, S Company.

	1.7.X1 $	31.12.X1 $
Shareholders' funds		
Issued capital	200	200
Retained earnings	600	800
	800	1,000
Percentage ownership acquired	50%	25%
Cost of percentage ownership acquired	450	240

¶1401

PIECEMEAL OR CREEPING ACQUISITION

Further, assume that ownership in excess of 50% is required for a subsidiary relationship to exist.

The two alternatives are as follows:

(A) Treat each investment separately, and eliminate each investment against the net assets acquired on each date, i.e. eliminate the cost of the 50% investment against net assets at 1.7.X1, and the cost of the 25% investment against net assets at 31.12.X1.

(B) Treat all investments prior to the subsidiary relationship together, and eliminate the total investment cost against the net assets of the subsidiary at the time it becomes a member of the group, i.e. eliminate the cost of the 75% investment against net assets at 31/12/X1.

By eliminating the 50% investment against net assets at 1.7.X1, alternative (A) assumes that 50% of all profits, etc. earned by S Company prior to that date are pre-acquisition, and that 50% of all profits earned after 1.7.X1 are post-acquisition, and therefore to be included in group profits.

However, S Company was not a member of the group until control was established, i.e. at 31.12.X1; profits earned by S Company prior to 31.12.X1 cannot be said to be earned by a group company.

Also, should the group have a year end between 30.6.X1 and 31.12.X1, say on 30.9.X1, the group profit reported at that date would not have included any profit earned by S Company (unless dividends were paid by S Company). If then, at 31.12.X1, 50% of the profits earned by S Company since 1.7.X1 are considered to be group profits, the group accounts at 30.9.X1 would have been "incorrect", and a correction would be made to opening retained earnings as at 1.10.X1. This is not an acceptable practice.

Therefore alternative (A) is not considered an acceptable approach, and should not be used.

The effect of the two approaches is illustrated as follows, using the information above:

	(Ai) $	Alternative A Dr (Cr) (Aii) $	(Ai) + (Aii) $	Alternative B Dr (Cr) (B) $
Dr Issued capital	100	50	150	150
Dr Retained earnings	300	200	500	600
Cr Investment	(450)	(240)	(690)	(690)
Dr Goodwill (discount)	50	(10)	40	(60)
	Nil	Nil	Nil	Nil

Alternative A:

A(i) is elimination of the cost of the 50% investment against 50% of the net assets at 1.7.X1.

A(ii) is elimination of the cost of the 25% investment against 25% of the net assets at 30.12.X1.

Therefore the net difference on consolidation is goodwill of $40.

¶1401

Alternative B:

B shows the elimination of the total cost of the 75% investment against 75% of the net assets at 31.12.X1, and results in a discount on acquisition of $60, a difference of $100 from that produced by alternative A.

This $100 results from the different amounts determined as pre-acquisition profits under the two approaches. Alternative A treats 50% of profits from 30.6.X1 to 31.12.X1 as post-acquisition, whereas alternative B treats all such profits as pre-acquisition.

	$
Retained earnings 31.12.X1	800
Retained earnings 30.6.X1	600
Profit between the two dates	200
Percentage treated by alternative A as post-acquisition 50%	
Profit treated by alternative A as post-acquisition	100

As can be seen from the above example, the effect on the group accounts of the alternative methods of treatment can be significant.

Alternative (B) is the only acceptable approach. Control is not achieved until more than 50% ownership is attained, and any profits earned by a subsidiary prior to that date should be considered to be pre-acquisition profits.

Equity accounting prior to acquisition

Should H Company account for its 50% investment in S Company using the equity method of accounting, 50% of the profits of S Company from the date of acquisition of that 50% investment would have been shown by the group as equity profits. Accordingly, use of alternative A would result in the application of the correct accounting treatment in that situation.

¶1402   Purchase of further shares from minority shareholders

When further shares are purchased from minority shareholders, a similar question arises as to what could be considered "pre" the latest acquisition.

What is acquired in a purchase of additional existing shares (for example, 10% of total issued capital of the subsidiary) is 10% of the share capital and reserves of the subsidiary company as at the date of the 10% investment.

The journal entry required to eliminate this latest investment will be similar to that which would be used for the initial investment, i.e. eliminate the cost of the 10% investment against 10% of shareholders' funds of the subsidiary company as at the date of the 10% investment.

¶1402

# PIECEMEAL OR CREEPING ACQUISITION 121

The overall effect is that the investment in the subsidiary must be related to the two acquisition dates for the purpose of calculating the total difference on consolidation, i.e. goodwill or discount.

An example will now be considered which covers both piecemeal acquisition to attain control, and the purchase of further existing shares.

Example 14.2

Piecemeal acquisition and purchase of further existing shares

H Company acquired shares in S Company at various times. The dates of acquisition and the share capital and reserves of S Company at those dates were as follows:

	31.12.X5 $	31.12.X7 $	31.12.X9 $
Issued capital	200	200	200
General reserve	200	200	400
Asset revaluation reserve	—	—	300
Retained earnings	100	200	300
	500	600	1,200
Interest acquired	30%	30%	30%
Cost of investment	100	150	400

The profit and loss account of S Company for the year ended 31.12.X9 was as follows:

	$
Operating profit after tax	50
Retained earnings 31.12.X8	250
Retained earnings 31.12.X9	300

Prepare journal entries necessary on consolidation with respect to the investment by H Company in S Company at each of the above dates. Assume that H Company *does not* follow the principles of equity accounting.

Suggested solution to Example 14.2

Journal Entries

31.12.X5 — No entries required on consolidation with respect to the investment by H Company in S Company

		$	$
31/12/X7	— Dr Issued capital (60% × $200)	120	
	Dr General reserve (60% × $200)	120	
	Dr Retained earnings	120	
	Cr Investment ($100 @ 31.12.X5 + $150 @ 31.12.X7)		250
	Cr Discount on acquisition		110

Elimination of investments in S Company made on 31.12.X5 and 31.12.X7

(The information given does not enable proper allocation of the journal entry to components of retained earnings.)

¶1402

ACCOUNTING FOR BUSINESS CONSOLIDATIONS

<u>31.12.X9</u> — 1. Entry as for 31.12.X7 is to be repeated, with Dr of $120 being against retained earnings brought forward rather than retained earnings

	$	$
2. Dr Issued capital (30% × $200)	60	
Dr General reserve (30% × $400)	120	
Dr Asset revaluation reserve (30% × $300)	90	
Dr Retained earnings brought forward (30% × $250)	75	
Dr Operating profit after tax (30% × $50)	15	
Dr Goodwill	40	
Cr Investment		400

Elimination of investment in S Company made on 31.12.X9

Analysis of retained earnings at 31/12/X9

Pre-acquisition re investments to 31.12.X7 (60% × $200)	120
Pre-acquisition re investment at 31.12.X9 (30% × $300)	90
Group share of retained earnings from 31.12.X7 to 31.12.X9 (60%)	60
Minority interest at 31.12.X9 (10% of $300)	30
Retained earnings 31.12.X9	300

¶1402

15

Sale of shares

Effect of sale of shares	¶1501
Components of journal entry re sale of shares	¶1502
Sale of all of wholly owned subsidiary	¶1503
Sale of all of partly owned subsidiary	¶1504
Part sale of partly owned subsidiary, still a subsidiary	¶1505
Part sale of partly owned subsidiary, no longer a subsidiary	¶1506
Subsequent equity accounting	¶1507

¶1501 Effect of sale of shares

Consideration needs to be given to a sale by a group of companies of shares which were issued by a member of the group.

A sale of shares will lead to a reduced shareholding, resulting in either:

(i) the investee company no longer being a subsidiary, with:
   (a) the holding company having no investment in the former subsidiary, or
   (b) the holding company retaining an investment in the former subsidiary;

¶1501

(ii) the investee company remaining a subsidiary but with the holding company holding a reduced percentage of the issued capital (with the issued capital formerly owned by, or attributable to, the group's holding company shareholders now owned by minority shareholders).

The effect of a sale transaction is to (i) decrease equity held by holding company shareholders, i.e. investment in subsidiary, and (ii) reduce the difference between the cost of shares in the subsidiary and the equity in net assets acquired (goodwill or discount on acquisition).

¶1502 Components of journal entry re sale of shares

The journal entry required to account for a sale or part sale of a subsidiary involves the following components:

(1) Dr Profit on sale in books of holding company

(profit on sale by holding company is irrelevant to group).

(2) Cr Profit on sale

(group profit on sale, calculated as the difference between consideration received and net assets of subsidiary disposed of at date of disposal).

(3) Dr Profit on sale

(value of initial goodwill, which was paid and has now been realised as a loss).

(4) Cr Retained earnings brought forward

(holding company share of post-acquisition profits of subsidiary, i.e. earned between date of purchase and date of previous consolidation. These earnings will have previously been included in the group accounts).

(5) Cr Operating profit

(holding company share of operating profit of subsidiary from date of previous consolidation to date of disposal, to recognise that during this period the group owned the subsidiary, and is entitled to report its profits).

(6) Dr Income tax expense

(group share of income tax expense on operating profit in (5) above).

(7) Cr either Profit on sale *or* Reserve account

(any post-acquisition asset revaluation reserve will not have been through the group profit and loss account; this reserve may be realised, in whole or in part, by the group on the sale of the subsidiary. To the extent that profit has been realised over the pre-revaluation amount, this profit should be either retained in the asset revaluation reserve or transferred to another reserve account).

SALE OF SHARES 125

(Entries (2), (3) and possibly (7) should be combined in one entry, but with sufficient supporting notation.)

¶1503   Sale of all of wholly owned subsidiary

When a wholly owned subsidiary is sold, it is necessary to ascertain the goodwill at the time of sale and the retained earnings since the original acquisition. This will give the information necessary for journal entry components (3) and (4) in ¶1502.

Example 15.1

Sale of All of Wholly Owned Subsidiary

Assume that Company A's 100% investment in B cost $600, and at the date this investment was acquired (during 19X6) B's share capital and reserves were as follows:

	$
Issued capital	300
Share premium reserve	20
Asset revaluation reserve	180
Retained earnings	(50)
	450

On 29 June 19X9 A sold all of its shares in B for $875, at which date B's share capital and reserves were as follows:

	$
Issued capital	300
Share premium reserve	20
Asset revaluation reserve	200
Retained earnings	300
	820

Profit after tax and extraordinary items for the year ended 29 June 19X9 was $85. Land owned by B was revalued in 19X8.

Company A's accounts show an extraordinary item of $275 profit on sale of its investment in Company B.

Prepare journal entry on consolidation with respect to the sale of shares in B.

Suggested Solution to Example 15.1

Journal Entry

	Note	Dr $	Cr $
Dr P/L — extraordinary item	1	275	
*Dr P/L — extraordinary item (re goodwill)	3	150	
Cr P/L — extraordinary item (net of tax)	5 & 6		85
*Cr P/L extraordinary item	2		55
Cr Retained earnings brought forward	4		265
*Cr P/L (or asset revaluation reserve)	7		20
		425	425

* These may be shown as one entry with details of calculations shown in the notation to the entry.

¶1503

Notes

The components of the above entry represent the various items listed in ¶1502, and are set out below.

1. Company A would have recorded a profit on sale as:
Cost of investment	600
Consideration received	875
	275

2. | | |
   |---|---:|
   | Consideration received | 875 |
   | Net assets at time of disposal | 820 |
   | | 55 |

3. Balance of goodwill at sale date is equal to initial goodwill less amortisation to date. Assuming no amortisation
Cost of investment	600
Net assets at acquisition date	450
Goodwill	150

4. | | | |
   |---|---:|---:|
   | Retained earnings at acquisition date | | (50) |
   | Retained earnings at sale date | 300 | |
   | *Less:* Profit earned during sale year | 85 | 215 |
   | | | 265 |

5. &
6. Profit earned during year of sale (the example does not give sufficient information to allocate this to operating profit before tax and income tax expense)

7. Post-acquisition asset revaluation reserve   20

¶1504   Sale of all of partly owned subsidiary

When a partly owned subsidiary is sold it is necessary to ascertain the goodwill at the time of sale and to determine the minority interests. In the following example the situation prior to the sale will be considered as a means of checking the journal entries used to record the sale.

Note also that in a sale of all of an investment the former subsidiary company will no longer be on the consolidation worksheet.

Example 15.2

Sale of All of Partly Owned Subsidiary

Assume that Company A purchased 80% of the issued capital of Company B at a cost of $700 on 30 June 19X1, at which time Company B's share capital and reserves were:

	$
Issued capital	100
Reserves	100
Retained earnings	600
	800

SALE OF SHARES

On 30 June 19X5 Company A sold all of its shares in Company B for $900.

Set out below are abbreviated balance sheets and profit and loss statements of Company A and Company B for the years ended 30 June 19X4 and 30 June 19X5.

Details as at 30.6.X4

	A Co. $	B Co. $	Debit $	Credit $	Group $
Issued capital	100	100			
Reserves	—	200			
Retained earnings	40	800			
	140	1,100			
Investment	700				
Other assets	(560)	1,100			
	140	1,100			
Operating profit	—	200			
Income tax expense	—	100			
	—	100			
Retained earnings brought forward	40	700			
Retained earnings	40	800			

Details as at 30.6.X5

	A Co. $	B Co. $	Debit $	Credit $	Group $
Issued capital	100	100			
Reserves	—	200			
Retained earnings	100	1,000			
	200	1,300			
Investment	—	—			
Other assets	200	1,300			
	200	1,300			
Operating profit	100	400			
Income tax expense	40	200			
	60	200			
Retained earnings brought forward	40	800			
Retained earnings	100	1,000			

Prepare consolidation worksheets as at 30 June 19X4 and as at 30 June 19X5.

¶1504

Solution to Example 15.2

Consolidation Entries as at 30.6.X4

		$	$
(a)	Dr Issued capital of B Co. (80% of $100)	80	
	Dr Reserves of B Co. (80% of $100)	80	
	Dr Retained earnings brought forward of B Co. (80% of $600)	480	
	Cr Investment in B Co.		700
	Dr Goodwill	60	
	Elimination of investment in B Co.		
(b)	Dr Issued capital of B Co. (20% of $100)	20	
	Dr Reserves of B Co. (20% of $200)	40	
	Dr Minority interest (P/L) (20% of $100)	20	
	Dr Retained earnings brought forward of B Co. (20% of $700)	140	
	Cr Minority interest brought forward		220
	Allocation of minority interest		

Worksheet as at 30.6.X4

	A Co.	B Co.	Debit	Credit	Group
	$	$	$	$	$
Issued capital	100	100	ª80 ᵇ20		100
Reserves	—	200	ª80 ᵇ40		80
Retained earnings	40	800	640	—	200
Minority interest				ᵇ220	220
	140	1,100	860	220	600
Investment	700			ª700	—
Goodwill			ª60		60
Other assets	(560)	1,100			540
	140	1,100	60	700	600
Operating profit	—	200			200
Income tax expense	—	100			100
	—	100			100
Minority interest			ᵇ20		20
	—	100	20		80
Retained earnings brought forward	40	700	ª480 ᵇ140		120
Retained earnings	40	800	640		200

¶1504

SALE OF SHARES

Consolidation Entries as at 30.6.X5

		$	$
(a)	Dr Operating profit (A Co.)	200	
(b)	Dr Profit on sale	140	
(c)	Dr Profit on sale	60	
(d)	Cr Retained earnings brought forward		160
(e)	Cr Operating profit		400
(f)	Dr Income tax expense	200	
(g)	Cr Profit on sale		80
(h)	Dr Minority interest (P/L)	40	
		640	640

Recognition of profit on sale of B Company

(a) Profit on sale in books of A Co.

		$
Investment cost		700
Consideration received		900
		200

(b) Group profit (loss) on sale

Net assets of subsidiary at date of disposal $1,300, A Co. share 80%	1040
Consideration received	900
Loss on sale	(140)

(c) Initial goodwill

Net assets at date of acquisition $800, amount acquired 80%	640
Cost of investment	700
Goodwill paid, now "written off"	60

(d)
Retained earnings at 30.6.X4	800
Retained earnings at acquisition date	600
	200
A Co. share 80%	160

(e) Current year profit — 400

(f) Current year income tax expense — 200

(g)
General reserve at date of acquisition	100
General reserve at date of sale	200
	100
A Co. share 80%	80

(h)
Current year after tax profit	200
Minority interest share 20%	40

¶1504

Note:

(1) Company B figures are not aggregated with those of Company A on the consolidation worksheet, as Company B is not a subsidiary at year end.

(2) Minority interests are entitled to a share of group profits during the year, and accordingly are shown as such in the profit and loss account even though there is no minority interest at year end. This disclosure is necessary to enable the group operating profit to be shown as including Company B's profit for the year on the "operating profit" line.

The alternative approach, showing only 80% of Company B's profit and no minority interest, is not acceptable, as it does not show the full result of the group's operations during the year.

(3) Retained earnings brought forward at 1 July 19X4 is equal to closing retained earnings at 30 June 19X4, as shown on the consolidation worksheet above.

(4) This example assumes no goodwill amortisation. If goodwill had been amortised, group retained earnings brought forward would be lower, and the loss on goodwill (entry (c)) would be lower by the same amount.

Worksheet as at 30.6.X5

	A Co. $	B Co. $	Debit $	Credit $	Group $
Issued capital	100	100			100
Reserves	—	200			
Retained earnings	100	1,000	640	640	100
	200	1,300	640	640	200
Investment	—	—			
Other assets	200	1,300			200
	200	1,300			200
Operating profit	100	400	ª200	ᵉ400	300
Income tax expense	40	200	ᶠ200		240
	60	200	400	400	
Extraordinary item			ᵇ140	ᵍ80	60
			ᶜ60		120
	60	200	600	480	(60)
Minority interest			ʰ40		(40)
	60	200	640	480	(100)
Retained earnings brought forward	40	800		ᵈ160	200
Retained earnings	100	1,000	640	640	100

Note: As B Company is not a subsidiary of A Company at 30 June 19X5, the B Company accounts are not added to A Company's accounts.

¶1505 Part sale of partly owned subsidiary, still a subsidiary

A sale which results in the subsidiary company's remaining a subsidiary is similar to the situations shown in Example 15.1 (¶1503) and Example 15.2 (¶1504). However, certain additional elements must be considered.

¶1505

SALE OF SHARES

Examine what has happened from a group point of view. The group remains in control of the subsidiary, and therefore all assets and liabilities stay within the group.

Consider the shareholders' funds of the subsidiary. The ownership of certain of these has moved from the holding company to "others". These "others" are disclosed as minority interests. Effectively, the group accounts will show a profit or loss on sale of the holding company shareholders' portion of the subsidiary, and an increase in the share of the subsidiary's shareholders' funds allocated to minority interests.

Example 15.3

Part Sale of Partly Owned Subsidiary, Still a Subsidiary

Consider the following example where H Company's shareholding in S Company is reduced from 80% to 70%.

H Company purchased shares in S Company when net assets of S Company were $1,000. Cost of this 80% was $900.

H Company sold 10% of S Company when net assets of S Company had increased to $1,500, including an asset revaluation reserve of $100 created post-acquisition.

Consideration received on the sale was $200.

Current year profit after tax of S Company is $100. (The sale took place at the end of the year.)

Set out below are abbreviated balance sheets and profit and loss statements of H Company and S Company immediately following H Company's initial investment in S Company.

Immediately Following Initial Investment

	H Co.	S Co.	Debit	Credit	Total
	$	$	$	$	$
Issued capital	100	100			
Asset revaluation reserve					
Retained earnings		900			
	100	1,000			
Investment in S Co.	900	—			
Other assets	—	1,000			
Liabilities	(800)	—			
	100	1,000			
Operating profit after tax	—	—			
Minority interest	—	—			
Retained earnings brought forward	—	900			
Retained earnings	—	900			

Prepare consolidation journal entries and consolidation worksheet as at the date of the investment by H Company in S Company and as at the date of sale of shares in S Company.

¶1505

Suggested Solution to Example 15.3

Journal Entries

1. *Initial elimination entry*

		$	$
(a)	Dr Issued capital (80% of $100)	80	
	Dr Retained earnings brought forward (80% of $900)	720	
	Cr Investment in S Co.		900
	Dr Goodwill	100	

2. *At time of sale*

In H Company's books the sale will have been recorded as follows:

Dr Bank	200	
Cr Investment in S Co. (⅛ of $900)		112.5
Cr Profit on sale (extraordinary item)		87.5

Therefore consolidation entries will be:

(a)	Dr Issued capital (70% of $100)	70	
	Dr Retained earnings brought forward (70% of $900)	630	
	Cr Investment in S Co. ($900 less $112.5)		787.5
	Dr Goodwill	87.5	

Elimination of investment

(b)	Dr Issued capital (30% of $100)	30	
	Dr Asset revaluation reserve (30% of $100)	30	
	Dr Retained earnings brought forward (30% of $1,200)	360	
	Dr Minority interest (P/L)	30	
	Cr Minority interest (B/S)		450

Recognition of minority interest

(c)	1. Dr Extraordinary item	87.5	
	2. Cr Extraordinary item		47.5
	3. Cr Retained earnings brought forward		30
	4. Cr Minority interest (P/L)		10

Recognition of profit on sale of shares in S Company

The components of journal (c)2. are as follows:

[*Note:* Rather than individual components (1), (4), (5) and (7) indicated in ¶1502, the journal entry needed may show only the credit of $47.5 to "extraordinary item", details of which will be shown in the notation to the journal entry.]

¶1505

SALE OF SHARES

		$
1.	Extraordinary item in books of H:	
	Cost of shares (80%)	900
	Amount sold (1/8 of 80%) = 1/8 × $900	112.5
	Consideration received	200.0
	Profit on sale	87.5

This is not relevant to the group, therefore it should be eliminated.

			$
2.	(a)	Group profit on sale is determined as follows:	
		Net tangible assets of S Co. at sale time	1,500
		10% of S Co. is sold	
		Net tangible assets of S Co. sold	150
		Consideration received	200
		Profit on sale	50

(b) The asset revaluation reserve created in the subsidiary (post-acquisition) was a recognition of an unrealised profit. 10% of this amount is now realised:

Reserve at acquisition — 30 June 19X1	100
Reserve at date of disposal — 30 June 19X5	200
Increase in reserve post-acquisition	100
Disposed — 10%	10

(c) Disposal of goodwill:
At the date of sale 1/8 of the initial goodwill is realised as a loss:

Initial goodwill	100.0
New goodwill [200 − (1/8 × 900)]	87.5
This is a debit to P/L extraordinary item	12.5

This gives a net profit on sale of $47.5 (i.e. $50 + $10 − $12.5).

3. To balance opening retained earnings: we have already taken as profit into retained earnings brought forward 80% of post-acquisition profits of S Company, i.e. 80% of $1,500-$1,000-$100 (asset revaluation reserve) − $100 current profit = $300. Now in the new elimination entry, we have so far shown only 70% of those earnings, by virtue of having allocated 30% to minority interest in journal (b). The amount allocated to minority interest in the balance sheet by journal (b) is correct; the minority shareholders *are* now entitled to 30% of the net assets of S Company. However, we also know that $300 of post-acquisition retained earnings of S Company had previously been included in the group accounts. The net result of journal entries (b) and (c) has been to show only $270 of those retained earnings. 10% has been allocated to minority interest, and eliminated from the "retained earnings brought forward" line in the profit and loss account. We therefore must adjust opening retained earnings by 10% of $300 = $30.

¶1505

4. The journal entry to recognise minority interest has given minority interest 30% of current year profits when in fact, during the period in which those profits were earned, minority interest had only a 20% interest therein. The share given to minority interest therefore must be adjusted.

As a check of the group profit on sale:

		$	$
(a)	Previously recognised by the group:		
	10% of $1,000 net tangible assets acquired	100	
	10% of $1,500 net tangible assets sold	150	
		50	
	Less: Post-acquisition asset revaluation reserve realised (10% of 100)	10	40
(b)	Amount realised on sale:		
	Paid	112.5	
	Received	200.0	87.5
	Profit on sale		47.5

Immediately Following Initial Investment

	H Co.	S Co.	Debit	Credit	Total
	$	$	$	$	$
Issued capital	100	100	ᵃ20		100
			ᵇ80		
Retained earnings		900	900	—	—
Minority interest				ᵇ200	200
	100	1,000	1,000	200	300
Investment in S Co.	900			ᵃ900	—
Goodwill			ᵃ100		100
Other assets	—	1,000			1,000
Liabilities	(800)	—			(800)
	100	1,000	100	900	300
Retained earnings			ᵃ180		
brought forward	—	900	ᵇ720	—	—
Retained earnings	—	900	900	—	—

¶1505

SALE OF SHARES

	At Date of Sale				
	H Co.	S Co.	Debit	Credit	Total
	$	$	$	$	$
Issued capital	100	100	ᵃ70		100
			ᵇ30		
Asset revaluation reserve		100	ᵇ30		70
Retained earnings	87.5	1,300	1,107.5	87.5	367.5
Minority interest				ᵇ450	450
	187.5	1,500	1,237.5	537.5	987.5
Investment in S Co.	787.5			ᵃ787.5	—
Goodwill			ᵃ87.5		87.5
Other assets	—	1,500			1,500
Liabilities	(600)	—			(600)
	187.5	1,500	87.5	787.5	987.5
Operating profit after tax		100			100
Extraordinary item	87.5	—	ᶜ87.5	ᶜ47.5	47.5
	87.5	100	87.5	47.5	147.5
Minority interest			ᵇ30	ᶜ10	20
	87.5	100	117.5	57.5	127.5
Retained earnings brought forward	—	1,200	ᵃ630	ᶜ30	240
			ᵇ360		
Retained earnings	87.5	1,300	1,107.5	87.5	367.5

continued over ...

¶1505

At End of Year Prior to Year of Sale

If we prepare a consolidated balance sheet and profit and loss account as at the end of the year immediately prior to the year of sale, we can prove that the retained earnings as at the beginning of the year of sale, as shown as brought forward in the "date of sale" profit and loss account, is correct.

	H Co.	S Co.	Debit	Credit	Total
	$	$	$	$	$
Issued capital	100	100	ª80		100
			ᵇ20		
Asset revaluation reserve		100	ᵇ20		80
Retained earnings		1,200	960		240
Minority interest				ᵇ280	280
	100	1,400	1,080	280	700
Investment in S Co.	900			ª900	—
Goodwill			ª100		100
Other assets	(800)	1,400			600
	100	1,400	100	900	700
Operating profit after tax	—	—			—
Extraordinary item	—	—			—
Minority interest	—	—			—
	—	—			—
Retained earnings brought forward	—	1,200	ª720 ᵇ240		240
Retained earnings	—	1,200	960	—	240

Journal entry a. Elimination of investment.
Journal entry b. Recognition of minority interest.

¶1506 Part sale of partly owned subsidiary, no longer a subsidiary

The following example demonstrates the entries involved for the part sale of a subsidiary that was only partly owned and that at the end of the year is no longer a subsidiary.

SALE OF SHARES

Example 15.4

General Automotive Products Limited (H Company) is a manufacturer of cars in Australia. On 31 March 19X7, H Company acquired a 60% interest in Auto Components Limited (S Company), the major manufacturer of car components in Australia, and also the major supplier to H Company. H Company's balance date for preparing annual accounts is 30 June.

The acquisition of H Company by S Company caused some concern within the car industry, and following pressure from the industry, H Company reduced its holding in S Company to 49% on 30 September 19X7. H Company was not aware at the time of preparing and finalising its accounts for the year ended 30 June 19X7 that it would dispose of part of its interest in S Company.

The shareholders' equity of S Company as at 31 March and 30 September 19X7 was as follows:

	31/3/X7	30/9/X7
	$000	$000
Share capital	750	750
Asset revaluation reserve	1,500	1,500
Retained profits	3,150	3,023
Shareholders' equity	5,400	5,273

The net assets of S Company as at the above dates were stated at fair values.

The interest in S Company sold by H Company on 30 September 19X7 was sold for a consideration of $979,500.

The balance sheets and profit and loss accounts of H Company and S Company as at 30 June 19X7 and 30 June 19X8 are shown on the following pages.

The following additional information is provided:

(a) The dividends provided for by H Company and S Company in both the year ended 30 June 19X7 and the year ended 30 June 19X8 have been provided on a proportional basis out of the profits earned during the year the dividend is proposed. H Company accounted for its share of the dividends proposed by S Company as at 30 June 19X7 by crediting the amount to operating profit.

(b) The extraordinary item recorded in the profit and loss account of H Company for the year ended 30 June 19X8 relates to the sale of the interest by H Company in S Company.

(c) Assume an average tax rate of 50%.

(d) H Company adopts the following accounting policies in preparing its group accounts:

- Group accounts are prepared as consolidated accounts.

- Goodwill arising on the acquisition of S Company is written off over a 20-year period commencing from the day after the date of acquisition.

- Consistent accounting policies are applied throughout the group.

¶1506

Balance Sheets as at 30.6.X7

	H Co. $000	S Co. $000	Dr $000	Cr $000	Group $000
TOTAL SHAREHOLDERS' EQUITY					
Share capital	1,500	750			
Reserves — asset revaluation reserve	3,000	1,500			
Retained profits	6,930	2,580			
Shareholders' equity attributable to members of the holding company	11,430	4,830			
CURRENT ASSETS					
Cash	750	420			
Receivables	5,400	3,840			
Inventories	10,920	5,690			
Other	1,770	220			
TOTAL CURRENT ASSETS	18,840	10,170			
NON-CURRENT ASSETS					
Investments — shares in S Co.	3,720	—			
— loans to S Co.	1,500	—			
Property, plant and equipment	6,700	4,690			
TOTAL NON-CURRENT ASSETS	11,920	4,690			
TOTAL ASSETS	30,760	14,860			
CURRENT LIABILITIES					
Creditors and borrowings	7,630	4,830			
Provisions	4,600	2,200			
Other	1,500	900			
TOTAL CURRENT LIABILITIES	13,730	7,930			
NON-CURRENT LIABILITIES					
Creditors and borrowings					
— loan from H Co.	—	1,500			
— other	4,000	—			
Provisions	1,200	600			
Other	400	—			
TOTAL NON-CURRENT LIABILITIES	5,600	2,100			
TOTAL LIABILITIES	19,330	10,030			
NET ASSETS	11,430	4,830			

¶1506

SALE OF SHARES

Profit and Loss Accounts as at 30.6.X7

	H Co.	S Co.	Dr	Cr	Group
	$000	$000	$000	$000	$000
Operating profit	5,200	3,480			
Income tax attributable to operating profit	2,280	1,740			
Operating profit after income tax	2,920	1,740			
Retained profits at 30.6.X6	6,010	1,840			
Total available for appropriation	8,930	3,580			
Dividends provided for	2,000	1,000			
Retained profits at 30.6.X7	6,930	2,580			

continued over ...

¶1506

Balance Sheets as at 30.6.X8

	H Co.	S Co.	Dr	Cr	Group
	$000	$000	$000	$000	$000
TOTAL SHAREHOLDERS' EQUITY					
Share capital	1,500	750			
Reserves — asset revaluation reserve	3,000	1,500			
Retained profits	7,350	4,270			
Shareholders' equity attributable to members of the holding company	11,850	6,520			
CURRENT ASSETS					
Cash	520	380			
Receivables	6,739	3,510			
Inventories	12,800	7,010			
Other	860	310			
TOTAL CURRENT ASSETS	20,919	11,210			
NON-CURRENT ASSETS					
Investments					
— shares in associated company	2,671	—			
— loans to associated company	1,000	—			
Property, plant and equipment	6,900	6,010			
TOTAL NON-CURRENT ASSETS	10,571	6,010			
TOTAL ASSETS	31,490	17,220			
CURRENT LIABILITIES					
Creditors and borrowings	7,520	5,400			
Provisions	4,900	2,400			
Other	1,300	1,200			
TOTAL CURRENT LIABILITIES	13,720	9,000			
NON-CURRENT LIABILITIES					
Creditors and borrowings	4,000	1,000			
Provisions	1,300	700			
Other	620	—			
TOTAL NON-CURRENT LIABILITIES	5,920	1,700			
TOTAL LIABILITIES	19,640	10,700			
NET ASSETS	11,850	6,520			

¶1506

SALE OF SHARES

Profit and Loss Accounts as at 30.6.X8

	H Co.	S Co.	Dr	Cr	Group
	$000	$000	$000	$000	$000
Operating profit	2,922	3,320			
Income tax attributable to operating profit	1,432	1,630			
Operating profit after income tax	1,490	1,690			
Profit on extraordinary items	380	—			
Profit on extraordinary items after income tax	380	—			
Operating profit after extraordinary items and income tax attributable to members of H Co.	1,870	1,690			
Retained profits at 30.6.X7	6,480	2,580			
Total available for appropriation	8,350	4,270			
Dividends provided for	1,000	—			
Retained profits at 30.6.X8	7,350	4,270			

Prepare consolidation journal entries and consolidated balance sheet and profit and loss account for the group for the year ended 30 June 19X7 and for the year ended 30 June 19X8.

Solution to Example 15.4

Journal Entries as at 30.6.X7

In H Company's accounts $ $

1. Dr Operating profit   450
   Cr Investment   450

   To show the dividend received from pre-acquisition profit as a return of investment (60% of $750)

On consolidation

2. Dr Issued capital (60% of $750)   450
   Dr Asset revaluation reserve of S Co. (60% of $1,500)   900
   Dr Retained earnings brought forward (60% of $1,840)   1,104
   Dr Operating profit before tax (60% of $2,620) 1,572
      Cr Income tax expense (60% of $1,310)   786
      Cr Dividend provided pre-acquisition   450
      Cr Investment in S Co. (cost $3,720 less $450)   3,270
   Dr Goodwill   480

   Elimination of investment in S Co.

¶1506

3. Dr Issued capital (40% of $750)   300
  Dr Asset revaluation reserve (40% of $1,500)   600
  Dr Retained earnings brought forward (40% of
   $1,840)   736
  Dr Minority interest (P/L) (40% of $1,740)   696
   Cr Dividend proposed (40% of $1,000)   400
   Cr Minority interest (B/S)   1,932

Allocation of minority interest
Check:
 Net tangible assets of S Co. at
  30.6.X7 $4,830
 Minority interest share   40%
         $1,932

4. Dr Operating profit   6
  Cr Goodwill   6

Amortisation for 3 months out of 20
years ($480 ÷ 20 ÷ 4)

5. Dr Loan from H Co.   1,500
  Cr Loan to S Co.   1,500

Elimination of inter-company loans

6. Dr Dividend received — H Co.   150
  Cr Dividend proposed — S Co.   150

Elimination of post-acquisition dividend

Note:

(1) *Operating profit and income tax expense*

              $
Retained earnings at acquisition date 31.3.X7   3,150
The information provided shows:
 Retained earnings brought forward at 1/7/X6   1,840
 Operating profit after income tax for 9 months to
  31.3.X7   1,310

The S Co. profit and loss account for the year ended
30.6.X7 included:
 Operating profit before tax   3,480
 Income tax expense   1,740
           1,740

 Average tax rate for year   50%

It can therefore be assumed that the same average tax
rate applied for the period to 31.3.X7
Accordingly:
Operating profit before income tax for the 9 months to
 31.3.X7   2,620
Income tax expense   1,310
Operating profit after income tax for 9 months to
 31.3.X7   1,310

¶1506

SALE OF SHARES

Retained earnings at 31.3.X7 were $3,150. This was before proposal of the dividend. The comparable retained earnings balance at 30.6.X7 is $3,580, i.e. before proposal of the dividend.

It can further be assumed that as the dividend was paid from profits earned during the year:

Profit for 9 months to 31.3.X7	$1,310
Profit for year to 30.6.X7	$1,740
Proportion of profit to 31.3.X7 75% (approx)	
Total dividend	$1,000
Dividend paid from profits earned prior to 31.3.X7	$ 750

Therefore the profit and loss account for the 3 months to 30.6.X7 is as follows:

Profit and Loss Accounts

	9 months 31.3.X7	Year to 30.6.X7
Operating profit	2,620	3,480
Income tax expense	1,310	1,740
Operating profit after income tax	1,310	1,740
Extraordinary items	—	—
Retained earnings brought forward	1,840	1,840
	3,150	3,580
Dividends proposed	750	1,000
Retained earnings	2,400	2,580

	Year to 30.6.X7	9 months to 31.3.X7	3 months to 30.6.X7
Operating profit	3,480	2,620	860
Income tax expense	1,740	1,310	430
	1,740	1,310	430

(2) *Check on goodwill*

Net tangible assets at acquisition date	$5,400
Net tangible assets acquired 60%	
	$3,240
Cost of investment	$3,720
Goodwill on acquisition	$ 480

¶1506

Worksheet as at 30.6.X7 (Balance Sheet)

	H Co.	S Co.	Dr	Cr	Group
	$000	$000	$000	$000	$000
TOTAL SHAREHOLDERS' EQUITY					
Share capital	1,500	750	²450		1,500
			³300		
Reserves — asset revaluation	3,000	1,500	²900		3,000
			³600		
Retained profits	6,930	2,580	4,714	1,786	6,582
Shareholders' equity attributable to members of H Co.	11,430	4,830	6,964		11,082
Minority interest in subsidiaries	—	—		³1,932	1,932
	11,430	4,830	6,964	3,718	13,014
CURRENT ASSETS					
Cash	750	420			1,170
Receivables	5,400	3,840			9,240
Inventories	10,920	5,690			16,610
Other	1,770	220			1,990
TOTAL CURRENT ASSETS	18,840	10,170	—	—	29,010
NON-CURRENT ASSETS					
Investments — shares in S Co.	3,720	—		²3,270	—
				¹450	
— loans to S Co.	1,500	—		⁵1,500	—
Property, plant and equipment	6,700	4,690			11,390
Intangibles —					
goodwill on consolidation	—	—	²480	⁴6	474
TOTAL NON-CURRENT ASSETS	11,920	4,690	480	5,226	11,864
TOTAL ASSETS	30,760	14,860	480	5,226	40,874
CURRENT LIABILITIES					
Creditors and borrowings	7,630	4,830			12,460
Provisions	4,600	2,200			6,800
Other	1,500	900			2,400
TOTAL CURRENT LIABILITIES	13,730	7,930			21,660
NON-CURRENT LIABILITIES					
Creditors and borrowings					
— loan from H Co.	—	1,500	⁵1,500		—
— other	4,000	—			4,000
Provisions	1,200	600			1,800
Other	400	—			400
TOTAL NON-CURRENT LIABILITIES	5,600	2,100	1,500	—	6,200
TOTAL LIABILITIES	19,330	10,030	1,500	—	27,860
NET ASSETS	11,430	4,830			13,014
Total of eliminations			8,944	8,944	

¶1506

SALE OF SHARES

Worksheet as at 30.6.X7 (Profit and Loss Account)

	H Co.	S Co.	Dr	Cr	Group
	$000	$000	$000	$000	$000
Operating profit	5,200	3,480	¹450		6,502
			²1,572		
			⁴6		
			⁶150		
Income tax attributable to operating profit	2,280	1,740		²786	3,234
Operating profit after income tax	2,920	1,740	2,178	786	3,268
Operating profit after extraordinary items and income tax	2,920	1,740	2,178	786	3,268
Minority interests in operating profit and extraordinary items after income tax	—	—	³696	—	696
Operating profit after extraordinary items and income tax attributable to members of H Co.	2,920	1,740	2,874	786	2,572
Retained profits at the beginning of the financial year	6,010	1,840	³736	—	6,010
			²1,104		
Total available for appropriation	8,930	3,580	4,714	786	8,582
Dividends provided for	2,000	1,000		³400	2,000
				⁶150	
				²450	
Retained profits at the end of the financial year	6,930	2,580	4,714	1,786	6,582

Journal Entries at 30.6.X8

Note:
During this year H Company sold ⅛ of ¹¹⁄₆₀ of its investment in S Company.

	$
Initial cost of investment (after receipt of dividend) ($3,720 − $450)	$3,270.00
Proportion sold ¹¹⁄₆₀	
Amount sold	599.50
Amount retained	$2,670.50
	$3,270.00

H Company has recorded a profit on sale of investment:
Cost of investment sold	$599.5
Consideration received	979.5
Profit on sale	$380.0

¶1506

			$	$
1.(a)	Dr Extraordinary item — H Co. profit on sale		380	
(b)	Cr Extraordinary item — group profit on sale			486.2
(c)	Dr Extraordinary item — group profit on sale		474	
(d)	Cr Retained earnings brought forward			102
(e)	Cr Operating profit			886
(f)	Dr Income tax expense		443	
(g)	Dr Minority interest (P/L)		177.2	
			1,474.2	1,474.2

Group profit on sale of part of investment in S Company

		$	$
2.	Dr Operating profit	6	
	Cr Extraordinary item — group profit on sale		6

Amortisation of goodwill for 3 months to 30 June 19X7

Notes:

(a) Extraordinary profit shown by H Company on sale of part of its investment in S Company is not relevant to the group.

		$
(b)	Net tangible assets of S Co. at date of sale	5,273.0
	Proportion held before sale 60%	
	Net tangible assets attributable to H Co. at date of sale	3,163.8
	Less: cost of investment retained	2,670.5
	Net tangible assets disposed of	493.3
	Consideration received	979.5
		486.2

(c) Balance of goodwill will not be recovered out of future profits.

(d) S Company's contribution to opening retained earnings, i.e. at 30 June 19X7

Net profit earned by S Co. post-acquisition	430
H Co. share 60%	
	258
Less: goodwill amortised	(6)
Less: dividend paid	(150)
	102

Check:

Retained earnings of H Co. per its accounts	6,930
Less: dividend credited to retained earnings, rather than to investment	(450)
	6,480
Group retained earnings	6,582
	102

¶1506

SALE OF SHARES

(e) Profit and loss accounts

The group owned 60% of S Company during the period to 30.9.X7 and should report the profit earned by S Company during that time as group profit.

	$
Retained earnings of S Co. at 30 June 19X7	2,580
Retained earnings of S Co. at 30 September 19X7	3,023
Profit for the period	443

	Year to 30.9.X7	9 months to 30.9.X7	3 months to 30.9.X7	H Co. share at 60%	MI share at 40%
	$	$	$	$	$
Operating profit	3,320	2,434	886	531.6	
Income tax expense	1,630	1,187	443	265.8	
	1,690	1,247	443	265.8	177.2

This assumes that no dividends were paid by S Company during the period.

Summary

When part of an investment in a subsidiary is sold to the extent that it is no longer a subsidiary, the consideration journal entry to record the sale is the same as that where all of the investment is sold, with the exception that the component in respect of "net assets less consideration" also takes into account the remaining investment.

continued over ...

¶1506

Balance Sheet as at 30.6.X8

	H Co.	Dr	Cr	Group
	$000	$000	$000	$000
TOTAL SHAREHOLDERS' EQUITY				
Share capital	1,500			1,500
Reserves — asset revaluation	3,000			3,000
Retained profits	7,350	1,480.2	1,480.2	7,350
Shareholders' equity attributable to members of H Co.	11,850	1,480.2	1,480.2	11,850
CURRENT ASSETS				
Cash	520.5			520.5
Receivables	6,739			6,739
Inventories	12,800			12,800
Other	860			860
TOTAL CURRENT ASSETS	20,919.5			20,919.5
NON-CURRENT ASSETS				
Investments				
— shares in associated company	2,670.5			2,670.5
— loans to associated company	1,000			1,000
Property, plant and equipment	6,900			6,900
TOTAL NON-CURRENT ASSETS	10,570.5			10,570.5
TOTAL ASSETS	31,490			31,490
CURRENT LIABILITIES				
Creditors and borrowings	7,520			7,520
Provisions	4,900			4,900
Other	1,300			1,300
TOTAL CURRENT LIABILITIES	13,720			13,720
NON-CURRENT LIABILITIES				
Creditors and borrowings				
— loan from H Co.	—			—
— other	4,000			4,000
Provisions	1,300			1,300
Other	620			620
TOTAL NON-CURRENT LIABILITIES	5,920			5,920
TOTAL LIABILITIES	19,640			19,640
NET ASSETS	11,850			11,850

¶1506

SALE OF SHARES

Profit and Loss Accounts as at 30.6.X8

	H Co. $000	Dr $000	Cr $000	Group $000
Operating profit	2,452	²6	¹886	3,332
Income tax attributable to operating profit	(962)	¹443		(1,405)
Operating profit after income tax	1,490	449	886	1,927
Profit on extraordinary items	380	¹380	¹486.2	18.2
		¹474	²6	
Income tax attributable to profit on extraordinary items	—			—
Profit on extraordinary items after income tax	380	854	492.2	18.2
Operating profit after extraordinary items and income tax	1,870	1,303	1,378.2	1,945.2
Minority interests in operating profit and extraordinary items after income tax	—	¹177.2		177.2
Operating profit after extraordinary items and income tax attributable to members of the holding company	1,870	1,480.2	1,378.2	1,768
Retained profits at the beginning of the financial year	6,480		¹102	6,582
Total available for appropriation	8,350	1,480.2	1,480.2	8,350
Dividends provided for	1,000			1,000
Retained profits at the end of the financial year	7,350	1,480.2	1,480.2	7,350

¶1507 Subsequent equity accounting

When an entity sells or disposes of part of its investment in a subsidiary, the remaining shareholding may not constitute a subsidiary relationship. In such cases it is necessary to consider whether the investment requires the application of the equity method of accounting. The following example demonstrates the entries involved in accounting for an investment in a company that requires the use of the equity method of accounting following the sale of part of a subsidiary.

To demonstrate the required approach to account for such a situation, and to enable a direct comparison of the result of a sale of a subsidiary to an equity accounting position with the result of a sale of a subsidiary to a non-equity accounting position, the following example uses the information from Example 15.4 (¶1506) with one change — it is assumed that H Company equity accounts for its investment of 49% in S Company.

¶1507

Example 15.5

Should H Company account for investments in associated companies using the equity method of accounting (and this is considered to apply in respect of the 49% investment in S Company), H Company's investment in S Company needs to be restated to its equity accounted value, rather than to cost as in ¶1506.

The consolidation entries to give effect to this are as follows (note the entries as at 30 June 19X7 in this example are the same as in Example 15.4):

Journal entry 1. at 30.6.X8 in Example 15.4, ¶1506 above remains the same, i.e.:

		$	$
1.	(Equity)		
	Dr Extraordinary item	380	
	Cr Extraordinary item		486.2
	Dr Extraordinary item	474.0	
	Cr Retained earnings brought forward		102.0
	Cr Operating profit		886.0
	Dr Income tax expense	443	
	Dr Minority interest (P/L)	177.2	
		1474.2	1474.2
2.	Dr Operating profit	6	
	Cr Extraordinary item		6

Amortisation of goodwill for 3 months to 30.9.X7

The credit in this entry has been made against the extraordinary profit on sale of part of the interest in S Company, rather than against goodwill, as the goodwill included in entry 1. above was before amortisation.

Had entry 3. been prepared before entry 1., entry 3. would show "credit goodwill" rather than "credit extraordinary item", and entry 1. would show a "credit extraordinary item" of $480.2 rather than $486.2, and a "debit extraordinary item" of $80.9 rather than $86.9.

		$	$
3.	Dr Investment	295.5	
	Cr Extraordinary item		295.5

To reinstate equity accounted profits not sold, although treated as sold in entry 1. above

4.	Dr Investment in S Co.	611	
	Cr Equity share of profit before tax		
	(49% of $3,320-$886)		1,193
	Dr Equity share of income tax expense		
	(49% of $1,630-$443)	582	

To recognise a share of profit for the 9 months to 30.6.X8

5.	Dr Equity share of operating profit	14.7	
	Cr Investment		14.7

Amortisation of goodwill for 9 months to 30.6.X8

¶1507

SALE OF SHARES

Notes: $

(1) Entry 3. — equity accounted profit since acquisition:
    Profit for 3 months to 30.6.X7   430
    Profit for 3 months to 30.9.X7   443
                                     873
                                     49%
                                     427.8

    Less: Goodwill amortised — 3 months to 30.6.X7
        ($6 × 49% ÷ 60)   (4.9)
        Goodwill amortised — 3 months to 30.9.X7   (4.9)
        Dividend received post acquisition ($250 × 49%)   (122.5)
                                       295.5

(2) *Value of investment*

The journal entries noted above result in H Company's investment in S Company as at 30.6.X8 being shown as:

	$
Value per H Co.'s balance sheet	2,670.5
Entry 3. above	295.5
Entry 4. above	611.0
Entry 5. above	(14.7)
	3,562.3

To check the result of these entries we can calculate the equity accounted value of the investment as at 30.6.X8.

	$	$
Original cost of investment (after pre-acquisition dividend)		2,670.5
S Co.'s profit after tax for 3 months to 30.6.X7	430	
S Co.'s profit after tax for year to 30.6.X8	1,690	
	2,120	
S Co. dividend paid post-acquisition	(250)	
	1,870	
	49%	916.3
Less: Goodwill amortised		
— 3 months to 30.6.X7		(4.9)
— year to 30.9.X7 ($4.9 × 4)		(19.6)
	3,562.3	

¶1507

(3) *Operating profit after tax*

H Company's shareholders' share of operating profit after tax (excluding extraordinary items) should include:

	$
Profit of H Co. — year to 30.6.X8	1,490.0
60% of profit of S Co. — 3 months to 30.9.X7	265.8
49% of profit of S Co. — 9 months to 30.6.X8 ($1,247 × 49%)	611.0
Less: Goodwill amortised — 3 months to 30.9.X7	(6.0)
— 9 months to 30.6.X8	(14.7)
	2,346.1

Profit and loss worksheet shows:

Group operating profit after tax	2,523.3
Minority interest	177.2
	2,346.1

(4) *Equity goodwill*

	$
Original goodwill	480
Proportion sold 11/60	
Amount sold ($480 ÷ 60 × 11)	88
Goodwill retained	392
	480
Goodwill retained	392
Amortisation period 20 years	
Amortisation amount per year	19.6
Amortisation for 3 months	4.9

¶1507

SALE OF SHARES

Worksheet as at 30.6.X8 (Balance Sheet)

	H Co. $000	S Co. $000	Dr $000	Cr $000	Group $000
TOTAL SHAREHOLDERS' EQUITY					
Share capital	1,500	750			1,500
Reserves — asset revaluation	3,000	1,500			3,000
Retained profits	7,350	4,270	2,076.9	2,968.7	8,241.8
Shareholders' equity attributable to members of H Co.	11,850	6,520	2,076.9	2,968.7	12,741.8
CURRENT ASSETS					
Cash	520	380			520
Receivables	6,739	3,510			6,739
Inventories	12,800	7,010			12,800
Other	860	310			860
TOTAL CURRENT ASSETS	20,919	11,210	—	—	20,919
NON-CURRENT ASSETS					
Investments — shares in associated company	2,670.5	—	[3]295.5 [4]611	[5]14.7	3,562.3
Loans to associated company	1,000.5	—			1,000.5
Property, plant and equipment	6,900	6,010			6,900.0
TOTAL NON-CURRENT ASSETS	10,571	6,010	906.5	14.7	11,462.8
TOTAL ASSETS	31,490	17,220	906.5	14.7	32,381.8
CURRENT LIABILITIES					
Creditors and borrowings	7,520	5,400			7,520
Provisions	4,900	2,400			4,900
Other	1,300	1,200			1,300
TOTAL CURRENT LIABILITIES	13,720	9,000	—	—	13,720
NON-CURRENT LIABILITIES					
Creditors and borrowings	4,000	1,000			4,000
Provisions	1,300	700			1,300
Other	620	—			620
TOTAL NON-CURRENT LIABILITIES	5,920	1,700	—	—	5,920
TOTAL LIABILITIES	19,640	10,700	—	—	19,640
NET ASSETS	11,850	6,520	906.5	14.7	12,741.8
Total of eliminations			2983.4	2983.4	

¶1507

Worksheet as at 30.6.X8 (Profit and Loss Account)
Incorporating Equity Accounting

	H Co.	S Co.	Dr	Cr	Group
	$000	$000	$000	$000	$000
Operating profit	2,922	3,320	²6	¹886	4980.3
			⁵14.7	⁴1,193	
Income tax attributable to operating profit	1,432	1,630	¹443 ⁴582		2457.0
Operating profit after income tax	1,490	1,690	1,045.7	2,079	2523.3
Profit on extraordinary items	380	—	¹380 ¹474	¹486.2 ²6 ³295.5	313.7
Income tax attributable to profit on extraordinary items	—	—			—
Profit on extraordinary items after income tax	380	—	854	787.7	313.7
Operating profit after extraordinary items and income tax	1,870	1,690			2837.0
Minority interests in operating profit and extraordinary items after income tax	—	—	¹177.2		177.2
Operating profit after extraordinary items and income tax attributable to members of the holding company	1,870	1,690	177.2		2659.8
Retained profits at the beginning of the financial year	6,480	2,580		¹102	6582.0
Total available for appropriation	8,350	4,270	177.2		9241.8
Dividends provided for	1,000	—			1,000.0
Retained profits at the end of the financial year	7,350	4,270	2076.9	2968.7	8,241.8

A comparison of the operating profit after tax, and minority interest, before extraordinary items, shows the following:

	Non-equity (¶1506)	Equity (¶1507)
	$	$
Profit of H Co. — year to 30.6.X8	1,490.0	1,490.0
60% of profit of S Co. — 3 months to 30.9.X7	265.8	265.8
49% of profit of S Co. — 9 months to 30.9.X8		611.0
Less: Goodwill amortised		
— 3 months to 30.9.X7	(6.0)	(6.0)
— 9 months to 30.6.X8		(14.7)
	1,749.8	2,346.1
Shown on worksheet as:	1,927.0	2,523.3
Operating profit after tax	177.2	177.2
	1,749.8	2,346.1

¶1507

16

Subsequent issue of shares by subsidiary

Effect of issue of shares	¶1601
No change in degree of ownership	¶1602
Increase in degree of ownership	¶1603
Decrease in degree of ownership through share issue — still a subsidiary	¶1604
Decrease in degree of ownership through share issue — company no longer a subsidiary	¶1605
Bonus share issue by subsidiary	¶1606
Bonus issue from intra-group asset revaluation reserve	¶1607

¶1601 Effect of issue of shares

Whenever an existing subsidiary company issues more shares, one of the following results will occur. There will be:

(a) no change in relative group interest in the subsidiary (¶1602);

(b) an increase in relative group interest in the subsidiary (¶1603);

(c) a decrease in relative group interest in the subsidiary (¶1604);

(d) a decrease in group interest to the extent that a subsidiary relationship no longer exists (¶1605).

The consolidation treatment required in each of these situations will be reviewed, using practical examples.

¶1602 No change in degree of ownership

No change in the degree of ownership will occur when shares issued by a subsidiary are taken up by existing shareholders in the same proportion as their existing shareholdings.

Example 16.1

H Company acquired 80% of the shares in S Company on 30 June 19X3 at a cost of $750, at which date S Company had issued capital of $500 in $1 shares and retained earnings of $300. On 30 June 19X6 S Company issued 100 shares at par, which were taken up by existing shareholders on a one for one basis.

Prepare consolidation journal entries as at 30 June 19X6.

Suggested Solution to Example 16.1

		Debit $	Credit $
(a)	Dr Issued capital (80% of $500)	400	
	Dr Retained earnings 1.7.X3 (80% of $300)	240	
	Dr Goodwill	110	
	Cr Investment at 30.6.X3		750
	Elimination of original investment		
(b)	Dr Issued capital (80% of $100)	80	
	Cr Investment at 30.6.X6		80
	Elimination of subsequent investment		

As the shares were taken up in proportion to existing shares, there are no complications on consolidation, apart from the need to eliminate that extra investment. It is recommended that this be done by making two entries, rather than by combining the two acquisitions into one entry.

Note that there is no goodwill or discount element in the second acquisition, as the shares were issued at par on a one for one basis, and accordingly H Company did not acquire any further interest in the shareholders' funds of S Company other than in the issued shares acquired.

¶1603 Increase in degree of ownership

The effect of acquiring additional shares in a subsidiary company from a share issue by that subsidiary company, if the additional share purchase increases the overall degree of ownership held by the holding company, is that the holding company is purchasing at the date of the second acquisition a further percentage ownership. The consolidation treatment is as follows:

(1) Eliminate the initial investment as if no further shares were acquired (i.e. using the existing elimination entry).

SUBSEQUENT ISSUE OF SHARES BY SUBSIDIARY 157

(2) Eliminate the second investment against:
   (a) issued capital acquired;
   (b) share premium reserve for the total amount of that reserve now "owned" (i.e. the same as the holding company's new proportionate ownership of the subsidiary). This will often be required, as new issues are not usually at par;
   (c) other reserves (including retained earnings) for the increase in percentage ownership.

What has the group done? The overall group financial position has not changed. However, the result of the holding company's subscription for an amount of shares in excess of its proportionate entitlement is that the holding company has increased its share at the expense of the minority.

Example 16.2

Increase in Degree of Ownership Through Share Issue

H Company owns 80% of the issued shares of S Company. One year later S Company makes an issue of 60,000 $1 shares at a premium of 50c, and H Company buys 50,000 of these shares.

Balance sheets of H Company and S Company immediately following each investment are set out below. Assume that S Company's assets are all non-monetary.

Balance Sheets
Immediately Following Initial Investment

	H. Co.	S. Co.	Debit	Credit	Group
	$000	$000	$000	$000	$000
Issued capital	1,000	100			
Retained earnings	1,000	400			
	2,000	500			
Investment in S Co.	750				
Other assets	1,300	600			
Other liabilities	(50)	(100)			
	2,000	500			
Operating profit after tax	200	100			
	200	100			
Opening retained earnings	800	300			
Retained earnings	1,000	400			

¶1603

ACCOUNTING FOR BUSINESS CONSOLIDATIONS

Balance Sheets
Immediately Following Subsequent Investment

	H. Co.	S. Co.	Debit	Credit	Group
	$000	$000	$000	$000	$000
Issued capital	1,000	160			
Retained earnings	1,000	800			
Share premium reserve		30			
General reserve		100			
	2,000	1,090			
Investment in S Co.	825				
Other assets	1,225	1,190			
Other liabilities	(50)	(100)			
	2,000	1,090			
Operating profit after tax		400			
Opening retained earnings	1,000	400			
Retained earnings	1,000	800			

Prepare consolidation worksheets and consolidation journal entries at each of the investment dates.

Suggested Solution to Example 16.2

Journal Entries

Journal entries required to prepare consolidated accounts immediately following original investment

	$000	$000
(a) Dr Issued capital (80% of $100)	80	
Dr Operating profit after tax (80% of $100)	80	
Dr Opening retained earnings (80% of $300)	240	
Cr Investment (at cost)		750
Dr Goodwill	350	

Elimination of initial investment

(b) Dr Issued capital (20% of $100)	20	
Dr Opening retained earnings (20% of $300)	60	
Dr Minority interest (P/L) (20% of $100)	20	
Cr Minority interest (B/S)		
(20% of net tangible assets of $500)		100

Allocation of minority interest

Journal entries required to prepare consolidated accounts immediately following second purchase of shares

H Company's degree of ownership has changed from 80% to 81.25% (i.e. H Company now owns 80,000 + 50,000 shares, and total shares issued is now 160,000), an increase of 1.25%.

	$000	$000
(a) Dr Issued capital (80% of $100)	80	
Dr Opening retained earnings	320	
Cr Investment		750
Dr Goodwill	350	

Elimination of initial investment

¶1603

SUBSEQUENT ISSUE OF SHARES BY SUBSIDIARY

(b) Dr Issued capital (at par)   50
    Dr Opening retained earnings ($400 × 1.25%)   5
    Dr Operating profit after tax ($400 × 1.25%)   5
    Dr Share premium reserve (81.25% × $30)   24.375
    Dr General reserve (1.25% × $100)   1.25
        Cr Investment   75
        Cr Discount on acquisition   10.625

Elimination of subsequent investment

(c) Dr Issued capital   30
    Dr Opening retained earnings   75
    Dr Minority interest (P/L)   75
    Dr Share premium reserve   5.625
    Dr General reserve   18.75
        Cr Minority interest (B/S)   204.375

Allocation of minority interest

(d) Dr Discount on acquisition   10.625
        Cr Assets   13.281
    Dr Minority interest (B/S)   2.656

To show assets acquired at cost to the group.
H Company received a discount
of $10.625 on acquisition of 80%

Worksheet Immediately Following Initial Investment

	H. Co.	S. Co.	Debit	Credit	Group
	$000	$000	$000	$000	$000
Issued capital	1,000	100	ᵃ80		1,000
			ᵇ20		
Retained earnings	1,000	400	400		1,000
Minority interest				ᵇ100	100
	2,000	500	500	100	2,100
Investment in S Co.	750			ᵃ750	—
Other assets	1,300	600			1,900
Other liabilities	(50)	(100)			(150)
Goodwill			ᵃ350		350
	2,000	500	350	750	2,100
Operating profit after tax	200	100	ᵃ80		220
Minority interest			ᵇ20		20
	200	100	100		200
Opening retained earnings	800	300	ᵃ240		800
			ᵇ60		
Retained earnings	1,000	400	400		1,000

¶1603

Worksheet Immediately Following Subsequent Investment

	H. Co.	S. Co.	Debit	Credit	Group
	$000	$000	$000	$000	$000
Issued capital	1,000	160	ª80		1,000
			ᵇ50		
			ᶜ30		
Retained earnings	1,000	800	480		1,320
Share premium		30	ᵇ24.375	—	
reserve			ᶜ5.625		
General reserve		100	ᵇ1.25		
			ᶜ18.75		80
Minority interest			ᵈ2.656	ᶜ204.375	201.719
Discount on					
acquisition			ᵈ10.625	ᶜ10.625	—
	2,000	1,090	703.281	215	2,601.719
Investment in S Co.	825			ª750	
				ᵇ75	
Other assets	1,225	1,190		ᵈ13.281	2,401.719
Other liabilities	(50)	(100)			(150)
Goodwill			ª350		350
	2,000	1,090	350	838.281	2,601.719
Operating profit					
after tax		400	ᵇ5		395
Minority interest			ᶜ75		75
		400	80		320
Opening retained			ª320		
earnings	1,000	400	ᵇ5		1,000
			ᶜ75		
Retained earnings	1,000	800	480		1,320

¶1604 Decrease in degree of ownership through share issue — still a subsidiary

¶1603 considered the accounting treatment required where a holding company purchases shares issued by an existing subsidiary in excess of its proportionate entitlement. We will now consider the opposite situation — where the holding company purchases less shares than its proportionate entitlement. The effect of this action on consolidation is to:

(1) reduce the percentage of the subsidiary company's issued capital and reserves that is owned by H Company;

(2) "give" to minority shareholders a portion of the profits of S Company that had previously been recognised by H Company.

¶1604

SUBSEQUENT ISSUE OF SHARES BY SUBSIDIARY

Example 16.3

Decrease in Degree of Ownership through Share Issue — Still a Subsidiary

H Company owns 80% of the issued shares of S Company, purchased on 30 June 19X4 at a cost of $750,000, at which time S Company had retained earnings of $400,000.

On 30 June 19X8 S Company issued a further 60,000 shares at a premium of 50c per share. H Company purchased 40,000 of these shares.

Balance sheets of each company at 30 June 19X7 and 19X8 were as follows:

Balance Sheets as at 30.6.X7

	H Co.	S Co.	Debit	Credit	Group
	$000	$000	$000	$000	$000
Issued capital	1,000	100			
Retained earnings	1,000	600			
	2,000	700			
Investment in S Co.	750				
Other assets	1,300	800			
Other liabilities	(50)	(100)			
	2,000	700			
Operating profit after tax	200	100			
Retained earnings 1.7.X6	800	500			
Retained earnings 30.6.X7	1,000	600			

Balance Sheets as at 30.6.X8

	H Co.	S Co.	Debit	Credit	Group
	$000	$000	$000	$000	$000
Issued capital	1,000	160			
Retained earnings	1,000	700			
Share premium reserve		30			
General reserve		100			
	2,000	990			
Investment in S Co.	810				
Other assets	1,240	1,090			
Other liabilities	(50)	(100)			
	2,000	990			
Operating profit after tax	—	100			
Retained earnings 1.7.X7	1,000	600			
Retained earnings 30.6.X8	1,000	700			

¶1604

ACCOUNTING FOR BUSINESS CONSOLIDATIONS

Prepare consolidation journals and consolidation worksheets as at 30 June 19X7 and 30 June 19X8.

Suggested Solution to Example 16.3

Consolidation Entries at 30.6.X7

		$000	$000
(a)	Dr Issued capital	80	
	Dr Opening retained earnings	320	
	Cr Investment		750
	Dr Goodwill	350	
(b)	Dr Issued capital	20	
	Dr Opening retained earnings	100	
	Dr Minority interest (P/L)	20	
	Cr Minority interest (B/S)		140

Worksheet as at 30.6.X7

	H Co.	S Co.	Debit	Credit	Group
	$000	$000	$000	$000	$000
Issued capital	1,000	100	ª80 ᵇ20		1,000
Retained earnings	1,000	600	440		1,160
Minority interest				ᵇ140	140
	2,000	700	540	140	2,300
Investment in S Co.	750			ª750	—
Other assets	1,300	800			2,100
Other liabilities	(50)	(100)			(150)
Goodwill			ª350		350
	2,000	700	350	750	2,300
Operating profit after tax	200	100			300
Minority interest				ᵇ20	20
	200	100	20		280
Retained earnings 1.7.X6	800	500	ª320 ᵇ100		880
Retained earnings 30.6.X7	1,000	600	440		1,160

Consolidation Entries at 30.6.X8

The consolidation entries required to account for a reduction in percentage ownership through a share issue are summarised below:

(i) Eliminate initial investment using "normal" entry, i.e. that which has been used in previous years.

(ii) Eliminate the subsequent investment against the issued capital that was acquired by virtue of this investment, and against the share premium reserve for the new proportionate ownership of the subsidiary by the group.

¶1604

SUBSEQUENT ISSUE OF SHARES BY SUBSIDIARY

Note that the group has not acquired any further interest in the retained earnings or other reserves (apart from the share premium reserve) of the subsidiary.

(iii) Eliminate the minority interest (current) portion of the share capital and reserves of the subsidiary company. The minority shareholders now have an increased interest in those items.

(iv) Adjust opening retained earnings. The minority interest in those profits has increased and this has been recognised in step (iii) above. However, the adjustment for this relinquishing of profits by the holding company must be made against current year profits rather than opening retained earnings, as opening retained earnings have already been reported and therefore cannot be altered.

(v) Net any goodwill and/or discount arising from the elimination of the two investments, or if considered appropriate eliminate discount against book value of non-monetary assets acquired.

Entries at 30.6.X8

The group interest in S Company has decreased by 5% from 80% to 75% as a result of the new share issue.

		$000	$000
(a)	Dr Issued capital	80	
	Dr Opening retained earnings	320	
	Cr Investment		750
	Dr Goodwill	350	

Elimination of initial investment

(b)	Dr Issued capital (par value of shares acquired)	40	
	Dr Share premium reserve (75% is "owned" by H Co.)	22.5	
	Cr Investment		60
	Cr Goodwill		2.5

Elimination of subsequent investment

(c)	Dr Issued capital (minority interest in the subsidiary is now 25%)	40	
	Dr Opening retained earnings	150	
	Dr Share premium reserve	7.5	
	Dr General reserve	25	
	Dr Minority interest (P/L)	25	
	Cr Minority interest (B/S)		247.5

Allocation of minority interest

(d)	Dr Minority interest (P/L)	30	
	Cr Opening retained earnings		30

To adjust opening retained earnings

¶1604

	Worksheet as at 30.6.X8				
	H Co.	S Co.	Debit	Credit	Group
	$000	$000	$000	$000	$000
Issued capital	1,000	160	ª80		1,000
			ᵇ40		
			ᶜ40		
Retained earnings	1,000	700	525	30	1,205
Share premium reserve		30	ᵇ22.5		
			ᶜ7.5		
General reserve		100	ᶜ25		75
Minority interest				ᵈ247.5	247.5
	2,000	990	740	277.5	2,527.5
Investment in S Co.	810			ª750	
				ᵇ60	—
Other assets	1,240	1,090			2,330
Other liabilities	(50)	(100)			(150)
Goodwill			ª350	ᵇ2.5	347.5
	2,000	990	350	812.5	2,527.5
Operating profit after tax		100			100
Minority interest			ᵈ30		55
			ᶜ25		
		100	55		45
Retained earnings 1.7.X7	1,000	600	ª320	ᵈ30	1,160
			ᶜ150		
Retained earnings 30.6.X8	1,000	700	525	30	1,205

¶1605 Decrease in degree of ownership through share issue — company no longer a subsidiary

The consolidation treatment required where there is a decrease in the ownership through a share issue is similar to that for a part sale of shares.

From a group point of view, control over the subsidiary has been relinquished for no consideration. In determining the loss on sale, consideration would be $nil.

Consider the following examples:

Example 16.4

Issue of Shares at Par

H Company acquired 100% of the shares in S Company on 30 June 19X5 at which time net assets of S Company included:

	$
Issued capital	100
Retained earnings	200
	300

SUBSEQUENT ISSUE OF SHARES BY SUBSIDIARY

On 30 June 19X9 S Company issued 100 shares at par to S Company.

Set out below are balance sheets and profit and loss statements for H Company and S Company at 30 June 19X8 and at 30 June 19X9.

Accounts as at 30.6.X8

	H Co. $	S Co. $	Debit $	Credit $	Group $
Issued capital	100	100			
Reserves	100				
Retained earnings	100	250			
	300	350			
Investment in S Co.	500	—			
Other assets	(200)	350			
	300	350			
Operating profit	100	180			
Income tax expense	40	80			
	60	100			
Opening retained earnings	40	150			
Retained earnings	100	250			

Accounts as at 30.6.X9

	H Co. $	S Co. $	Debit $	Credit $	Group $
Issued capital	100	200			
Reserves	100				
Retained earnings	100	390			
	300	590			
Investment in S Co.	500	—			
Other assets	(200)	590			
	300	590			
Operating profit	—	200			
Income tax expense	—	60			
	—	140			
Opening retained earnings	100	250			
Retained earnings	100	390			

Prepare consolidation journal entries and consolidation worksheets as at 30 June 19X8 and 30 June 19X9.

¶1605

Suggested Solution to Example 16.4

Accounts as at 30.6.X8
Journal Entry

	$	$
Dr Issued capital	100	
Dr Opening retained earnings	200	
Cr Investment in S Co.		500
Dr Goodwill	200	

Elimination of investment in S Co.

Accounts as at 30.6.X8

	H Co. $	S Co. $	Debit $	Credit $	Group $
Issued capital	100	100	100		100
Reserves	100				100
Retained earnings	100	250	200		150
	300	350	300	—	350
Investment in S Co.	500	—		500	—
Goodwill			200		200
Other assets	(200)	350			150
	300	350	200	500	350
Operating profit	100	180			280
Income tax expense	40	80			120
	60	100			160
Minority interest	—	—			
	60	100			160
Opening retained earnings	40	150	200		(10)
	100	250			150
Dividends paid	—	—			
Retained earnings 30.6.X4	100	250	200		150

Journal Entries 30.6.X9

			$	$
(a)	Cr Extraordinary item			10
(b)	Dr Extraordinary item		200	
(c)	Cr Opening retained earnings			50
(d)	Cr Operating profit			200
(e)	Dr Income tax expense		60	
			260	260

¶1605

SUBSEQUENT ISSUE OF SHARES BY SUBSIDIARY

Notes:

		$
(a)	Net tangible assets of S Co. immediately prior to share issue	490
	Less: Cost of investment retained	500
	Net tangible assets disposed of	(10)
	Consideration received	—
	Gain	10
(b)	Goodwill will not be recovered	
(c)	Retained earnings at acquisition date	200
	Retained earnings at 1 July 19X8	250
		50

(d)-
(e) S Co. was a subsidiary of H Co. for all of the year. All profits earned by S Co. during the year are to be reported on by H Co. group.

Note that the amount of opening retained earnings in the 30.6.X9 accounts is equal to the closing balance of retained earnings as at 30.6.X8.

Consider what has happened from a group point of view. H Company group is no longer entitled to control the post-acquisition increases in shareholders' funds of S Company that were previously reported as being earned by H Company group.

H Company controlled S Company at the time of the new share issue, and in the absence of information to the contrary we must assume that H Company willingly instructed S Company to make that share issue. The results of this decision should be reported in the profit and loss account of H Company group.

	$
Net tangible assets of S Co. prior to share issue	490
Net tangible assets of S Co. at acquisition date	300
Amount "given up" by H Co. group	190

The consolidation worksheet as at 30.6.X9 shows the recognition of $190 as a loss.

continued over ...

¶1605

ACCOUNTING FOR BUSINESS CONSOLIDATIONS

Worksheet as at 30.6.X9

	H Co.	S Co.	Debit	Credit	Group
	$	$	$	$	$
Issued capital	100	200			100
Reserves	100				100
Retained earnings	100	390	260	260	100
	300	590	260	260	300
Investment in S Co.	500	—			500
Other assets	(200)	590			(200)
	300	590			300
Operating profit	—	200		200	200
Income tax expense	—	60	60		60
	—	140	60	200	140
Minority interest	—	—			
	—	140	60	200	140
Extraordinary item			200	10	190
	—	140	260	210	(50)
Opening retained earnings	100	250		50	150
	100	390			100
Dividends paid	—	—			—
Retained earnings	100	390	260	260	100

Note: S Company is no longer a subsidiary, and its accounts are not added to those of H Company.

Example 16.5

Issue of Shares at a Premium

Now consider Example 16.4 above, assuming that the shares issued by S Company on 30 June 19X9 were issued at a premium of $4.00 per share.

Prepare consolidation journals as at 30 June 19X9.

Suggested Solution to Example 16.5

Journal Entries

	$	$
Cr Extraordinary item		*10
Dr Extraordinary item	*200	
Cr Opening retained earnings		50
Cr Operating profit		200
Dr Income tax expense	60	

i.e. Net loss = *$200 less *$10 = $190

This is the same entry as if the shares were issued at par, as shown in Example 16.4 above. Accordingly the consolidation worksheet will be identical to that in the suggested solution to Example 16.4.

¶1605

Net asset backing

Consider what has happened to the net asset backing of H Company group's investment in S Company:

	Prior to issue	Subsequent to issue	Difference
Net tangible assets of S Co.	$490	$990	
H Co. interest	100%	50%	
	$490	$495	$5

The net asset backing of H Company's investment has increased, yet the profit and loss account of H Company shows a loss of $190 as a result of the share issue.

This anomaly is due to the fundamental concept of historical cost accounting.

Historical cost financial statements are designed to show assets at cost, not at their net asset backing. Any increases in net assets of outside entities in which an entity or group has an interest are considered unrealised from a historical cost point of view, and are not reported upon. In the above example, the historical cost financial statements as shown by the suggested solution show a loss of $190. The increase in net asset backing of the investment will only be included in the group accounts when realised.

While S Company was part of the H Company group, and H Company controlled S Company, the profits earned by S Company were earned as a result of decisions by H Company. H Company had the power to distribute those profits to itself as dividends. Accordingly those profits were reported as being earned and available for distribution by the H Company group. However, now that H Company no longer has control of S Company those profits are "unrealisable" from H Company group's point of view and should not be shown as distributable by H Company. They are therefore removed from H Company group's net assets by way of being shown as a loss.

Appropriation or loss

Some practitioners argue that the above-mentioned reduction in retained earnings available for distribution should be shown as an appropriation of retained earnings. For example:

	$
Operating profit after tax	x
Extraordinary items	x
	x
Opening retained earnings	x
Amount available for appropriation	x
Appropriations	
Dividend paid	(x)
Release of retained earnings of former subsidiary company on issue of shares by that former subsidiary	(x)
Retained earnings	x

¶1605

Proponents of this approach consider that the group has not suffered a loss as a result of issue of shares. The appropriation recognises that the group has forgone the right to control retained earnings of the former subsidiary company.

Recognition of a loss may be considered preferable to recognition of an appropriation.

Had H Company group moved from 100% ownership of S Company to 50% ownership by way of selling shares, H Company would have given part of its investment in S Company and received cash, i.e. it would have changed one asset into another. When H Company moves to 50% ownership by way of share issue, it does so without that direct exchange of cash; however, the end result is similar.

H Company made the decision to issue shares to B Company, and any result of a transaction controlled by the group should be reported in the group accounts.

¶1606 Bonus share issue by subsidiary

The effect of a bonus issue of shares must be considered from three perspectives.

1. *What is a bonus issue?*

A bonus issue is a dividend that has been declared and satisfied by the issue of shares. A bonus issue may be made from retained earnings or from a reserve account, including an asset revaluation reserve or a share premium reserve.

2. *What effect does this have on a recipient company?*

According to *Stroud's Judicial Dictionary* the word "bonus" on a share certificate is evidence that the shares concerned have been issued gratis, i.e. the shares have been acquired at no cost to the purchaser.

Thus a receipt of bonus shares should be recorded in the accounts of the investor company by memorandum only, and the cost of the investment should not be changed.

Some sources argue that the par value of the shares issued is the amount of a dividend received by the investor, and that the receipt of a bonus issue should be recorded in the investor company's accounts by a debit to investment account and a credit to dividends received; however, this approach is not considered acceptable for two reasons:

  (i) Investments must be valued at cost or at valuation, and if at valuation the credit would be to an asset revaluation reserve rather than to the profit and loss account.

  (ii) By crediting the bonus issue to dividends received, the dividend becomes part of the distributable profits of the investor company, which is not correct. Shares cannot be distributed.

SUBSEQUENT ISSUE OF SHARES BY SUBSIDIARY

3. *What effect does a bonus issue have on the company making the bonus issue?*

The subsidiary company has "locked in" part of its reserves. By creating additional paid-up capital out of retained earnings, these reserves are no longer available for the payment of dividends.

Thus a bonus issue should be recorded in the accounts of the subsidiary company as follows:

    Dr Retained earnings (or whatever reserve is the source of the dividend)
        Cr Issued capital

No journal entry is required in the recipient company's accounts; a note is needed only to show that the number of shares held has increased.

Accounting treatment of bonus issue

Alternative 1

Treat the bonus issue as a cash dividend which is used to purchase shares.

    Therefore on receipt of dividends:
        In H Co. — Dr Inter-company account
                      Cr Dividends received (P/L)
        In S Co. — Dr Dividends paid
                      Cr Inter-company account

    Then H Co. purchases shares:
        In H Co. — Dr Investment in S
                      Cr Inter-company account
        In S Co. — Dr Inter-company account
                      Cr Issued share capital

Alternative 2

This is considered the preferred approach.

        In S Co. — Dr Dividend paid
                      Cr Issued capital
    In H Co. — nothing; note by memorandum only
    On consolidation—
            Dr Issued capital
                Cr Dividends paid

The notes to the group accounts should include a note such as:

"Consolidated retained earnings includes an amount of $X not available for distribution, as they have arisen on a bonus issue of shares by a subsidiary."

Example 16.5

Assume that H Company owns 320,000 shares in S Company, purchased on 30 June 19X0 at a cost of $750,000. At that time the shareholders' funds of S Company were:

	$000
Issued capital	400
Retained earnings	200
	600

¶1606

On 30 June 19X4 S Company issued 100,000 bonus shares, out of retained earnings, at par.

Set out below are balance sheets as at 30 June 19X4.

	H Co. $000	S Co. $000	Debit $000	Credit $000	Group $000
Issued capital	1,000	500			
Retained earnings	1,000	400			
	2,000	900			
Investment in S Co.	750				
Other assets	1,300	1,000			
Other liabilities	(50)	(100)			
	2,000	900			
Operating profit after tax	200	100			
	200	100			
Retained earnings 1.7.X3	800	400			
Dividends satisfied by bonus issue		(100)			
Retained earnings 30.6.X4	1,000	400			

Prepare consolidation journal entries and consolidation worksheet as at 30 June 19X4.

Suggested Solution to Example 16.5

		$000	$000
(a)	Dr Issued capital	320	
	Dr Opening retained earnings	160	
	Cr Investment		750
	Dr Goodwill	270	

Elimination of original investment

(b)	Dr Issued capital	80	
	Dr Opening retained earnings	80	
	Dr Minority interest (P/L)	20	
	Cr Minority interest (B/S)		180

Recognition of minority interest at 30 June 19X4

(c)	Dr Issued capital	100	
	Cr Dividend paid		100

Transfer to retained earnings of shares issued by way of bonus. This entry eliminates the dividend paid within the group.

¶1606

SUBSEQUENT ISSUE OF SHARES BY SUBSIDIARY   173

	Accounts as at 30.6.X4				
	H Co.	S Co.	Debit	Credit	Group
	$000	$000	$000	$000	$000
Issued capital	1,000	500	a320 b80 c100		1,000
Retained earnings	1,000	400	260	100	1,240
Minority interest				b180	180
	2,000	900	760	280	2,420
Investment in S Co.	750			a750	
Other assets	1,300	1,000			2,300
Other liabilities	(50)	(100)			(150)
Goodwill			a270		270
	2,000	900	270	750	2,420
Operating profit after tax	200	100			300
Minority interest			b20		20
	200	100	20		280
Retained earnings 1.7.X3	800	400	a160 b80		960
Dividends paid		(100)		c100	
Retained earnings 30.6.X4	1,000	400	260	100	1,240

A note may be included in the group accounts advising that part of group retained earnings is "locked in". For example:

"*Note:* Included in group retained earnings is $100 of non-distributable profits arising from a bonus issue of shares by a subsidiary company."

¶1607   Bonus issue from intra-group asset revaluation reserve

Asset revaluation reserves are "unrealised" reserves. They arise from a decision by directors to adjust the book value of an asset or assets. No transaction takes place with an outside party.

A holding company may revolve its investment in a subsidiary company, and may "pay" a bonus issue from that reserve. This gives a particular problem to consolidation accountants, as illustrated in the following example.

Example 16.6

A Company has held its 100% investment in S Company for a number of years. The net assets of S Company have increased substantially during that period. On 30 June 19X7 A Company revalues its investment in S Company, from cost of $10 (including no goodwill) to $1,000. The journal entry in A Company's financial statement is:

¶1607

	$	$
Dr Investment in S Co.	990	
Cr Asset revaluation reserve		990

A Company then uses this asset revaluation reserve to make a bonus issue to its shareholders. The journal entry in A Company's books is as follows:

	$	$
Dr Asset revaluation reserve	990	
Cr Issued capital		990

On consolidation as at 30 June 19X7 the net assets of A Company and S Company will be:

	A Co. $	S Co. $
Issued capital	1,090	100
Asset revaluation reserve	—	—
Retained earnings	2,000	900
	3,090	1,000

Consolidation Elimination Entries

	$	$
1. Dr Issued capital S Co.	100	
Cr Investment in S Co.		100
Elimination entry carried forward from prior years		
2. Dr Asset revaluation reserve	990	
Cr Investment in S Co.		990
Reversal of intra-group revaluation		

This leaves the investment in S Company at $nil, and group issued capital equal to A Co.'s issued capital.

However, asset revaluation reserve now has a debit balance of $990. This cannot remain; how do we remedy this situation?

Consider what the group has done. Two transactions were entered into by group members:

(1) *a revaluation* — this is an inter-company transaction and has correctly been eliminated; and

(2) *a bonus issue of shares* — a bonus issue is a dividend; however, at present the group accounts show no dividend paid.

From where was the dividend "paid"?

From a group point of view the dividend could not have been paid from an asset revaluation reserve, since from a group point of view no such reserve existed. Therefore the dividend must have been "paid" from another reserve. The only other reserve account of the company making the bonus issue is retained earnings, and we must assume that it was from this account that the group has paid the dividend.

¶1607

The journal entry required is as follows:

	$	$
Dr Profit and loss account — dividends paid	990	
Cr Asset revaluation reserve		990

No internally generated goodwill

Some authorities contend that the debit in the above journal entry should go to goodwill, being a recognition of the increase in net worth of S Company.

However, this amounts to the recognition of internally generated goodwill, which is not only a contradiction of the whole basis of historical cost accounting and the stewardship notion of financial reporting, but is also in contravention of Approved Accounting Standard ASRB 1013: Accounting for Goodwill and Statement of Accounting Standards AAS 18 of the same title, both of which specify that internally generated goodwill is not to be brought to account.

17

Preference shares

Nature of preference shares ——— ¶1701
General principles of consolidation
   relating to preference shares — ¶1702
Preference dividends in arrears — ¶1703

¶1701 Nature of preference shares

Preference shares can be issued in almost unlimited forms.

In most cases preference shareholders are not entitled to vote at general meetings and are not entitled to participate in a distribution of profits beyond a specified proportion. This proportion is usually specified as a percentage per annum of par value, or par value plus premium contributed, of the preference shares, e.g. "x% preference shares".

As the name implies, preference shares receive preferential treatment over ordinary shares — this will normally be in the form of full entitlement to dividends for preference shareholders before any entitlement to dividends is given to ordinary shareholders. What does this mean with regard to consolidation?

Investments in subsidiary companies are eliminated against the shareholders' funds in which an interest is acquired by virtue of that investment. In most cases an investment in ordinary shares entitles the holder to an interest in all shareholders' funds of the investee. However, this will not be so if those shareholders' funds include preference shares.

An investment in preference shares in most cases only entitles an investor to a specified proportion of shareholders' funds, and it is against this proportion that an investment in preference shares is eliminated.

¶1701

PREFERENCE SHARES 177

An investment in only preference shares would not, in most cases, result in a subsidiary relationship, as the entitlement of the investor is limited and holders of the issued ordinary shares in that investee will control the investee.

¶1702 General principles of consolidation relating to preference shares

The following principles apply where preference shares are non-participating (i.e. x% preference shares):

1. Eliminate the investment in the ordinary issued share capital in the usual way without taking into account preference shares issued as part of net tangible assets.

2. Eliminate the cost of investment in preference shares against the par value of the preference shares acquired.

3. Allocate to minority interest and to H Company (in the ratio of the ownership of preference shares) part of the current year profits for preference dividends if not already provided for in the accounts. If insufficient profits were earned, allocate sufficient retained earnings brought forward; if retained earnings are still insufficient, use reserves (distributable reserves only) to recognise preference dividends. If there are insufficient reserves, then show in a note the amount of preference dividends payable.

4. Allocate to minority interest their share of current year's operating profit after tax (and after preference dividends) in the ratio of ownership of ordinary share capital.

5. Allocate to minority interest their share of retained earnings brought forward (after allowing for any preference dividends still payable from those retained earnings and giving minority interest a share of those preference dividends).

6. Allocate to minority interest their share of ordinary share capital and reserves which remain.

7. Allocate to minority interest their share of preference share capital.

Consider the following example:

Example 17.1

H Company owns 80% of the issued ordinary capital of S Company. This interest was acquired on 31 December 19X0 at a cost of $500,000.

On 31 December 19X5 H Company subscribed for 200,000 $1 par, 6% preference shares in S Company, at a premium of 50¢ per share.

Set out below are abbreviated balance sheets and profit and loss statements for H Company and S Company as at 31 December 19X6.

¶1702

	H Co.	S Co.	Debit	Credit	Group
	$000	$000	$000	$000	$000
Issued capital					
— ordinary	500	100			
— preference	—	250			
Reserves					
— general	500	—			
— share premium	—	125			
Retained earnings	500	995			
Minority interest	—	—			
	1,500	1,470			
Investment in S Co.	800				
Other assets	700	1,470			
	1,500	1,470			
Operating profit	600	250			
Income tax expense	250	140			
	350	110			
Retained earnings brought forward	250	900			
	600	1,010			
Dividends paid					
— ordinary	100	—			
— preference	—	15			
Retained earnings	500	995			

Prepare consolidation journal entries as at 31.12.X6 using the following information.

1. Net assets of S Company at acquisition dates were as follows:

	31/12/X0	31/12/X5
	$000	$000
Issued capital — ordinary	100	100
— preference	—	250
Share premium reserve	—	125
Retained earnings	600	900
	700	1,375

2. All non-monetary assets of S Company in existence at 31.12.X0 were sold prior to 31.12.X5.

¶1702

PREFERENCE SHARES

Suggested Solution to Example 17.1

Elimination Entries

	$000	$000
1. Dr Ordinary issued capital (80% of $100)	80	
Dr Retained earnings brought forward (80% of $600)	480	
Cr Investment in ordinary shares		500
Cr Discount on acquisition		60
Elimination of investment in ordinary shares		
2. Dr Preference issued capital	200	
Cr Investment in preference shares		300
Dr Share premium reserve	100	
Elimination of investment in preference shares		
3. Dr Issued capital — ordinary (20% of $100)	20	
Dr Issued capital — preference	50	
Dr Share premium reserve (20% of $125)	25	
Dr Retained earnings brought forward (20% of $900)	180	
Dr Minority interest (P/L) (20% of $110)	22	
Cr Preference dividends paid to minority interest ($50 × 6%)		3
Cr Minority interest (B/S)		294
Allocation of minority interest		
4. Dr Preference dividend received by H Co.	12	
Cr Preference dividend paid by S Co.		12
Elimination of inter-company dividend		
5. Dr Discount on acquisition	60	
Cr Retained earnings brought forward		60
To recognise that discount related to non-monetary assets which have been sold outside the group in prior years		

As can be seen from the consolidation worksheet:

(1) All issued capital of S Co. has been eliminated

(2) All investments in S Co. have been eliminated

(3) Minority interest at balance date equals:
    (i) 20% of S Company's "ordinary" capital and reserves
        i.e. issued ordinary shares   20
            share premium reserve   25
            retained earnings   199   244
    (ii) 20% of "preference" share capital   50   50
                      294

¶1702

Accounts as at 31.12.X6

	H Co.	S Co.	Debit	Credit	Group
	$000	$000	$000	$000	$000
Issued capital					
— ordinary	500	100	¹80		500
			³20		
— preference	—	250	²200		—
			³50		
Reserves					
— general	500	—			500
— share premium	—	125	³25		—
			²100		
Retained earnings	500	995	694	75	876
Minority interest	—	—		³294	294
	1,500	1,470	1,169	369	2,170
Investment in S Co.	800			¹500	—
				²300	
Other assets	700	1,470			2,170
Discount on acquisition			⁵60	¹60	—
	1,500	1,470	60	860	2,170
Total of eliminations			1,229	1,229	
Operating profit	600	250	⁴12		838
Income tax expense	250	140			390
	350	110	12		448
Minority interest			³22		22
	350	110	34		426
Retained earnings					
brought forward	250	900	¹480	⁵60	550
			³180		
	600	1,010	694	60	976
Dividends paid					
— ordinary	100	—			100
— preference	—	15		³3	—
				⁴12	
Retained earnings	500	995	694	75	876

¶1703 Preference dividends in arrears

Complexities arise where preference dividends are in arrears, i.e. not paid and not provided for. This situation is possible only where an expectation that preference dividends will be payable cannot be demonstrated. The following treatments may be appropriate.

- If insufficient profit or reserves are available to pay preference dividends, show the amount in arrears either as a note or as a liability, then allocate profits as they are earned to the preference shareholders before any profits are allocated to ordinary share owners.

- Where preference dividends are in arrears at the date of acquisition, this will increase the equity acquired, as the shares will be purchased "cum-div". In calculating goodwill the investment cost should not be reduced, the equity acquired should be increased. However, in later years after arrears of dividends are paid, the investment cost should be reduced.
- If preference shares are in arrears at the date of acquisition of ordinary shares, establish a liability for preference dividends out of retained earnings at the acquisition date, and then calculate goodwill.

18

Reduction in shareholders' funds of subsidiary

Loss-making subsidiary	¶1801
Negative shareholders' funds at acquisition	¶1802
Loss in a particular year	¶1803
Return to positive shareholders' funds	¶1804
Post-acquisition reduction in pre-acquisition asset revaluation reserve of subsidiary	¶1805

¶1801 Loss-making subsidiary

A loss-making subsidiary company poses several unusual problems in consolidations. There are three basic situations:

(1) At the date of acquisition — negative shareholders' funds in the subsidiary are acquired.
(2) Subsequent to acquisition — post-acquisition losses result in negative net assets.
(3) The subsidiary returns to a profit-making situation from a loss-making position.

Each of these situations is examined in the following paragraphs.

¶1801

¶1802 Negative shareholders' funds at acquisition

When a company purchases 100% of the issued capital of another company which has negative shareholders' funds, the only effect on consolidation will usually be that the initial elimination entry will show a credit to accumulated losses in place of the more usual debit to retained earnings.

However, where a partial acquisition takes place, a problem as to recognition of minority interest arises.

Minority interest is shown in group accounts on the balance sheet at an amount equal to the minority shareholders' proportionate ownership of the share capital and reserves of the subsidiary company or companies concerned.

Where the minority shareholders' proportionate ownership of the share capital and reserves is negative (usually when accumulated losses are greater than the total of issued capital and reserves) minority interest would in theory become negative. However, most authorities believe that, because of the limited liability of shareholders, minority interest cannot be shown as negative, and therefore the holding company shareholders must "bear" any amount of that deficiency above the amount of capital issued to minority shareholders. For example, where shareholders' funds of an 80% owned subsidiary are deficient by $500 and the issued capital of that subsidiary is $100, the minority interest in that subsidiary will be shown as $nil in the group balance sheet.

Let us assume that the $500 deficiency is made up of $100 of issued capital (fully paid) and $600 of accumulated losses. Minority interest will eliminate $20 of that issued capital and, because of limited liability, only $20 of the accumulated losses, the remainder being borne by holding company shareholders.

Can minority interest be negative?

The approach outlined above is based on the theory that minority interest disclosed in group accounts represents the minority shareholders' legal entitlement to the net assets of subsidiaries concerned. However, consolidated financial statements are not prepared on the basis of representing the financial position of a legal entity. A group is not a legal entity.

Consolidated financial statements are designed to demonstrate the financial position of a notional economic entity.

A minority shareholder's legal entitlement is shown in the financial statements of the individual company in which that minority has an interest.

Certain transactions which are unquestionably "legal" transactions are excluded from consolidated financial statements, e.g. sale of inventory within the group. The idea that group minority interest is related to legal entitlement is incorrect.

¶1802

If a subsidiary has negative shareholders' funds, the minority interest therein should be able to be shown as negative.

However, as this "incorrect" theory is espoused by International Accounting Standard IAS 27, and various U.S., U.K. and Canadian accounting standards, and as we have as yet no Australian accounting standard dealing with the matter, the examples and discussion shown hereinafter will adopt the approach that minority interest cannot be negative.

¶1803 Loss in a particular year

Where a loss is earned by a partially owned subsidiary company in a particular year, the minority's share of that loss will be shown as a credit in the profit and loss account of the group, and this will have a debit effect on the minority interest in the balance sheet.

Assuming that minority interst cannot be negative, care must be taken to ensure that the share of current year losses allocated to the minority does not result in a debit balance of minority interest in the balance sheet.

Consider the following situation:

H Company owns 75% of S Company.

The balance sheet of S Company shows net tangible assets of $400,000 at 30 June 19X8 (of which the minority interest share as per the group balance sheet is $100,000).

S Company sustains a loss of $800,000 after tax during 19X9.

The journal entry to take up the minority interest's share of the loss at 30 June 19X9 is as follows:

	$	$
Dr Minority interest (B/S)	$100,000	
Cr Minority interest (P/L)		$100,000

This will be part of the "second" journal entry (see ¶906) to allocate minority interest.

¶1804 Return to positive shareholders' funds

When a subsidiary returns to making profits to such an extent that its deficiency of shareholders' funds is eliminated, a further complication arises.

Because the holding company has borne a greater share of the subsidiary company losses than its ownership percentage, it will require a return of the losses borne by it on behalf of the minority shareholders before it will allocate any profits of the subsidiary to the minority. This is shown in the following example:

¶1803

REDUCTION IN SHAREHOLDERS' FUNDS OF SUBSIDIARY

Example 18.1

Loss-making Subsidiary

H Company owns 75% of S Company's issued capital of $100.

Share capital and reserves of S Company for each of the years 19X0 to 19X5 were as follows:

	19X0	19X1	19X2	19X3	19X4	19X5
Issued capital	100	100	100	100	100	100
Retained earnings	200	(200)	(300)	(400)	(100)	900
	300	(100)	(200)	(300)	—	1,000
Current year profits	50	(400)	(100)	(100)	300	1,000

Suggested Solution to Example 18.1

Retained earnings and current year profits should be allocated as follows:

	19X0	19X1	19X2	19X3	19X4	19X5
Retained earnings						
H Co. share	150	(150)	(225)	(300)	(75)	675
Minority interest share	50	(50)	(75)	(100)	(25)	225
	200	(200)	(300)	(400)	(100)	900
H Co. — allocated	150	(175)	(275)	(375)	(75)	850
Minority interest — allocated	50	(25)	(25)	(25)	(25)	50
	200	(200)	(300)	(400)	(100)	900
Cumulative difference between amounts of retained earnings allocated to minority interest and amounts which should have been borne by minority interest	—	(25)	(50)	(75)	nil	175
Current year profits						
H Co. share	37.5	(300)	(75)	(75)	225	750
Minority interest share	12.5	(100)	(25)	(25)	75	250
	50	(400)	(100)	(100)	300	1,000
H Co. — allocated	37.5	(325)	(100)	(100)	300	750
Minority interest — allocated	12.5	(75)	—	—	—	250
	50	400	(100)	(100)	(300)	1,000
Difference between amount of profits allocated to minority interest and share which should have been borne by minority interest	—	(25)	(25)	(25)	75	Nil

¶1804

Journal entries for recognition of minority interest in each of those years are as follows:

*Debit (Credit)

	19X0	19X1	19X2	19X3	19X4	19X5
Issued capital	25	25	25	25	25	25
Retained earnings brought forward	37.5	50	(25)	(25)	(25)	(25)
Minority interest (P/L)	12.5	(75)	—	—	—	250
Minority interest (B/S)	(75)	—	—	—	—	(250)

Allocation of retained earnings

	Retained earnings		Allocation
Opening balance	200	H Co.	150
		Minority interest	50
19X1 result	(400)	H Co.	(325)
		Minority interest	(75)
Balance end 19X1	(200)	H Co.	(175)
		Minority interest	(25)
19X2 result	(100)	H Co.	(100)
		Minority interest	—
Balance end 19X2	(300)	H Co.	(275)
		Minority interest	(25)
19X3 result	(100)	H Co.	(100)
		Minority interest	—
Balance end 19X3	(400)	H Co.	(375)
		Minority interest	(25)
19X4 result	300	H Co.	300
		Minority interest	—
Balance end 19X4	(100)	H Co.	(75)
		Minority interest	(25)
19X5 result	1,000	H Co.	750
		Minority interest	250
Balance end 19X5	900	H Co.	675
		Minority interest	225

¶1805 Post-acquisition reduction in pre-acquisition asset revaluation reserve of subsidiary

Approved Accounting Standard ASRB 1010: Accounting for the Revaluation of Non-Current Assets and Statement of Accounting Standards AAS 10 of the same title provide that, where a devaluation of assets reverses a previous revaluation within the same class of assets, the revaluation decrement should be debited to the revaluation reserve to the extent possible (i.e. the reserve should not become negative). These

REDUCTION IN SHAREHOLDERS' FUNDS OF SUBSIDIARY

standards also provide that a revaluation decrement should be debited to the profit and loss account where it relates to a class of assets not previously revalued.

A situation requiring some thought is where a subsidiary has, at acquisition date, an asset revaluation reserve, and subsequent to acquisition this reserve is reduced.

On consolidation, if we simply continue to use the investment elimination entry used in prior years, which includes a debit to the asset revaluation reserve existing at acquisition date, the amount debited to the pre-acquisition asset revaluation reserve of the subsidiary will be more than the current value of that asset revaluation reserve, and will leave a debit balance in the asset revaluation reserve account.

The object of consolidation is to present the accounts of a group, and when in doubt as to the course of action to be taken one should consider the situation from the group point of view.

Considering a pre-acquisition asset revaluation reserve of a subsidiary, from a group point of view no revaluation of the assets of the subsidiary has ever taken place. As the revaluation occurred prior to acquisition, the revaluation reserve has never been shown in the group accounts, having been eliminated from the accounts of the subsidiary on consolidation. This in effect is a reserve that has been "paid for" by the group.

Therefore, the revaluation decrement should, in the consolidated accounts, be debited to the profit and loss account, with consideration to be given to the disclosure of this amount as an extraordinary item. The result of this is that the group shows a loss on devaluation of an asset from its "cost" to the group.

This would be achieved by applying the elimination entry as used in previous years, and then debiting the profit and loss account and crediting the asset revaluation reserve with the revaluation decrement.

Example 18.2

H Company acquired all of the issued capital of S Company on 30 June 19X0 for $500,000. On 30 June 19X5 S Company had its land and buildings revalued by an independent valuer. This valuation showed that the slump in property prices during the years 19X2 to 19X5 had seriously affected the value of the land and buildings, and a revaluation downwards of $100,000 was required.

The accounts of S Company at each of the relevant dates were as follows:

¶1805

ACCOUNTING FOR BUSINESS CONSOLIDATIONS

	30.6.X0	30.6.X5
	$000	$000
Issued capital	100	100
Asset revaluation reserve	300	200
Retained earnings	100	500
	500	800
Land and buildings	300	200
Other assets (net of liabilities)	200	600
	500	800
Operating profit before tax		350
Income tax expense		100
		250
Retained earnings brought forward		250
Retained earnings		500

The journal entries required on consolidation at 30 June 19X5 are as follows:

1. Dr Issued capital   100
   Dr Asset revaluation reserve   300
   Dr Retained earnings brought forward   100
       Cr Investment in S Co.   500

   Elimination of investment in S Co.

2. Dr Operating profit before tax   100
       Cr Asset revaluation reserve   100

   S Company has applied the revaluation decrement against the revaluation reserve. The group must apply this decrement against profit and loss account.

With minority interest

The following example considers a similar situation to that in Example 18.2, with the addition of a minority interest.

Example 18.3

The existence of minority shareholders in Example 18.2 above would require adjustment of the minority interest in current year profit of S Company to reflect the fact that S Company is now contributing less profit to the group.

If we assume that in the above example H Company had paid $400,000 to acquire 80% of the issued capital of S Company, and that S Company earned a profit of $250,000 during 19X5, the consolidation entries would be as follows:

		$	$
(a)	Dr Issued capital	80	
	Dr Asset revaluation reserve	240	
	Dr Retained earnings brought forward	80	
	Cr Investment		400
	Elimination of investment in S Company		
(b)	Dr Issued capital	20	
	Dr Asset revaluation reserve	40	

¶1805

REDUCTION IN SHAREHOLDERS' FUNDS OF SUBSIDIARY

Dr Minority interest (P/L)	50	
Dr Retained earnings brought forward	50	
Cr Minority interest (B/S)		160

Recognition of minority interest

(c) Dr Operating profit 100
Cr Asset revaluation reserve 100

To show what the group has done in devaluing assets

(d) Dr Asset revaluation reserve 20
Cr Minority interest (P/L) 20

To recognise a reduced minority share of current year profit as a result of different treatment of devaluation on consolidation to that applied in subsidiary company accounts

Check the amount disclosed as minority interest:

Net assets of S Co. at 30.6.X5	$800
Minority share	20%
Balance of minority interest	$160

Assuming the information shown below for H Company, the completed consolidation worksheet is shown below.

Accounts as at 31.12.X5

	H Co.	S Co.	Debit	Credit	Group
	$	$	$	$	$
Issued capital	1,000	100	ª80		1,000
			ᵇ20		
Asset revaluation reserve		200	ª240	ᶜ100	—
			ᵇ40		
			ᵈ20		
Retained earnings	—	500	280	20	240
Minority interest				ᵇ160	160
	1,000	800	680	280	1,400
Land and buildings	—	200			200
Investment in S Co.	400			ª400	—
Other assets (net of liabilities)	600	600			1,200
	1,000	800		400	1,400
Operating profit before tax	—	350	ᶜ100		250
Income tax expense	—	100			100
Operating profit	—	250	100		150
Minority interest	—		ᵇ50	ᵈ20	30
	—	250	150	20	120
Retained earnings 1.7.X4	—	250	ª80		120
			ᵇ50		
Retained earnings 30.6.X5	—	500	280	20	240

¶1805

19

Indirect interests

Wholly owned subsidiaries ——— ¶1901
Partly owned subsidiaries ——— ¶1902
Examples of group shareholding
    situations which may occur —— ¶1903
Summary ————————————— ¶1904

¶1901 Wholly owned subsidiaries

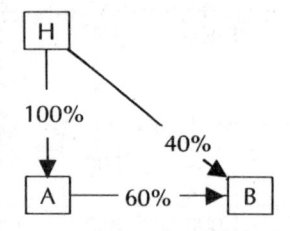

```
        H
       / \
   100%   40%
    ↓      ↘
    A ─60%→ B
```

Shareholdings within groups are often not "in a straight line".

In the above example, B Company is a wholly owned subsidiary of H Company.

The investment by H Company in B Company is not in itself sufficient to generate a subsidiary relationship. However, when viewed in the light of A Company's investment in B Company it is an investment in a group company.

H Company will control A Company and can therefore control the shares in B Company held by A Company. Combining this 60% with the 40% owned directly by H Company gives H Company control over 100% of B Company.

¶1901

INDIRECT INTERESTS

Timing of investment by H Company in B Company

H Company may invest in B Company:

(a) before A Company invests in B Company;

(b) at the same time as A Company invests in B Company;

(c) after A Company invests in B Company.

Each of these situations is treated in the same way as a piecemeal acquisition (see Chapter 14).

¶1902 Partly owned subsidiaries

Consideration of indirect investments involving partly owned subsidiaries from a group point of view enables these often complex looking structures to be dealt with in consolidation accounting. Each acquisition should be considered with the question "What has the group done?" Minority interest should also be considered at the time of preparing consolidated accounts, again from a group point of view.

A general "rule" can be used in this regard. In most situations the indirect minority is allocated a share of shareholders' funds of the subsidiary in which it has an indirect interest only from the date that subsidiary comes into the group. It is only from this date that the indirect minority, and the group, have any interest in the subsidiary. Of course, any direct minority interest will be allocated a share of all shareholders' funds of the subsidiary.

¶1903 Examples of group shareholding situations which may occur

Example 19.1

Blue Invests in Green before Red Invests in Blue

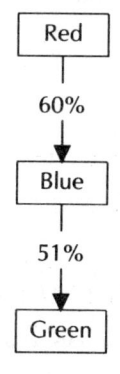

```
    Red
     |
    60%
     ↓
    Blue
     |
    51%
     ↓
   Green
```

(1) Red acquired its interest in Blue on 30 June 19X1 for $480,000.

(2) Blue acquired its interest in Green on 30 June 19X0 for $300,000.

The respective balance sheets of the companies as at 30 June 19X0 are as follows:

¶1903

	Red $000	Blue $000	Green $000
Share capital and reserves			
Ordinary capital ($1 each)	1,000	500	400
Retained earnings	550	200	100
	1,550	700	500
Represented by			
Investment in ordinary shares in subsidiary	500	300	—
Other assets net of liabilities	1,050	400	500
	1,550	700	500

The profit and loss accounts of the three companies for the year ended 30 June 19X0 were as follows:

	Red $000	Blue $000	Green $000
Operating profit	400	200	60
Income tax	250	100	20
Profit after tax	150	100	40
Opening retained earnings	600	100	60
Available for appropriation	750	200	100
Less dividends paid	200	—	—
Retained earnings 30.6.X0	550	200	100

The profit and loss accounts of the three companies for the year ended 30 June 19X1 were as follows:

	Red $000	Blue $000	Green $000
Operating profit	300	100	250
Income tax expense	150	50	125
Profit after tax	150	50	125
Retained earnings 1.7.X0	550	200	100
Available for appropriation	700	250	225
Less dividends paid	300	—	—
Retained earnings 30.6.X1	400	250	225

Assume that no other transactions occurred during 19X1.

(a) Prepare consolidation journals as at 30 June 19X0 in respect of Blue's investment in Green.

(b) Prepare consolidation journals and consolidation worksheet of Red group as at 30 June 19X1.

(c) Show how profits for the year ended 30 June 19X1 are allocated.

¶1903

INDIRECT INTERESTS

Suggested Solution to Example 19.1

In this situation the "Red Group" is investing in "Blue plus Green".

In this situation, a question arises in relation to the treatment of consolidation goodwill which exists in the accounts of a group acquired. Do we:

(a) eliminate Red's investment in Blue group, using (effectively) Blue group's consolidated accounts; or

(b) eliminate Red's investment in Blue using Blue's individual company accounts?

Elimination of Red's investment against the net assets of Blue alone ignores the fact that Blue is entitled to receive as a dividend 51% of profits earned by Green during the period since the date Blue acquired its investment in Green. We must assume that Red was aware of this at the time of its investment in Blue, and that such an entitlement was taken into account in determining the price Red was willing to pay to acquire Blue.

Also, the investment by Red in Blue brings both Blue and Green into the "Red group" for the first time as from 30 June 19X1. Accordingly all profits earned by Green prior to 30 June 19X1 must be eliminated as pre-acquisition; the Red group did not earn those profits.

Consolidation Journal as at 30.6.X0

		$000	$000
1.	Dr Share capital of Green	204	
	Dr Retained earnings brought forward	30.6	
	Dr Operating profit	30.6	
	Cr Income tax expense		10.2
	Cr Investment in subsidiary		300
	Dr Goodwill	45	

Elimination of Blue's investment in Green against 51% of shareholders' funds of Green at 30.6.X0

2.	Dr Share capital of Green	196	
	Dr Retained earnings brought forward	29.4	
	Dr Minority interest (P/L)	19.6	
	Cr Minority interest (B/S)		245

Recognition of direct minority share (49%) of net assets of Green at date of consolidation, i.e. 30.6.X1

Consolidation Journal as at 30.6.X1

1.	Dr Share capital of Green	204	
	Dr Retained earnings brought forward	51	
	Cr Investment in subsidiary		300
	Dr Goodwill	45	

Elimination of Blue's investment in Green as at 30 June 19X1

Note that this is the same entry as for 30.6.X0, with a time adjustment for components of retained earnings.

¶1903

2. Dr Share capital of Green 196
   Dr Retained earnings brought forward (4% of
      $100) 49
   Dr Minority interest (P/L) (49% of $125) 61.25
      Cr Minority interest (B/S)
         (49% of $625 ($500 + $125)) 306.25

Allocation of direct minority interest in Green

3. Dr Share capital of Blue 300
   Dr Retained earnings brought forward — Blue 120
   Dr Operating profit — Blue 60
      Cr Income tax expense — Blue 30
   Dr Operating profit — Green (60% of 51% of
      $250) 76.5
      Cr Income tax expense — Green (60% of
         51% of $125) 38.25
      Cr Investment 500
   Dr Goodwill on consolidation — Red's
      investment in Blue 11.75

Elimination of Red's investment in Blue

(Note: Profits earned by Green since its acquisition by Blue have been "acquired" by Red, not "earned" by Red.)

4. Dr Share capital 200
   Dr Retained earnings brought forward 80
   Dr Minority interest (P/L) 20
      Cr Minority interest (B/S) 300

Direct minority share of Blue as at 30.6.X1 being 40% of net assets of Blue as at 30.6.X1

5. Dr Minority interest (P/L) (49% of 51% of
      $125) 25.5
      Cr Minority interest (B/S) 25.5

Allocation of indirect minority share of Green. The indirect minority only "shares" in the profits earned by Green since that minority "acquired" its interest in Green, i.e. on the day that Blue invested in Green.

¶1903

INDIRECT INTERESTS

Consolidation Worksheet as at 30.6.X1

	Red	Blue	Green	Debit	Credit	Group
	$000	$000	$000	$000	$000	$000
Issued capital	1,000	500	400	[1]204 [2]196 [3]300 [4]200		1,000.00
Retained earnings	400	250	225	543.25	68.25	400.00
Minority interest					[2]306.25 [4]300 [5]25.5	631.75
	1,400	750	625	1,443.25	700	2,031.75
Investment	500	300	—		[1]300 [3]500	—
Goodwill	—	—	—	[1]45 [3]11.75		56.75
Other assets	900	450	625			1,975.00
	1,400	750	625	56.75	800	2,031.75
Total of eliminations				1,500	1,500	
Operating profit	300	100	250	[3]60 [3]76.5		513.50
Income tax expense	150	50	125		[3]30 [3]38.25	256.75
	150	50	125	136.5 [2]61.25 [4]20 [5]25.5	68.25	256.75
Minority interest						106.75
	150	50	125	243.25	68.25	150.00
Retained earnings brought forward	550	200	100	[1]51 [2]49 [3]120 [4]80		550.00
	700	250	225	543.25	68.25	700.00
Dividends paid	300	—	—			300.00
	400	250	225	543.25	68.25	400.00

¶1903

Note: Allocation of profits — year ended 30.6.X1

		$000
Green		
Profit of Green for 19X1 is		125.00
This is allocated as follows:		
49% to Green's direct minority shareholders		61.25
51% to Red group	63.75	
Less: 40% of that amount to Blue's direct minority shareholders	25.50	25.50
60% of 51% eliminated as being pre-Red's acquisition	38.25	38.25
		125.00
Blue		
Profit of Blue for 19X1 is		50.00
This is allocated as follows:		
40% to Blue's direct minority shareholders		20.00
60% eliminated as pre-Red's acquisition		30.00
		50.00
In summary, total profit earned by each company in the Red group is:		
Red	150	
Blue	50	
Green	125	325.00
and is allocated as follows:		
To Red group — from Red	150	150.00
Pre-acquisition — Blue	30.00	
— Green	38.25	68.25
To minority: direct — Green	61.25	
— Blue	20.00	
indirect — Green	25.50	106.75
		325.00

¶1903

INDIRECT INTERESTS   197

Example 19.2

Red Invests in Blue before Blue Invests in Green

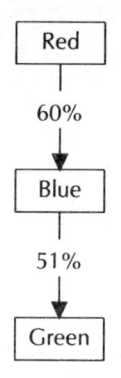

```
     Red
      │
     60%
      ▼
     Blue
      │
     51%
      ▼
    Green
```

1. Eliminate the investment by Red in Blue in the normal manner, i.e. the cost of investment against the net assets of Blue at the acquisition date.
2. Eliminate the investment by Blue in Green in the usual way. In this situation Red group, consisting of Red and Blue, is investing in Green. The cost of the group's investment happens to sit in the accounts of Blue — this is no different from the situation where the group investment sits in the accounts of Red, as far as elimination of the investment is concerned.
3. Allocate the post-acquisition profits of Blue in the usual way, i.e. 40% to minority interest.
4. Allocate the post-acquisition profits of Green in the normal manner, i.e. as for 3. above. This will be done in the "second" journal entry (see ¶906), wherein the 40% minority interest is allocated a share of all the shareholders' funds of Blue as at the balance date.
5. Allocate the post-acquisition profits of Green based on indirect minority interest.

Therefore, minority interest in Red group =
 40% of all Blue + 49% of all of Green
 + 40% of 51% of post-acquisition profit of Green.

Example 19.3

Red Invests in Blue, Red Invests in Green, Blue Invests in Green

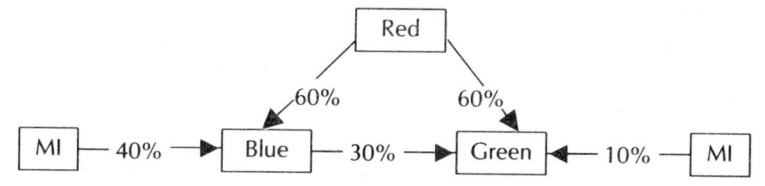

```
              Red
            /     \
          60%     60%
          ▼         ▼
 MI─40%→ Blue ─30%→ Green ←10%─ MI
```

1. Eliminate the investment by Red in Blue in the usual way.
2. Eliminate the investment by Blue in Green in the usual way.
3. Eliminate the investment by Red in Green in the usual way.

¶1903

4. Minority interest allocation is as follows:

> 40% of all of Blue's net assets
>
> plus 10% of all of Green's net assets
>
> plus 40% of 30% of Green's post-acquisition increases in net assets, i.e. from the date Blue invests in Green.
>
> Green's increases in reserves will be allocated as follows:

60% to Red group	60%
60% of 30% = 18% to Red group	18%
40% of 30% = 12% to Blue's minority interest	12%
10% to Green's minority interest	10%
	100%

Example 19.4

Blue Invests in Green, Red Invests in Blue, Red Invests in Green

This is treated in the same fashion as Example 19.3 above. The additional investment by Red in Green is accounted for in the normal manner.

Minority interest is allocated as follows:

> 40% of all Blue
> plus 40% of 30% of Green, post-Red's investment in Blue
> plus 10% of all Green.

Green's increase in reserves will be allocated as follows:

60% to Red group	60%
plus 60% of 30% to Red group, subsequent to Red's investment in Blue	18%
plus 40% of 30% to Blue's direct minority subsequent to Red's investment in Blue	12%
plus 10% of all of Green	10%
	100%

¶1904 Summary

An investment in a subsidiary company involving indirect interests should be eliminated against the net assets of the subsidiary as at acquisition date.

Direct minority interests should be allocated a share equal to their direct ownership percentage in all of the share capital and reserves of the subsidiary at balance date.

Indirect minority interests should be allocated a share of the movements in the reserves of the subsidiary from the later of:

(a) the date on which the subsidiary became part of the group, or

(b) the date on which the company in which the indirect minority has a direct interest acquired its investment in the subsidiary.

20

Adjustments to pre-acquisition situation

Post-acquisition information ¶2001
Pre-acquisition inventory and fixed asset sales ¶2002
Post-acquisition recognition of future income tax benefits not recognised at acquisition date ¶2003

¶2001 Post-acquisition information

Should information come to hand subsequent to acquisition that assets or liabilities were understated or overstated as at acquisition date, adjustments should be made to the difference on consolidation previously determined.

Example 20.1

Assume that at 31 December 19X5 H Company purchased 100% of S Company at a cost of $500,000. H Company considered the assets of S Company to be fairly stated.

The consolidated accounts of H group included goodwill of $100,000 with respect to that investment.

If subsequent information obtained on 30 December 19X6 shows that, e.g., certain provisions in S Company were overstated as at 31 December 19X5 by $20,000, the goodwill should be shown as $80,000 in the December 19X6 accounts.

The reversal of these provisions would involve a credit to profit in the accounts of S Company, being a reversal of the debit to profit made on creation of the provision. As the provision was created prior to acquisition date, the original debit to the profit and loss account would have been to pre-acquisition profits. Any subsequent adjustment to that provision, be it to increase or decrease the provision, as a result of the provisions being incorrect as at acquisition date, must also be considered to be against pre-acquisition profits.

Example 20.2

Let us consider the above example, and assume that the provision for reorganisation in the accounts of S Company at acquisition date related to an internal reorganisation being undertaken by S Company. This reorganisation was not affected by the acquisition by H Company. The provision stood at $150,000 at acquisition date; the reorganisation was subsequently completed at a cost of $130,000.

The following consolidation elimination entry at acquisition date would have been made:

	$	$
Dr Net assets	400,000	
Cr Investment in S Co.		500,000
Dr Goodwill	100,000	

If the adjustment to the provision was made in a year different from that of the acquisition, the profit and loss account disclosure will need to be considered.

Subsequent to acquisition, S Company would have written back to the profit and loss account $20,000, being the provision not required:

	$	$
Dr Provision for reorganisation	20,000	
Cr Operating profit		20,000

As the operating profit credited is the pre-acquisition operating profit, the consolidation elimination entry would need to become:

	$	$
Dr Net assets	420,000	
Cr Investment in S Co.		500,000
Dr Goodwill	80,000	

The respective abbreviated balance sheets of H Company and S Company at 31 December 19X5 and 31 December 19X6 were as follows:

¶2001

ADJUSTMENTS TO PRE-ACQUISITION SITUATION

Accounts as at 31.12.X5

	H Co.	S Co.	Debit	Credit	Group
	$000	$000	$000	$000	$000
Issued capital	100	100			
Reserves	100	—			
Retained earnings	100	300			
	300	400			
Goodwill	—	—			
Investment in S Co.	500	—			
Provision for reorganisation	—	(150)			
Other assets		550			
Other liabilities	(200)				
	300	400			
Operating profit	—	200			
Income tax expense	—	80			
	—	120			
Retained earnings brought forward	100	180			
Retained earnings	100	300			

Accounts as at 31.12.X6

	H. Co.	S. Co.	Debit	Credit	Group
	$000	$000	$000	$000	$000
Issued capital	100	100			
Reserves	100	—			
Retained earnings	100	320			
	300	420			
Goodwill	500	—			
Investment in S Co.	—	—			
Provision for reorganisation	—	—			
Other assets		420			
Other liabilities	(200)				
	300	420			
Operating profit	—	20			
Income tax expense	—	—			
	—	20			
Retained earnings brought forward	100	300			
Retained earnings	100	320			

¶2001

Suggested Solution to Example 20.2

Elimination Entry at 31.12.X5

	$	$
Dr Issued capital	100	
Dr Operating profit	200	
Cr Income tax expense		80
Dr Retained earnings brought forward	180	
Cr Investment		500
Dr Goodwill	100	

Accounts as at 31.12.X5

	H Co.	S Co.	Debit	Credit	Group
	$000	$000	$000	$000	$000
Issued capital	100	100	100	—	100
Reserves	100	—	—	—	100
Retained earnings	100	300	380	80	100
	300	400	480	80	300
Goodwill	—	—	100	—	100
Investment in S Co.	500	—	—	500	—
Provision for reorganisation	—	(150)	—	—	(150)
Other assets	—	550	—	—	350
Other liabilities	(200)	—	—	—	—
	300	400	100	500	300
Operating profit	—	200	200	—	—
Income tax expense	—	80	—	80	—
	—	120	—	—	—
Retained earnings brought forward	100	180	180	—	100
Retained earnings	100	300	380	80	100

Elimination Entry at 31.12.X6

	$000	$000
Dr Issued capital	100	
Dr Retained earnings brought forward	300	
Dr Operating profit	20	
Cr Investment		500
Dr Goodwill	80	

¶2001

ADJUSTMENTS TO PRE-ACQUISITION SITUATION

Note:

(1) The entry to debit retained earnings brought forward as at 31.12.X6 reflects the sum of the entries made at 31.12.X5 against the profit and loss account components:

	$000
Operating profit	200
Income tax expense	(80)
Retained earnings brought forward	180
	300

(2) The debit to operating profit in the elimination entry reflects that an entry has been made in S Company's "operating profit" account which relates to pre-acquisition profits. In order to eliminate pre-acquisition profits at the specific account level, our elimination entry must go against the specific account in which those pre-acquisition profits are now recorded.

Accounts as at 31.12.X6

	H Co.	S Co.	Debit	Credit	Group
	$000	$000	$000	$000	$000
Issued capital	100	100	100	—	100
Reserves	100	—	—	—	100
Retained earnings	100	320	320	—	100
	300	420	420	—	300
Goodwill	—	—	80	—	80
Investment in S Co.	500	—	—	500	—
Provision for reorganisation	—	—	—	—	—
Other assets	—	420	—	—	220
Other liabilities	(200)	—	—	—	—
	300	420	80	500	300
Operating profit	—	20	20	—	—
Income tax expense	—	—	—	—	—
	—	20	—	—	—
Retained earnings brought forward	100	300	300	—	100
Retained earnings	100	320	320	—	100

¶2002 Pre-acquisition inventory and fixed asset sales

Different opinions exist as to the accounting treatment required where profit is made on the sale of inventory or fixed assets between:

(a) a group member, and

(b) an outside party who subsequently becomes a group member,

when the assets are still on hand.

¶2002

Possible treatments are:

(a) to treat the profit as unrealised, or

(b) to treat the profit as realised.

Those who consider that the profit should be unrealised argue that the group holds assets at a cost higher than that paid by individual members of the group and that therefore adjustment is required.

Those who consider that the profit should not be considered unrealised argue that the group as it stood at the time of the transaction purchased or sold the assets to an outside party and that therefore the transaction is one which should be reported on by the group. Subsequent entry into the group of that outside party is considered not to alter the fact that the transaction in question was between the group and an outside party.

Where the transaction for sale and the entering into the group of the outside party are related decisions, it is preferable that the profit be considered unrealised; this will effectively reduce the net assets of the new group member at the time of acquisition. This will be so whether the new member had sold the asset, in which case the profit will be considered unrealised, or has purchased the asset, in which case the asset will be considered to be overvalued.

I consider that where the transaction for sale and the transaction for acquisition of the former outside party are not related, the profit is realised, and no adjustment is necessary on consolidation.

¶2003 Post-acquisition recognition of future income tax benefits not recognised at acquisition date

Future income tax benefits "available" to entities are sometimes not recognised as assets, due to uncertainty of recovery. Future income tax benefits will only be realised if the entity makes taxable profits in the future, and other conditions are met.

As a result, a subsidiary acquired may not show an existing future income tax benefit as an asset at acquisition date. Subsequent to acquisition date, the subsidiary may fulfil the conditions necessary and realise the benefit of that undisclosed asset.

This has implications for the goodwill determined on acquisition — the assets of the subsidiary are a component of the goodwill calculation; any subsequent change in those assets *may* affect goodwill.

Example 20.3

H Company has purchased 100% of S Company. H Company invested in S Company on 31 December 19X2. Details of net assets of S Company at that date were:

	$
Issued capital	100
Retained earnings	100
	200

ADJUSTMENTS TO PRE-ACQUISITION SITUATION

The notes to the accounts of S Company at 31 December 19X2 noted that future income tax benefits of $100 had not been recognised in those accounts due to their realisability not being assured.

The investment in S Company cost H Company $350.

On acquisition, H Company would also assume that the future income tax benefits were not assured of realisation, and the investment elimination entry at 3 December 19X2 would be:

		$	$
(a)	Dr Issued capital	100	
	Dr Retained earnings	100	
	Cr Investment		350
	Dr Goodwill	150	

Assume that during the year ended 31 December 19X3 circumstances were such that the future income tax benefit was able to be recognised.

If the circumstances giving rise to the recognition of the future income tax benefit related solely to the activities of the subsidiary, i.e. its realisation was not affected by group activities contemplated at the time of the acquisition, the future income tax benefit should be recognised as a "pre-acquisition" asset. Had the benefit been recognised in the accounts as at 31/12/X2 the corresponding credit to income tax expense would have increased retained earnings by $100, i.e.: the acquisition elimination entry would have been, and should now become:

		$	$
(b)	Dr Future income tax benefit	100	
	Cr Income tax expense		100
(c)	Dr Issued capital	100	
	Dr Retained earnings	100	
	Dr Income tax expense	100	
	Cr Investment		350
	Dr Goodwill	50	

If the future income tax benefit is now able to be recognised as a result of activities of the group which were not contemplated at the time of acquisition, the benefit should be considered post-acquisition, and a credit recorded to group income tax expense. No change will be required in respect of the acquisition elimination entry.

The worksheets below provide balance sheets and profit and loss accounts for H Company and S Company as at 31.12.X3, showing the elimination entries:

(a) assuming no realisation of the future income tax benefit; and

(b) assuming realisation of the future income tax benefit.

The adjustment entries shown are those noted above.

Note that entry (b) above is included in the accounts of S Company itself; it is not a consolidation adjustment.

¶2003

(a) *Assuming no realisation of future income tax benefit*

Accounts as at 31.12.X3

	H Co.	S Co.	Debit	Credit	Group
	$	$	$	$	$
Issued capital	100	100	100		100
Retained earnings	100	100	100		100
	200	200	200		200
Investment in S Co.	350			350	—
Other assets		200			200
Other liabilities	(150)				(150)
Goodwill			150		150
Future income tax benefit		100			100
	200	200	150	350	200
Operating profit	—	—			—
Income tax expense (credit)	—	—			—
	—	—			—
Retained earnings brought forward	100	100	100		100
Retained earnings	100	200	100	—	100

¶2003

ADJUSTMENTS TO PRE-ACQUISITION SITUATION

(b) *Assuming realisation of "pre-acquisition" future income tax benefit during the year ended 31.12.X3*

Accounts as at 31.12.X3

	H Co.	S Co.	Debit	Credit	Group
	$	$	$	$	$
Issued capital	100	100	100		100
Retained earnings	100	200	200	—	100
	200	200	300	—	200
Investment in S Co.	350			350	—
Other assets		200			200
Other liabilities	(150)				(150)
Goodwill			50		50
Future income tax benefit		100			100
	200	200	50	350	200
Operating profit	—	—			—
Income tax expense (credit)	—	(100)	100		—
	—	100	100		—
Retained earnings brought forward	100	100	100		100
Retained earnings	100	200	200	—	100

¶2003

21

Statements of sources and applications of funds

Accounting standards ———— ¶2101
Aim of funds statements ———— ¶2102
Consolidated funds statements —— ¶2103

¶2101 Accounting standards

Statement of Accounting Standards AAS 12, "Statement of Sources and Applications of Funds" requires the preparation of a statement of sources and applications of funds ("a funds statement") as part of each set of financial statements for any reporting entity in the private sector, other than companies, and any public sector reporting entity which uses an accrual basis of accounting.

Approved Accounting Standard ASRB 1007: Financial Reporting of Sources and Applications of Funds requires all companies to prepare a funds statement to be entitled a "summary of sources and applications of funds", and to be presented as a note to the financial statements. "Funds" is defined in the standard as meaning "cash and cash equivalents (credit or barter)".

Funds statements are required to be prepared as part of consolidated financial statements. Under both accounting standards, where consolidated financial statements are prepared it is only necessary to prepare a consolidated funds statement; it is not necessary to also include a funds statement for the holding entity.

STATEMENTS OF SOURCES AND APPLICATIONS OF FUNDS

¶2102 Aim of funds statements

The purpose of a funds statement is to present the activities of the entity or group in a manner which portrays what funds were received during the year and how those funds were applied. It is basically a summary of movements in account balances during the year, adjustments having been made where necessary to balance sheet and profit and loss account movements so that movements of funds are shown rather than accounting movements, although there are few differences between the two. Particular areas where balance sheet and profit and loss account movements are adjusted in presentation from an accounting basis to a funds basis include the following.

Funds from operations

A note to the funds statement is necessary to show the differences between operating profit and funds from operations.

Income tax

Payment of income tax is considered a fund movement. Tax-effect accounting adjustments and provision for income tax are considered non-fund movements.

Fixed assets

Movements in fixed asset balances from one year to the next are shown separately in funds statements as follows:

		$	
	Opening balance	x	
Plus	Purchases at cost	x	— Application of funds
Less	Depreciation and amortisation	x	— Non-fund movement, in reconciliation of funds from operations
Plus	Profit on sale	x	— Non-fund movement[1]
Less	Loss on sale	x	— Non-fund movement[1]
Less	Consideration received and receivable	x	— Source of funds[1] in funds from operations
Equals	Closing balance	x	

Note 1. The reconciliation of funds from operations includes:
   (a) consideration received on sale as a revenue, or fund, item; and
   (b) book value of fixed assets sold, as a non-fund item, being the difference between consideration received and profit or loss on sale.

Provisions

Payments from provisions, excluding provisions for annual leave and doubtful debts, are considered fund movements, while amounts set aside or written back from those provision accounts are non-fund movements. The total movements in the annual leave and doubtful debt provisions are considered fund movements.

¶2102

Consolidated funds statements

Preparation of consolidated funds statements is generally a matter of examining movements in balance sheet and profit and loss accounts, and showing these movements as either sources or applications of funds, after adjusting for non-fund items and different funds disclosures required as shown above.

¶2103 Consolidated funds statements

Particular situations requiring consideration in the preparation of consolidated funds statements include the following.

Acquisition of subsidiaries

From a funds statement point of view the acquisition of a subsidiary is shown as the acquisition of the particular assets and liabilities of that subsidiary, and the "payment" of any goodwill to acquire those assets and liabilities is shown as an application of funds.

As goodwill represents the difference between cost and net assets (or assets less liabilities) acquired, the inclusion of assets, liabilities and goodwill in a funds statement will result in the sources of funds shown from the acquisition being equal to the applications of funds.

The assets and liabilities acquired are not shown separately in the funds statement, but are included with other movements of the group. For example:

1.1.X0	Group opening balance of receivables	$100,000
31.3.X0	Subsidiary acquired — balance of receivables at acquisition date	$50,000
31.12.X0	Group closing balance of receivables, including that for all entities in the group including the newly acquired subsidiary	$175,000

The funds statement in this situation will show as an application of funds an increase in receivables of $75,000, from $100,000 to $175,000.

A note to the funds statement is required to show the fair value of assets and liabilities acquired by the group on acquisition of a subsidiary, with the difference between those assets and liabilities shown as equal to the goodwill on acquisition.

Sale of subsidiaries

As for acquisition of subsidiaries, movements shown in a group funds statement will include the removal from the group of the individual assets and liabilities of a subsidiary sold. Consideration received and/or receivable on the sale will be shown as a source of funds.

A note to the funds statement will show the assets and liabilities disposed of, the consideration received, and the difference as being the profit or loss on the sale.

¶2103

Foreign subsidiaries

Any gain (or loss) on translation of foreign subsidiary financial statements will be shown as a source (or application) of funds. The overall gain or loss on translation reflects the effect of the movements in exchange, with balances on all assets and liabilities combined.

A complication arises in respect of non-current assets, such as fixed assets. As noted above (¶2102), all movements of non-current assets are separately disclosed in the funds statement. Should some fixed assets be held overseas, one of the movements in the balance of fixed assets from one year to the next will be the exchange rate movement. For example:

	$A
Opening balance	100
+ Cost of additions	40*
− Depreciation	(12)*
+ Profit on sale	2*
− Consideration received on sale	(8)*
+ Translation difference	10
Closing balance in $A	132

Each of the above movements marked * is expected to be seen in a funds statement.

Compare fixed assets disclosure with accounts receivable disclosure. Assuming that there were no movements in the foreign currency balance of receivables during the year, but that the exchange rate moved favourably, the following movement may occur in the $A translation of the foreign subsidiary financial statements:

	$A
Opening balance of receivables	100
Closing balance of receivables	110

The movement of $10 is the result of a translation.

The consolidated funds statement would show a $10 movement in accounts receivable.

The translation difference in respect of the fixed assets as shown in the table above and the receivables is a gain, and the total gain of $20 (i.e. $10 translation difference shown in the table above plus $10 movement in accounts receivable) will be shown as a source of funds.

What happens to the other side of this entry?

The accounts receivable increase is shown simply as $10, and is mixed with all other group accounts receivable movements. The types of movements are not disclosed.

However, each movement illustrated above in respect of fixed assets *is* disclosed separately. Accordingly, the translation adjustment relating to fixed assets, included in the group gain of $20 above, should also be disclosed separately. The same applies for all non-current assets.

¶2103

A review of published accounts for a number of Australia's major public companies which are known to have significant assets overseas shows that none of these companies disclosed separately in their summaries of sources and applications of funds the movement on translation of fixed assets. One can only assume that the movement has been "lumped in" with other fixed asset movements. The probable reason for this treatment is that correct disclosure does not appear to be in line with "normal" funds statements. This cannot be used as justification for an accounting practice.

Minority interest

The minority interest shown in the group accounts reflects an allocation of a share of shareholders' funds of relevant subsidiaries.

Funds statements should show movements from the point of view of the group. Accordingly allocations to minority interest are not relevant and should be ignored for the purpose of preparation of the funds statement.

22

Overseas subsidiaries

Accounting for overseas subsidiaries	¶2201
Inter-company balances	¶2202
Acquisition elimination entry	¶2203
Inter-company inventory sale	¶2204

¶2201 Accounting for overseas subsidiaries

Subsidiary entities operating in other countries are as much a part of a group as local entities.

To enable consolidation into financial statements of an Australian group the individual financial statements of overseas entities need first to be converted to Australian currency.

Approved Accounting Standard ASRB 1012: Foreign Currency Translation, and Statement of Accounting Standards AAS 20 of the same title, set out rules as to how this conversion is to be done. Two methods of conversion are recognised by the standards, and the situations in which they are to be used are described. No choice exists as to which method can be used — a certain method is required to be used in each particular situation.

Current rate method

This method is prescribed for foreign entities which effectively operate independently of the Australian group.

All assets and liabilities are transferred at balance day rates, profit at rates of the day when the profit is earned, and issued capital and other reserve movements at historical rates. The difference resulting on translation is shown in a translation reserve account.

Temporal method

When a foreign entity operates effectively as a branch of the Australian group, financial statements are translated to Australian currency in conformity with the requirements of Statement of Accounting Standards AAS 20A and Approved Accounting Standard ASRB 1012. The following is an extract from AAS 20A:

"(i) monetary items are translated at the exchange rate current at balance date;

(ii) non-monetary items are translated at exchange rates current at the dates as at which those items were first recognised in the accounts or, where those items have been revalued (upwards or downwards), at exchange rates current at the dates of revaluation;

(iii) owners' equity at the date of acquisition (including, in the case of a corporation, share capital at acquisition and pre-acquisition reserves) is translated at the exchange rate current at acquisition date;

(iv) post-acquisition movements in owners' equity (other than retained profits or accumulated losses) are translated at the exchange rates current at the dates as at which those movements were recognised in the accounts, except that where such movements represent transfers between items within owners' equity, the movements are translated at the exchange rates current at the date that the amounts transferred were originally recognised in owners' equity;

(v) distributions from retained profits (that is, dividends paid or proposed) are translated at the exchange rates current at the dates when the distributions were paid or proposed, as is applicable;

(vi) post-acquisition movements in retained profits or accumulated losses, because of transfers from the profit and loss account or its equivalent, are recognised as a result of applying (vii) below for each reporting period; and,

(vii) revenue and expense items are translated at the exchange rates current at the dates as at which those items were recognised in the accounts, except that items (including depreciation) that relate to non-monetary items are translated at the rates used to translate those non-monetary items."

¶2202 Inter-company balances

When preparing consolidated financial statements we expect inter-company account balances (i.e. amounts owed by companies in the group to other companies in the group) to offset each other exactly. However, this will usually not be the case if one party is an overseas subsidiary. Consider the following illustration:

Example 22.1

On 31 December 19X0 Subsidiary A in Australia lends $A1 million to Subsidiary X in Japan.

¶2202

OVERSEAS SUBSIDIARIES

Assume the exchange rate on 31 December 19X0 was $A1 = Yen 1, and on 31 December 19X1 was $A1 = Yen 1.50.

Subsidiary X pays interest monthly in advance, so that at 31 December 19X1 the balance in Subsidiary A's accounts is $A1 million.

As the Australia/Japan exchange rate has moved during the year, the liability shown in the accounts of Subsidiary X will not be Yen 1 million as it was on the date of the transaction, but Yen 1.5 million. This will be so using either the current rate or temporal methods.

The Japanese subsidiary will show in its accounts a loss of Yen 500,000.

A loss has also been made from a group point of view. The group has placed $A1 million offshore. To return these funds to Australia as at 31 December 19X1 would result in only $A666,667 being received in Australia. The group has placed itself in a position of risk in relation to the Australia/Japan exchange rate, and will record either a profit or a loss as that exchange rate moves.

The result is that a loss or a profit can be made on an inter-company balance.

¶2203 Acquisition elimination entry

Acquisition elimination entries do not usually change from year to year.

Some authorities consider that when a foreign subsidiary is acquired the acquisition entry may change from year to year if goodwill is involved and the current rate method is used. The investment, in $A, is eliminated against net assets using a conversion rate which does not change from that at acquisition date; however, goodwill is an asset, and under the current rate method is converted using the exchange rate ruling at balance date. Accordingly the value of goodwill can change from year to year with an amount equal to the change being shown in the foreign currency translation reserve.

Example 22.2

Subsidiary A (Australian) acquires an investment in Subsidiary J (Japanese) on 31 December 19X0. Subsidiary A controls Subsidiary J as if it were a branch of the Australian operations.

Assume the following exchange rates:

    31.12.X0 $A1 = Yen 1.00
    31.12.X1 $A1 = Yen 1.25

Assume that the consolidation elimination entry with respect to the investment in subsidiary J as at 31 December 19X0 was determined as follows:

	$A	$A	
Dr Issued capital	100		($A1 = Yen1)
Dr Retained earnings	100		($A1 = Yen 1)
Cr Investment		250	
Dr Goodwill	50		

The corresponding entry at 31 December 19X1 would be:

	$A	$A	
Dr Issued capital	100		(historic rate $A1 = Yen 1)
Dr Retained earnings brought forward	100		(historic rate $A1 = Yen 1)
Cr Investment		250	
Dr Goodwill	40		($A1 = Yen 1.25)
Dr Translation reserve	10		

This approach is based upon an assumption that the goodwill is an overseas asset, relating to future benefits to flow from the foreign operations.

Other authorities believe that goodwill is an asset in the currency of the investor. The accounts of the investor, Subsidiary J, in Example 22.2 above, show the investment in $A. This investment cost includes a goodwill component, upon which a return in $A is expected. The fact that the benefits in respect of that goodwill will be earned overseas is only relevant to the extent that changes may be required to be made to the period of amortisation.

The asset goodwill is represented by future benefits to flow from assets and liabilities in a foreign country.

We can assume that the decision to invest in Subsidiary J was made with an awareness of the risks to the return of that investment from movements in exchange rates. The return on that investment should therefore be measured after taking into account the gain or loss from exchange rate movements. Using the situation of the above example, Subsidiary A would have invested an "extra" $A50 in Subsidiary J, expecting profits from Subsidiary J to be of sufficient Japanese yen to return that $A50. As the return of funds is dependent on exchange rates, the exchange rate factor would also have been taken into account in making the decision to invest. If the expected level of yen profits is achieved, but the exchange rate moves unfavourably, the goodwill will not be recovered as expected, and should therefore be reduced. Any reduction in goodwill is effectively a loss on the investment, and should be recorded as such by way of the overall translation adjustment. This would also apply where a foreign subsidiary invests in another foreign subsidiary.

¶2204 Inter-company inventory sale

The group profit and loss account can be affected by the sale of inventory betweeen two group members if the inventory is acquired by a group member overseas.

Example 22.3

A Company — Australian — owns 100% of NZ Company — New Zealander.

On 1 July 19X6 A Company sold inventory to NZ Company. This inventory cost A Company $100, and was sold to NZ Company for $120. NZ Company still held the inventory at 30 June 19X7. Exchange rates were as follows:

OVERSEAS SUBSIDIARIES

1.7.X6 — $A1 = $NZ1.00
30.6.X7 — $A1 = $NZ1.25

Assume an Australian income tax rate of 39%.

What consolidation elimination entry is required on 30.6.X7?

The inventory will be acquired by NZ Company at a cost of $NZ120. This will be converted to $A on 30.6.X7 as $A96 (i.e. $NZ120 ÷ 1.25).

Elimination entry required:	$	$
Dr Operating profit A Co.	20	
Cr Inventory		20
Dr Future income tax benefit	7.8	
Cr Income tax expense		7.8

Elimination of unrealised inventory profit

This results in inventory in the group accounts with a value of:

Per consolidation worksheet, from	
NZ Co. accounts	$A96
Less: Adjustment from elimination entry	$A20
	$A76

Had A Company transferred the stock to NZ Company at no profit, the inventory would have been recorded in the accounts of NZ Company on 1 July 19X6 at $NZ100. On 30 June 19X7 this would have been converted to $A80 ($NZ 100 ÷ 1.25).

We now have a different value for inventory in the group because of the value at which it was transferred. The following is the true position.

Consider the payment side of the transaction. Assume NZ Company had paid for the inventory on 1 July 19X6. The amount required would have been $NZ120 to equate to $A120. The group therefore has the asset "cash" in Australia. Had the cash been left in New Zealand and sent to Australia on 30 June 19X7, it would have realised $A96. By bringing the cash to Australia on 30 June 19X6, the cash has *not* reduced its $A value by $24.

Income tax

The income tax rate to be applied in accounting for a sale of inventory to an overseas subsidiary needs to be considered.

Using the information in the above Example 22.3, the tax effect of the entry is to be at Australian tax rates.

Income tax expense is directly related to operating profit. The operating profit on the transaction was recorded in A Company and therefore the tax effect of the profit is 39%. On elimination of this profit, the related income tax expense recorded in the accounts of A will also be eliminated. Income tax will be paid on the unrealised profit in the year of the transaction, and will be paid in Australia.

Accordingly, any unrealised profit eliminated which relates to a transaction between two group members should be tax effected at the rate of tax paid by the group member which made the sale.

¶2204

23

Current Australian statutory requirements for companies

General	¶2301
Requirement to prepare group accounts	¶2302
Definitions	¶2303
Form and content of group accounts	¶2304
Financial years	¶2305
Acquisition of holding company shares by subsidiary company	¶2306
Relief from preparation of accounts	¶2307
Statement by directors	¶2308
Directors' report	¶2309
True and fair view	¶2310
Audit of group accounts	¶2311
Schedule 7	¶2312

¶2301 General

The statutory requirements in Australia relating to group accounts of companies are included in the Companies Code ("the Code"), in

CURRENT STATUTORY REQUIREMENTS FOR COMPANIES

Schedule 7 to the Companies Regulations ("Schedule 7") and in Approved Accounting Standards issued by the Accounting Standards Review Board ("ASRB") These ASRBs have the force of law by virtue of sec. 266 of the Code. A brief summary of these requirements is set out in the following paragraphs.

¶2302 Requirement to prepare group accounts

The directors of a holding company are required by sec. 269(3) of the Code to have made out for presentation at its annual general meeting group accounts dealing with—

"(a) the profit or loss of the company and its subsidiaries for their respective last financial years; and

(b) the state of affairs of the company and its subsidiaries as at the end of their respective last financial years."

Such group accounts are in addition to the accounts of the holding company itself.

However, sec. 269(6) provides relief to wholly owned "Australian" holding companies from the requirements to prepare group accounts. "Australian" holding companies are those incorporated in any State or Territory of Australia.

For example, consider the group organisation chart below:

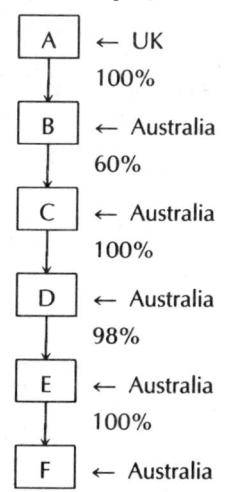

```
    A   ← UK
    ↓ 100%
    B   ← Australia
    ↓ 60%
    C   ← Australia
    ↓ 100%
    D   ← Australia
    ↓ 98%
    E   ← Australia
    ↓ 100%
    F   ← Australia
```

Group accounts are required for the following groups:

(1) E and F
(2) C, D, E and F
(3) B, C, D, E and F.

The group comprising D, E and F is not required to prepare group accounts due to the relief granted by sec. 269(6).

¶2302

¶2303 Definitions

The terms "holding company", "subsidiary company" and "related company" are defined in sec. 7 of the Companies Code as follows:

Subsidiary company

"7(1) For the purposes of this Code, a corporation shall, subject to sub-section (3), be deemed to be a subsidiary of another corporation if —

(a) that other corporation —

   (i) controls the composition of the board of directors of the first-mentioned corporation;

   (ii) is in a position to cast, or control the casting of, more than one-half of the maximum number of votes that might be cast at a general meeting of the first-mentioned corporation; or

   (iii) holds more than one-half of the issued share capital of the first-mentioned corporation (excluding any part of that issued share capital that carries no right to participate beyond a specified amount in a distribution of either profits or capital); or

(b) the first-mentioned corporation is a subsidiary of any corporation that is that other corporation's subsidiary (including a corporation that is that other corporation's subsidiary by another application or other applications of this paragraph)."

The key point in sec. 7(1)(a)(i) is the word "composition". As clarified by sec. 7(2), it is not control of board meetings currently held that determines the relationship between companies, rather the power to decide the appointment and removal of directors.

Section 7(1) also does not preclude a situation where a company can be a subsidiary of two separate companies, although this is very rare.

Section 7(6) provides that the holding/subsidiary relationship is maintained through indirect relationships, e.g.:

$$\boxed{A} - 51\% \rightarrow \boxed{B} - 51\% \rightarrow \boxed{C} - 51\% \rightarrow \boxed{D} - 51\% \rightarrow \boxed{E}$$

In the above situation Company E is a subsidiary of Company A. Notwithstanding that Company A's share of any dividends paid by Company E is 6.77% (i.e. 51% of Company B × 51% of Company C × 51% of Company D × 51% of Company E), Company A through its control of the "intermediary" companies (B, C and D) controls Company E.

Company A can control Company B through Company A's 51% ownership. Company A can therefore control 51% of Company C, and similarly of Company D and Company E.

The other ("minority") shareholders of Company B have no power to control any of Company A's votes in Company C. The same applies to the minority shareholders in C, D and E.

CURRENT STATUTORY REQUIREMENTS FOR COMPANIES 221

Holding company

"7(4) A reference in this Code to the holding company of a company or other corporation shall be read as a reference to a corporation of which that last-mentioned company or that other corporation is a subsidiary."

A corporation can have more than one holding company. For example, in the chart shown above, Company E has four holding companies, viz. A, B, C and D. This is a common occurrence in practice. A holding company which is not itself also a subsidiary company is often referred to as the "ultimate holding company". Holding companies which are also subsidiary companies are often referred to as "intermediate holding companies".

Related corporations

"7(5) Where a corporation—

(a) is the holding company of another corporation;

(b) is a subsidiary of another corporation; or

(c) is a subsidiary of the holding company of another corporation,

that first-mentioned corporation and that other corporation shall, for the purposes of this Code, be deemed to be related to each other."

Broadly, this section of the Code can be interpreted as providing that, wherever a holding/subsidiary relationship exists, whether directly or indirectly, all such companies are said to be related.

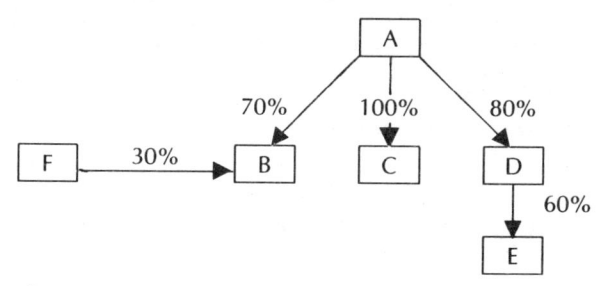

```
              A
       70% / 100% \ 80%
F  30%→ B     C     D
                    | 60%
                    E
```

In the above organisational chart, Companies A, B, C, D and E are related to each other. Company F is not related to any of the other companies shown above.

¶2304 Form and content of group accounts

Section 266 of the Code defines "group accounts" as including all forms of combinations of the accounts of individual companies within a group, e.g. full consolidation; two or more sets of consolidated accounts; individual accounts; or a combination of one or more sets of consolidated accounts and one or more sets of individual accounts. The basic aim of the legislation is that all group accounts should be in the form of one set of consolidated accounts, although in certain circumstances some other combination is acceptable, provided the directors comply with Schedule 7.

¶2304

¶2305 Financial years

The directors of a holding company that is not a foreign subsidiary or a recognised company are required by sec. 268 of the Code to take such steps as are necessary to ensure:

(i) that within 12 months after a corporation becomes a subsidiary the financial year of that corporation coincides with the financial year of the holding company; and

(ii) that the financial year of each of its other subsidiaries coincides with the financial year of the holding company.

¶2306 Acquisition of holding company shares by subsidiary company

"A corporation cannot be a member of a company that is its holding company ..."

Section 36(1) of the Code contains the above provision and renders void any acquisition of shares in a holding company by a subsidiary (subject to some minor exclusions).

¶2307 Relief from preparation of accounts

Pursuant to sec. 273(5) of the Code, on 2 April 1986 the National Companies and Securities Commission ("NCSC") issued a class order relieving the directors of wholly owned subsidiary companies from the requirements to prepare accounts, provided that, among other things, the directors of the holding company execute a deed guaranteeing the debts of the subsidiary companies concerned.

¶2308 Statement by directors

Directors of a holding company for which group accounts are prepared are required by sec. 269 of the Code to prepare a statement on those group accounts. This statement refers to the state of affairs and the result for the period of both the holding company and the group and the ability of the holding company to pay its debts.

¶2309 Directors' report

Section 270(2) of the Code requires the directors to attach to group accounts made under sec. 269(3) a directors' report containing information required by that subsection. This information is identical to that required for an individual company except that it is to relate to the group.

¶2310 True and fair view

The directors of a holding company must not cause the group accounts or their report to be made out unless they have available sufficient information in relation to each subsidiary to ensure that the group accounts will give a true and fair view.

¶2305

¶2311 Audit of group accounts

Group accounts of holding companies (other than exempt proprietary companies) must be audited not less than 14 days before the annual general meeting of the holding company. This requirement is imposed by sec. 275 and 285(1) and (2) of the Code.

¶2312 Schedule 7

The presentation of group accounts is governed by Schedule 7 of the Companies Regulations.

The provisions of Schedule 7 covering group accounts are applicable to all companies, including exempt proprietory companies. The relevant clauses from Schedule 7 concerning specific disclosures required to be made in the group accounts are set out below.

"Group accounts not consolidated or whose grouping differs from previous accounts

35   The group accounts shall be accompanied by a note specifying—

(a) where the group accounts are prepared otherwise than as one set of consolidated accounts covering the group—

   (i) the reasons why the preparation of one such set of consolidated accounts is impracticable or why it is preferable for the group accounts to be in the form in which they are prepared, as the case may be; and

   (ii) the extent to which the group accounts are significantly affected by transactions and balances between the corporations covered by those accounts, other than to the extent stated in any notes to those accounts;

(b) where the group accounts of a holding company in respect of a financial period include accounts whose grouping differs from the grouping of the accounts included in the group accounts of that company in respect of the immediately preceding financial period, the first-mentioned group accounts shall, except where they have been prepared as one set of consolidated accounts include a notice containing a statement by the directors of the company specifying the nature of the grouping of those accounts that so differs and the reasons for that difference.

Subsidiaries acquired or disposed of

36(1)   Where during a financial period a subsidiary has been acquired by a company or by a corporation in a group of companies, the group accounts of that company or that relate to that group, as the case may be, in respect of that period shall include a note specifying in relation to each subsidiary so acquired—

(a) its name;

(b) the proportion of shares acquired in the subsidiary;

(c) the consideration of those shares; and

(d) the fair value of its net tangible assets at the time of that acquisition.

36(2) Where during a financial period a subsidiary has been disposed of by a company or by a corporation in a group of companies, the group accounts of that company or that relate to that group, as the case may be, in respect of that period, shall include a note specifying in relation to each subsidiary so disposed of—

(a) its name;

(b) the operating profit or loss and extraordinary items attributable to members of the holding company arising on disposal of that subsidiary;

(c) the fair value of its net tangible assets at the time of that disposal; and

(d) the remaining interest (if any) held in it by a corporation or corporations in that group.

Particulars in relation to subsidiaries

37(1) In this clause "share" means a share in the issued share capital of a corporation (excluding any part of that issued share capital that carries no right to participate beyond a specified amount in a distribution of either profits or capital).

37(2) The group accounts of a holding company in respect of a financial period shall include a note specifying in relation to each subsidiary of the company—

(a) particulars of—

   (i) its name;

   (ii) its country of formation or incorporation; and

   (iii) its relationship with other corporations in the group of companies,

as at the end of that financial period;

(b) the amount of its contribution to the profit or loss of the group of companies during that period;

(c) if its financial year differs from that of the holding company — particulars of its financial year; and

(d) if any of its business was carried on during that period in a country outside Australia — the name of that country.

37(3) In respect of a subsidiary that has issued share capital, the particulars referred to in sub-paragraph (2)(a)(iii) shall include, in relation to the shares held in the subsidiary by the holding company and each other corporation in the group of companies—

(a) the amount at which the shares so held are recorded in the books of that corporation; and

(b) the percentage of the shares so held in relation to all the shares of the subsidiary.

¶2312

CURRENT STATUTORY REQUIREMENTS FOR COMPANIES

Elimination of transactions and balances

38(1) In the preparation of consolidated accounts, any transactions and balances between corporations covered by those accounts shall be eliminated, as appropriate, in determining the amounts to be stated in those accounts.

38(2) Without limiting the effect that sub-clause (1) would otherwise have, that sub-clause applies in relation to the matters provided for by clauses 17, 22 and 23.

Form of accounts of holding company and subsidiaries

39(1) Subject to sub-clause (2), where the group accounts of a holding company include separate accounts for one of its subsidiaries, the account of the subsidiary shall, as far as practicable, be in the same form as the accounts of the holding company.

39(2) In the case of a subsidiary that is incorporated outside the State, it is sufficient compliance with the provisions of sub-clause (1) if the accounts of the subsidiary—

(a) are in such form;

(b) are reported on by an auditor in such manner;

(c) contain such particulars; and

(d) include or are accompanied by such documents (if any),

as is or are required by the law of the place in which it is formed or incorporated being the law concerning accounts to be laid before the subsidiary in a general meeting.

Divergent accounting periods

40 A reference in this Schedule to a financial period in relation to group accounts of a holding company is, where the financial period of any one or more of the corporations in the group of companies does not end on the date on which the financial period of the holding company ends, a reference to the financial period of the holding company and the financial period of each other corporation in the group of companies that does not end on that date."

The financial statements of "Example Public Company Limited" reproduced in Appendix II show the disclosures required by Schedule 7.

¶2312

24

Cross holdings

Nature of cross holdings	¶2401
Methods of accounting for cross holdings	¶2402
Summary	¶2403

¶2401 Nature of cross holdings

The situations considered so far in this text have involved investments by entities in other entities.

We will now look at situations where an entity has an investment in another entity and that second entity also has an investment in the first entity. For example:

```
┌───────────┐    80% ──→    ┌───────────┐
│ Company A │               │ Company B │
└───────────┘    ←── 20%    └───────────┘
```

These situations are referred to as "cross holdings" or "reciprocal shareholdings".

Section 36 of the Companies Code requires a subsidiary company to dispose of any shares it holds in its holding company within one year of the establishment of the holding/subsidiary relationship. As a result the relationship shown in the example above in respect of corporate cross shareholdings can only exist for a maximum of one year.

The Companies Code, however, does not prohibit the holding of shares between subsidiaries, hence situations such as that shown below can exist indefinitely.

¶2401

CROSS HOLDINGS

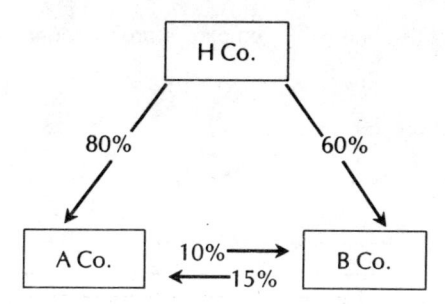

```
            H Co.
          /       \
       80%         60%
        ↓           ↓
      A Co.  10%→  B Co.
             ←15%
```

The elimination of each investment, including cross held investments, is as explained in previous chapters. For example, using the group structure shown above, the book value of the 10% investment in B Company by A Company is eliminated against 10% of the net assets of B Company as at acquisition date. No consideration of cross holdings is necessary in determining the elimination entry, as the cross holdings do not affect the share capital and reserves acquired.

The problem for consolidation accountants presented by the above situation lies in determining the "after cross holding" profits of each company; i.e. given that A Company and B Company have investments in each other, how are post-acquisition profits allocated? This problem arises because each company has its own profits, plus an interest in the other. The "other" company has its own profits, plus an interest in the first company — a "circular" problem. Before consolidation can commence, the "after cross holding" or "real" profits of each company must be determined. This will apply to all periods since the acquisition of the cross holding, and therefore may involve both current year profits and retained earnings brought forward from the prior year.

Example 24.1

Assume the following investments are held:

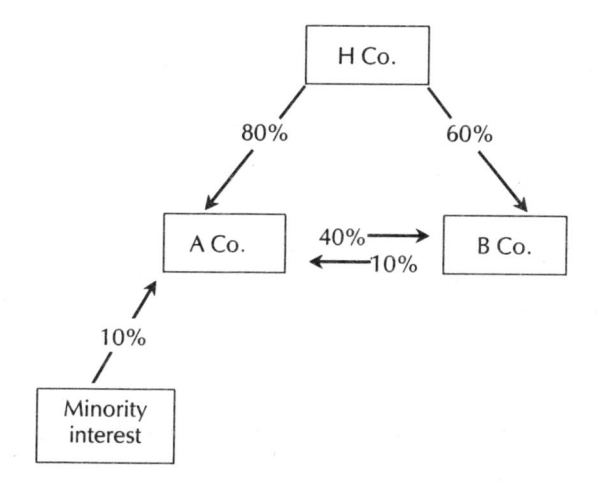

```
              H Co.
            /       \
         80%         60%
          ↓           ↓
        A Co.  40%→  B Co.
               ←10%
          ↑
         10%
          /
      Minority
      interest
```

¶2401

Examine the entitlements to A Company's profits during each of the periods noted below:

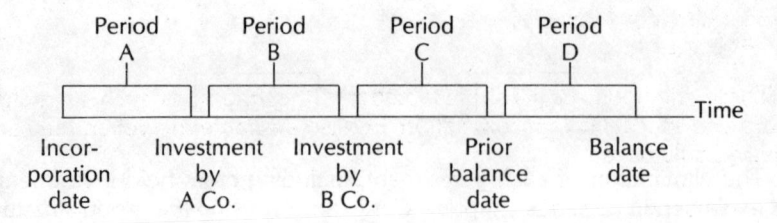

```
      Period        Period        Period        Period
        A             B             C             D
        |             |             |             |
  ┌─────────────┬─────────────┬─────────────┬─────────────┐
  │             │             │             │             │_____ Time
  └─────────────┴─────────────┴─────────────┴─────────────┘

  Incor-      Investment    Investment     Prior        Balance
  poration       by            by         balance        date
   date         A Co.         B Co.        date
```

Retained earnings of A Company earned during each period are allocated as follows:

Period A:

"Pre" the acquisition by H Co.	80%
Direct minority interest	10%
"Pre" the acquisition by B Co.	10%
	100%

No adjustment is needed for cross holdings during Period A, as no cross holdings existed during Period A.

Period B:

"Post" the acquisition by H Co.	80%
Direct minority interest	10%
"Pre" the acquisition by B Co.	10%
	100%

Again no adjustment is needed for cross holdings during Period B.

Period C:

During this period the cross holding is effective. The "real" profit of A Company must be determined, and allocated as follows:

"Post" the acquisition by H Co.	80%
Direct minority interest	10%
"Post" the acquisition by B Co.	10%
	100%

Period D:

The "real" profit of A Company will be allocated in the same proportions as for Period C.

¶2401

CROSS HOLDINGS 229

¶2402 Methods of accounting for cross holdings

Authorities on the subject of cross holdings note two alternative methods commonly used in determining the "real" profits of each company, i.e. after taking into account cross holdings:

(1) Simultaneous equations

(2) Geometric progressions.

These methods are illustrated below. Other methods such as matrix algebra and successive approximation are also available; however, they are not commonly used.

Example 24.2

Assume that in the group structure illustrated in ¶2401 Example 24.1 the profit of A Company for the year was $100, and the profit of B Company for the year was $200.

(1) *Simultaneous equations*

Let:

a = Real profit of A Co.
b = Real profit of B Co.
$\$A$ = Recorded profit of A Co.
$\$B$ = Recorded profit of B Co.

$a = \$A + 40\%b$
$b = \$B + 10\%a$

This formula can be applied in the situation assumed in this Example:

$a = \$100 + .4b$
$b = \$200 + .1a$

$a = \$100 + .4(\$200 + .1a)$
$ = \$100 + \$80 + .04a$

$a = \$100 + \$80 + \dfrac{4}{100}a$

$\dfrac{100a}{100} - \dfrac{4}{100a} = \$100 + \$80 + \dfrac{4}{100a} - \dfrac{4}{100a}$

$\dfrac{96a}{100} = \$180$

$a = \dfrac{100}{96} \times 180$

$a = \$187.50$

$b = \$200 + .1a$
$ = \$200 + .1 \times \$187.50$
$ = \$218.75$

Having determined the real profits of A Company and B Company, consolidation proceeds, and real profits are allocated using the methodology explained in Example 24.1.

¶2402

(2) *Geometric progressions*

$$a = \frac{x}{1-r}$$

$$b = \frac{y}{1-r}$$

x = Recognised profit of A Co. + Direct interest in B Co.
y = Recognised profit of B Co. + Direct interest in A Co.
r = Direct interest in A Co. × Direct interest in B Co.

Applying these formulas to the situation in this Example:

r = Direct interest in A Co. × Direct interest in B Co.
r = 10% × 40%
r = 4%

x = $100 + 40% × $200
  = $180
y = $200 + 10% × $100
  = $210

$$a = \frac{x}{1-r}$$

$$= \frac{180}{1-.04}$$

$$= \frac{180}{.96}$$

= $187.50

$$b = \frac{y}{1-r}$$

$$= \frac{210}{.96}$$

= $218.75

¶2403 Summary

The problem for consolidation accountants faced with cross holdings lies in the determination of amounts of profit to be allocated to outside equity interests.

To enable such an allocation, the "real" profits of each company must be determined, and usual consolidation techniques applied to allocate those "real" profits.

¶2403

Appendix A

Example covering various aspects of consolidation

A Ltd. is a holding company, owning 90% of the share capital of B Ltd. and 80% of the share capital of C Ltd.

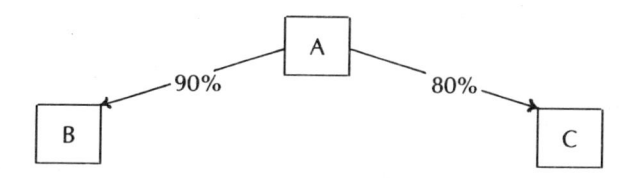

```
          A
    90%/    \80%
    B          C
```

B Ltd. holds $40,000 of debentures in C Ltd. Share capital and reserves of the subsidiary companies at the date of acquisition were as follows:

	B Ltd. $	C Ltd. $
Paid-up capital	100,000	40,000
Reserves	2,500	4,500
Profit and loss appropriation account	37,500	20,500
	$140,000	$ 65,000

App. A

Trial balances were extracted from the books of these companies at 31 December 19X8 as follows:

	A Ltd. $	B Ltd. $	C Ltd. $
Inventory on hand at 1 January 19X8	60,000	70,000	25,000
Other assets	203,000	40,000	58,000
Machinery	150,000	50,000	50,000
Debentures of C Ltd.		40,000	
Shares in B Ltd. (at cost)	130,000		
Shares in C Ltd. (at cost)	50,000		
Purchases	140,000	90,000	65,000
Manufacturing, selling and administration expenses	130,000	87,000	58,000
Debenture interest paid	10,000		2,500
Dividends paid (from current earnings)	10,000	7,500	4,500
	$883,000	$384,500	$263,000
Sundry liabilities	52,650	35,000	13,500
Debentures	200,000		50,000
Issued capital	200,000	100,000	40,000
Reserves	60,000	2,500	4,500
Profit and loss appropriation account at 1 January 19X8	40,000	45,000	25,000
Sales	320,000	200,000	130,000
Debenture interest received		2,000	
Dividends received	10,350		
	$883,000	$384,500	$263,000

Additional information

		A Ltd.	B Ltd.	C Ltd.
1.	Inventory on hand at 31 December 19X8	$70,000	$65,000	$30,000

including profits on inter-company sales as follows:
Inventory on hand A Ltd.: Profit of $4,000 on goods obtained from B Ltd. and $4,000 on goods obtained from C Ltd

Inventory on hand B Ltd.: Profit of $3,000 on goods obtained from C Ltd.

2. The inventory on hand at 1 January 19X8 did not include any unrealised profits.
3. Sales during the year include sales of $50,000 from C Ltd. to B Ltd.; $20,000 from C Ltd. to A Ltd.; $40,000 from B Ltd. to A Ltd.; and machinery from B Ltd. to A Ltd. of $25,000 on which B Ltd. had made a profit of $2,000. This sale of machinery took place on 1 January 19X8.
4. No tax entries have been raised in the current year. Tax rate = 50%. Assume no permanent differences, other than dividends received being fully rebatable.
5. Ignore amortisation of goodwill.

App. A

EXAMPLE ASPECTS OF CONSOLIDATION

6. Assume that the non-monetary assets to which the discount on acquisition of C Ltd. related have been sold outside the group in prior years.
7. Depreciation on machinery is charged at 10% p.a. straight-line.

Required

Prepare consolidated worksheets, consolidation journal entries, and the consolidated balance sheet and profit and loss account.

Suggested Solution

Journal Entries Required

	Dr (Cr)	A Ltd. $000	B Ltd. $000	C Ltd. $000
Dr Income tax expense		25	10	4.75
Cr Sundry liabilities				
— provision for income tax		(25)	(10)	(4.75)

50% of operating profit before tax and before dividends received

Detailed Profit and Loss Accounts

	A Ltd. $000	B Ltd. $000	C Ltd. $000
Sales	320	200	130
Less: Cost of sales			
Inventory 1.1.X8	60	70	25
Purchases	140	90	65
Inventory 31.12.X8	(70)	(65)	(30)
	130	95	60
Gross profit	190	105	70
Other expenses	(130)	(87)	(58)
Debenture interest paid	(10)		(2.5)
Dividends received	10.35		
Debenture interest received		2	
	60.35	20	9.5
Income tax expense	25	10	4.75
	35.35	10	4.75
Retained earnings 1.1.X8	40	45	25
	75.35	55	29.75
Dividends paid	(10)	(7.5)	(4.5)
Retained earnings 31.12.X8	65.35	47.5	25.25

App. A

Consolidation Journal Entries

		$000	$000
(a)	Dr Issued capital (90% of $100,000)	90	
	Dr Reserves (90% of $2,500)	2.25	
	Dr Retained earnings brought forward (90% of $37,500)	33.75	
	Cr Investment in B Ltd.		130
	Dr Goodwill	4	

Elimination of investment in B Ltd.

(b)	Dr Issued capital (10% of $100,000)	10	
	Dr Reserves (10% of $2,500)	0.25	
	Dr Retained earnings brought forward (10% of $45,000)	4.5	
	Dr Minority interest (P/L) (10% of $10,000)	1	
	Cr Minority interest (B/S)		15.75

Allocation of minority interest in B Ltd. at 31.12.X8

(c)	Dr Issued capital (80% of $40,000)	32	
	Dr Reserves (80% of $4,500)	3.6	
	Dr Retained earnings brought forward (80% of $20,500)	16.4	
	Cr Investment in C Ltd.		50
	Cr Discount on acquisition		2

Elimination of investment in C Ltd. at 31.12.X8

(d)	Dr Discount on acquisition of C Ltd.	2	
	Cr Retained earnings brought forward		2

Elimination of discount on acquisition

(e)	Dr Issued capital (20% of $40,000)	8	
	Dr Reserves (20% of $4,500)	0.9	
	Dr Retained earnings brought forward (20% of $2,500)	5	
	Dr Minority interest (P/L) (20% of $4,750)	0.95	
	Cr Minority interest (B/S)		14.85

Allocation of minority interest in C Ltd. at 31.12.X8

(f)	Dr P/L — Closing inventory	4	
	Cr Inventory		4
	Dr Future income tax benefit	2	
	Cr Income tax expense		2
	Dr Minority interest (B/S)	0.2	
	Cr Minority interest (P/L)		0.2

Elimination of unrealised profit on stock sold by B Ltd. to A Ltd.

App. A

EXAMPLE ASPECTS OF CONSOLIDATION

(g)	Dr P/L — Closing inventory	3	
	Cr Inventory		3
	Dr Future income tax benefit	1.5	
	Cr Income tax expense		1.5
	Dr Minority interest (B/S)	0.3	
	Cr Minority interest (P/L)		0.3

Elimination of unrealised profit on stock sold by C Ltd. to B Ltd.

(h)	Dr P/L — Closing inventory	4	
	Cr Inventory		4
	Dr Future income tax benefit	2	
	Cr Income tax expense		2
	Dr Minority interest (B/S)	0.4	
	Cr Minority interest (P/L)		0.4

Elimination of unrealised profit on stock sold by C Ltd. to A Ltd.

(i)	Dr Sales — C Ltd.	70	
	Cr Purchases — B Ltd.		50
	Cr Purchases — A Ltd.		20
	Dr Sales — B Ltd.	40	
	Cr Purchases — A Ltd.		40

Elimination of inter-company inventory sales and purchases

(j)	Dr Debentures of C Ltd.	40	
	Cr Debentures in C Ltd. held by B Ltd.		40

Elimination of inter-company indebtedness

(k)	Dr Interest received by B Ltd.	2	
	Cr Interest paid by C Ltd.		2

Elimination of inter-company interest

(l)	Dr Operating profit — sales	2	
	Cr Machinery		2
	Dr Future income tax benefit	1	
	Cr Income tax expense		1
	Dr Minority interest (B/S) (20% × after-tax effect)	0.2	
	Cr Minority interest (P/L)		0.2

Elimination of inter-company profit on sale of machinery

(m)	Dr Provision for depreciation	0.2	
	Cr Depreciation expense		0.2
	Dr Income tax expense	0.1	
	Cr Future income tax benefit		0.1

Adjustment for depreciation on machine sold from B Ltd. to A Ltd. — additional depreciation on cost of $2,000 at 10% p.a.

App. A

(n) Dr Dividends received by A Ltd.   6.75
     Dr Minority interest (B/S)   0.75
        Cr Dividend paid by B Ltd.   7.5
     Elimination of inter-company dividend paid

(o) Dr Dividends received by A Ltd.   3.6
     Dr Minority interest (B/S)   0.9
        Cr Dividend paid by C Ltd.   4.5
     Elimination of inter-company dividend paid

Consolidated Worksheet
Balance Sheets as at 31.12.X8

	A Ltd.	B Ltd.	C Ltd.	Debit	Credit	Group
	$000	$000	$000	$000	$000	$000
Issued capital	200	100	40	ᵃ90 ᵇ10 ᶜ32 ᵉ8		200
Reserves	60	2.5	4.5	ᵃ2.25 ᵇ0.25 ᶜ3.6 ᵉ0.9		60
Retained earnings	65.35	47.5	25.25	85.05	21.8	74.85
Minority interest				ᶠ0.2 ᵍ0.3 ʰ0.4 ⁱ0.2 ⁿ0.75 ᵒ0.9	ᵇ15.75 ᶜ14.85	27.85
	325.35	150	69.75	234.8	52.4	362.7
Machinery	150	50	50		ʲ2	248
Debentures of C Ltd.		40		ʲ40		—
Investments in B Ltd.	130				ᵃ130	—
Investments in C Ltd.	50				ᶜ50	—
Goodwill				ᵃ4		4
Inventory	70	65	30		ᶠ4 ᵍ3 ʰ4	154
Other assets	203	40	58	ᶠ2 ᵍ1.5 ʰ2 ⁱ1	ᵐ0.1	307.4
Sundry liabilities	77.65	45	18.25	ᵐ0.2		140.7
Discount on acquisition				ᵈ2	ᶜ2	—
Debentures	200		50		ʲ40	210
	325.35	150	69.75	52.7	235.1	362.7
Total of Eliminations				287.5	287.5	

App. A

EXAMPLE ASPECTS OF CONSOLIDATION

Consolidated Worksheet
Profit and Loss Acounts as at 31.12.X8

	A Ltd. $000	B Ltd. $000	C Ltd. $000	Debit $000	Credit $000	Group $000
Dividends received	10.35	—	—	ⁿ6.75 ᵒ3.6		—
Operating Profit	50	20	9.5	ᶠ4 ᵍ3 ʰ4 ⁱ2	ᵐ0.2	66.7
Income tax expense	25	10	4.75	ᵐ0.1	ᶠ2 ᵍ1.5 ʰ2 ⁱ1	33.35
	35.35	10	4.75			33.35
Minority interest	—	—	—	ᵇ1 ᵉ0.95	ᶠ0.2 ᵍ0.3 ʰ0.4 ⁱ0.2	0.85
	35.35	10	4.75			32.5
Retained earnings brought forward	40	45	25	ᵃ33.75 ᵇ4.5 ᶜ16.4 ᵉ5	ᵈ2	52.35
	75.35	55	29.75			84.85
Dividend paid	10	7.5	4.5		ⁿ7.5 ᵒ4.5	10
Retained earnings	65.35	47.5	25.25	85.05	21.8	74.85

App. A

Appendix B
Example consolidated financial statements

It is necessary for the final result of consolidation accounting to present fairly the results of the group's transactions.

An example set of consolidated financial statements, including notes thereto, has been prepared by KPMG Peat Marwick, Chartered Accountants. These financial statements show the results of the consolidation process, and are reproduced hereunder. All companies and persons mentioned in the example are fictitious. Any resemblance to any companies or persons, living or dead, is purely coincidental.

References

The following abbreviations are used in the Example statements to indicate the reference source of the disclosure requirements, followed by the particular section, clause or paragraph.

- AAS: Statements of Accounting Standards issued jointly by the Australian accounting bodies.
- AGR: Accounting Guidance Releases issued jointly by the Australian accounting bodies.
- APS: Statements on Conformity with Statements of Accounting Standards issued jointly by the Australian accounting bodies.
- ASRB: Approved Accounting Standards issued by the Accounting Standards Review Board.
- D1.1: Statement on Accounting Practice: Presentation of Balance Sheet, issued by The Institute of Chartered Accountants in Australia.
- Reg.: Regulations contained in the Companies Regulations.
- Sch. 7: Schedule 7 to the Companies Regulations.
- Sec.: Sections of the Companies Code.
- SE: Australian Stock Exchange Official Listing Rules.

EXAMPLE CONSOLIDATED FINANCIAL STATEMENTS

EXAMPLE PUBLIC COMPANY LIMITED AND SUBSIDIARIES
FINANCIAL STATEMENTS AND REPORT 30 JUNE 19X9

Example Public Company Limited is incorporated in New South Wales.

(Note: Section 509 of the Companies Code requires that where a company issues its annual report outside its State or Territory of incorporation, the name of its State or Territory of incorporation must appear in legible characters on the annual report.)

Contents

	Page
Directors' Report	239
Profit and Loss Accounts for the year ended 30 June 19X9	246
Balance Sheets as at 30 June 19X9	247
Notes to and Forming Part of the Accounts for the year ended 30 June 19X9, including	249
Consolidated Summary of Sources and Applications of Funds	294
Supplementary Equity Financial Statements	297
Statement by Directors	302
Auditors' Report to the Members	302
Supplementary Information	303

EXAMPLE PUBLIC COMPANY LIMITED AND SUBSIDIARIES
DIRECTORS' REPORT

Sec. 270(2)   The Directors present their report together with the accounts of Example Public Company Limited and the consolidated accounts of the group for the year ended 30 June 19X9 and the auditors' report thereon.

Sec. 270(2)(a)(i)   **Directors**
The Directors of the holding company in office at the date of this report are:

Sec. 270(3A)(a)*   Mr William Michael
Chairman (Non-Executive Director)
Age 63
Chairman of EFT Limited, FORX Limited and Example Public Company (Manufacturing) Pty. Limited
Bachelor of Engineering (University of Sydney)
Director since 19U6 — appointed Chairman 19V9.

Mr Garry Andrews
Managing Director
Age 59
Wide management and engineering experience in Australia and overseas
Chairman of Example Public Company (Construction) Pty. Limited
Bachelor of Civil Engineering (University of Queensland)
Director since 19V0 — appointed Managing Director 19X0.

Sec. 270(13)   * *Details of directors' qualifications, experience and special responsibilities are only required to be disclosed by a public company which is not a wholly owned subsidiary of an Australian corporation at the end of the financial year.*

App. B

Mr Harold James
Director — Property Development
Age 51
Formerly Managing Director of L.J. Estate Limited, 19U9 to 19X2
Associate of the Real Estate and Stock Institute of Victoria
Director since 19X3.

Mr Kym Johns
Director — Mining
Age 68
Formerly Managing Director of Eastern Mining Limited, 19V5 to 19X1
Associate of the Australian Institute of Mining and Metallurgy and Fellow of the Australian Institute of Management. Directorships include Deep Mines NL, ABC Energy Ltd., and Example Public Company (Mining and Exploration) Pty. Limited.

Mr Don Marks
Director — Finance
Age 45
Fifteen years' service including General Manager 19V8 to 19X1
A Director since 19X1
Fellow of The Institute of Chartered Accountants in Australia
Master of Economics (University of Sydney).

Mr Stephen Martin
Director — Construction
Age 49
Bachelor of Civil Engineering
Twenty-five years' service including six as a Director.

Mr Alexander Stewart
Director — Hardware and Other Industries
Age 50
Twenty-nine years' experience in an operational and management capacity in the Nuts and Bolts group of companies
A Director since 19X3
Director of Example Public Company (Hardware) Pty. Limited.

Mr Ronald Thomas
Alternate Director since 19X0 representing Mr Don Marks
Age 48
Nineteen years' service in an accounting and management capacity
Certified Public Accountant
Bachelor of Commerce (University of N.S.W.).

In accordance with the holding company's articles of association, Messrs G. Andrews and H. James retire from the Board of Directors and, being eligible, offer themselves for re-election.

Mr R. Stephens retired as a Director of the holding company during the year.

(Note: It is recommended that details of directors who must vacate their office by virtue of sec. 226 of the Companies Code (i.e., those who have

EXAMPLE CONSOLIDATED FINANCIAL STATEMENTS

attained 72 years of age) be disclosed also. It is also recommended that details of directors who have vacated their office during the year or subsequent to balance date be disclosed.)

Sec. 270(2)(a)(ii) **Principal Activities**

The principal activities of the corporations in the group during the course of the financial year were the manufacture and sale of bricks, pipes, windows, ropes and wires; exploration, development and mining of iron ore and coal; construction; and the development of properties.

As a result of the acquisition of Example Public Company (Hardware) Pty. Limited (formerly Hardware Distributors Pty. Limited) late in the financial year, the group's activities have been extended to include the distribution of hardware products.

The boat building division of Example Public Company (Manufacturing) Pty. Limited was closed during the year and Example Public Company (Holdings) Pty. Limited was liquidated.

During the year there were no other significant changes in the nature of the activities of the corporations in the group.

Sec. 270(2)(a)(iii) **Group Result**

The group profit for the year attributable to the shareholders of Example Public Company Limited was:

	19X9 $000	19X8 $000
Operating profit after income tax	4,600	2,951
Interest of minority shareholders	(428)	(359)
	4,172	2,592
Extraordinary items after income tax	(249)	(335)
Interest of minority shareholders	—	(26)
	(249)	(309)
Operating profit and extraordinary items after income tax attributable to members of Example Public Company Limited	3,923	2,283

The contribution by each corporation in the group to the net profit is set out in Note 30 to the accounts.

Sec. 270(2)(b) **Review of Operations***

Manufacture of Building Products

The demand for the new PVC and polyethylene pipes has far exceeded expectations. Our Smith Street factory has taken on another 400 people and is now operating at full capacity in a bid to fill the backlog of orders from both Australia and overseas. With

Sec. 270(11) * *Not required for a Directors' Report of a wholly owned subsidiary of an Australian corporation.*

App. B

the continued growth of its bathroom division Example Public Company (Manufacturing) Pty. Limited has increased its contribution to group profit by 97% to $1,255,000. This is an outstanding result even in light of the increased level of activity in new housing and home improvements. It represents the rewards of investing additional resources in the development of fibre cement and PVC products. The result reflected the company's ability to increase sales volume whilst improving margins.

Based on independent valuations, the freehold land and buildings employed in this division were revalued by $3.4m in March 19X9.

Mining

Example Public Company (Mining and Exploration) Pty. Limited is the mining and exploration company of the group. The company contributed $419,000 to group profit, an increase of 50.2%. Ore mined during the year increased by 67,885 tonnes to 249,840 tonnes. The additional tonnage was principally due to the discovery and commencement of production of the No. 3 Orebody in Western Australia. However, production output fell by an estimated 36,000 tonnes as a result of industrial disputes during the year.

Although the output of steaming coal increased by 22%, the company's revenue was up only 13% due to the impact of competition on prices. In addition the result was significantly affected by the write-off of $953,000 in exploration expenditure due to the abandonment of an area of interest.

Construction

Example Public Company (Construction) Pty. Limited is the design, construction and project management company of the group. The company contributed $1,198,000 to group profit. This represents an increase of 75.2% on the result for the previous year. Turnover for the year was up $5.7m to $25.8m.

The company continued to win a significant share of the major contracts around Australia particularly in remote areas. The 19X9 year was marked by a number of impressive construction performances headed by completion of the Timbucktoo Casino complex eight months ahead of time and $980,000 below budget.

Based on independent valuations, the freehold land and buildings of this company were revalued by $2.7m on 31 March 19X9.

Property Development

The division's contribution to profit was $1,084,000. In comparison with 19X8 this represents a downturn of 17% which the Directors consider to be primarily attributable to the reduced level of activity in new housing in the last quarter of the year. A total of 503 lots were sold during the year as against 610 in the previous year. The largest downturn was in Queensland where only 10 lots were sold, 150 fewer than 19X8.

EXAMPLE CONSOLIDATED FINANCIAL STATEMENTS

The holding company's 50% interest in Property Development Partnership returned a profit of $21,000 which was satisfactory in light of the rental market for commercial properties.

The first quarter of the 19Y0 financial year has seen an increase in demand. A continuance of this trend is expected in the remainder of 19Y0.

Other Industries

The acquisition in the latter part of the year of Example Public Company (Hardware) Pty. Limited (formerly Hardware Distributors Pty. Limited) proved to be a success. The company's contribution to group profit was $165,000 for the period since acquisition. This represents a return of approximately 21%. With the improving factory efficiencies the Directors believe that the company is well placed for expansion. Further cost cutting in the next 12 months should enable the company to increase its margins whilst continuing to secure a larger share of the domestic market.

Sec. 270(2)(a)(iv) **Dividends**

The amounts paid or declared by way of dividend by the holding company since the end of the previous financial year were:

(i) as proposed and provided for in last year's report, a final ordinary dividend of 8 cents per share amounting to $230,000 in respect of the year ended 30 June 19X8, paid on 30 November 19X8;

(ii) as proposed and provided for in last year's report, a preference dividend of 3.5% per share amounting to $35,000 in respect of the year ended 30 June 19X8, paid on 30 November 19X8.

An interim ordinary fully franked dividend of 8 cents per share in respect of the year ended 30 June 19X9 was paid on 31 January 19X9. $230,000

The final dividends recommended by the Directors of the holding company in respect of the year ended 30 June 19X9 are:

(i) an ordinary fully franked dividend of 8 cents per share amounting to $250,000

(ii) a preference fully franked dividend of 3.5% per share amounting to $35,000

The total dividends provided for or paid in respect of the year ended 30 June 19X9 are therefore $515,000

(Notes:

• This disclosure of dividends may be omitted if this information is not applicable, or a statement to that effect may be included.

• Dates on which dividends are paid are shown as a matter of best practice.)

App. B

244 ACCOUNTING FOR BUSINESS CONSOLIDATIONS

Sec. 270(2)(c) **State of Affairs***

In the opinion of the Directors there were no significant changes in the state of affairs of the group that occurred during the financial year under review not otherwise disclosed in this report or the group accounts.

Sec. 270(2)(d) **Events Subsequent to Balance Date***

There has not arisen in the interval between the end of the financial year and the date of this report any item, transaction or event of a material and unusual nature likely, in the opinion of the Directors of the holding company, to affect significantly the operations of the group, the results of those operations, or the state of affairs of the group, in subsequent financial years — except that the holding company has entered into a contract to purchase for cash all of the issued shares in Super Tiles Pty. Limited, a manufacturer of indoor and outdoor tiles. The cost of purchase is $890,000.

Sec. 270(2)(e) **Likely Developments***

The group will continue to pursue its policy of increasing its strength in its major business sectors during the next financial year. This will require further investment in areas such as manufacture of building products and construction which have performed well over recent years and offer sound opportunities for future development.

If interest rates fall from current levels the group will be able to pursue suitable opportunities for growth by acquisition.

Several developments in the operations of the group existing at the date of this report are likely to be realised during 19Y0. These include:

(i) the proposed acquisition of a further 30% of the issued capital in Example Public Company Assoc. (Transport) Pty. Limited — a company which has a large share of the transport market in Victoria;

(ii) the planned development of the iron ore deposit discovered and evaluated by Example Public Company (Mining and Exploration) Pty. Limited in Western Australia.

These developments alone are expected to increase group revenue by at least 10% in 19Y0. Providing the group is successful in containing costs, profits should increase proportionately.

Sec. 270(3) *(Note: If the directors believe that it would prejudice the interests of the company to provide information about likely developments, they need not provide it but must state that such information has been omitted.)*

Sec. 270(11) * *Not required for a Directors' Report of a wholly owned subsidiary of an Australian corporation.*

App. B

Directors' Interests and Benefits**

Sec. 270(3A)(b)
SE 3C(3)(c)

The relevant interest of each Director in the ordinary share capital of the company shown in the Register of Directors' Shareholdings as at the date of this report is:

Mr W. Michael	1,010 shares
Mr G. Andrews	13,280 shares
Mr H. James	2,810 shares

Sec. 270(3A)(c)
Sec. 270(7)

Since the end of the previous financial year no Director of the holding company has received or become entitled to receive any benefit (other than a benefit included in the aggregate amount of emoluments received or due and receivable by Directors shown in the group accounts) by reason of a contract made by the holding company or a related corporation with the Director or with a firm of which the Director is a member, or with a company in which the Director has a substantial interest, other than in respect of Mr H. James, a partner in the firm of James & Co., Real Estate Agents, which firm renders professional services to the group in the ordinary course of business.

Sec. 271
Reg. 58(5)

Rounding off of amounts

As the holding company is of a kind referred to in reg. 58(6) of the Companies Regulations, the Directors have chosen to round off amounts in this report and the accompanying accounts to the nearest one thousand dollars in accordance with sec. 271 of the Companies Code and reg. 58 of the Companies Regulations.

Dated at [City] this .... day of 19X9

Signed in accordance with a resolution of the Directors:

....W. MICHAEL
:Directors
.... G. ANDREWS

Sec. 270(4) to (6)

(Notes:

• If applicable, details of options granted by corporations in the group over their unissued shares should also be disclosed. A suggested note in respect of options is contained in Example Private Company Pty. Limited.

• The above report is an example of the report to be made out by directors of a company which is a holding company at the end of the financial year. An example of a Directors' Report for a company which is not a holding company at the end of the financial year is contained in the specimen financial statements entitled Example Private Company Pty. Limited.

• A Class Order issued by the National Companies and Securities Commission on 4 May 1988 broadly provides that a company or a group with total assets in excess of $1 billion may round off amounts to the nearest one hundred thousand dollars. Reference to the Class Order should be made for full details.)

** Details of shareholdings registered in the Register of Directors' Shareholdings are only required to be disclosed by a public company which is not a wholly owned subsidiary of an Australian corporation at the end of the financial year.

App. B

EXAMPLE PUBLIC COMPANY LIMITED AND SUBSIDIARIES
Profit and Loss Accounts for the Year Ended 30 June 19X9

			Consolidated		Holding Company	
Sch 7. cl. 3(1)(a)			19X9	19X8	19X9	19X8
		Note	$000	$000	$000	$000
Sch. 7 cl. 5(1)	Operating profit	3, 4	6,310	5,072	1,230	791
Sch. 7 cl. 5(1) ASRB 1018.21	Income tax attributable to operating profit	5	1,710	2,121	90	156
Sch. 7 cl. 5(1)	Operating profit after income tax .		4,600	2,951	1,140	635
	Minority interests in operating profit		(428)	(359)	—	—
			4,172	2,592	1,140	635
Sch. 7 cl. 5(1) ASRB 1018.20	Profit/(loss) on extra-ordinary items	6	(408)	(160)	(4)	576
Sch. 7 cl. 5(1)	Income tax attributable to profit or loss on extraordinary items	6	(159)	175	(159)	175
Sch. 7 cl. 5(1) ASRB 1018.40	Profit/(loss) on extraordinary items after income tax		(249)	(335)	155	401
Sch. 7 cl. 5(1)	Minority interests in extraordinary items		—	(26)	—	—
			(249)	(309)	155	401
Sch. 7 cl. 5(1)	Operating profit and extraordinary items after income tax attributable to members of the holding company		3,923	2,283	1,295	1,036
Sch. 7 cl. 5(1)	Retained profits at the beginning of the financial year		7,287	5,514	4,761	4,025
Sch. 7 cl. 5(1) ASRB 1018.51	Aggregate of amounts transferred from reserves	7		381	24	166
Sch. 7 cl. 5(1)	Total available for appropriation		11,210	8,178	6,080	5,227
Sch. 7 cl. 5(1) ASRB 1018.50	Dividends paid and proposed	8	515	466	515	466
Sch. 7 cl. 5(1) ASRB 1018.51	Aggregate of amounts transferred to reserves	7	34	—	—	—
Sch. 7 cl. 5(1)	Other appropriations	9	—	425	—	—
			549	891	515	466
Sch. 7 cl. 5(1)	Retained profits at the end of the financial year		10,661	7,287	5,565	4,761

App. B

EXAMPLE CONSOLIDATED FINANCIAL STATEMENTS

D1.1(39) The profit and loss accounts are to be read in conjunction with the notes to and forming part of the accounts set out on page 249ff.

Sch. 7
cl. 5(1), (2)
(Notes: The headings set out in Sch. 7 shall be used to the extent they are relevant. The headings shown comprise all of the headings contained in Sch. 7, with the exception that Sch. 7 does not make reference to the notes to and forming part of the accounts.

Where a company changes an accounting policy in order to comply with a statutory requirement or an accounting standard and the change specifically requires an initial adjustment to be made directly against retained profits at the beginning of the financial period, the adjustment shall appear in the profit and loss account directly below the line "retained profits at the beginning of the financial year". Suitable wording to describe the adjustment may be as follows:

"Adjustment to retained profits at the beginning of the financial year due to initial adoption of [accounting standard adopted]."

The item shall be cross referenced to the note to the accounts which provides details of the change in accounting policy.)

EXAMPLE PUBLIC COMPANY LIMITED AND SUBSIDIARIES
Balance Sheets at at 30 June 19X9

			Note	Consolidated 19X9 $000	Consolidated 19X8 $000	Holding Company 19X9 $000	Holding Company 19X8 $000
Sch. 7 cl. 3(1)(b)							
Sch. 7 cl. 6(1), Sec. 269(7)(b)		CURRENT ASSETS					
Sch. 7 cl. 6(1)		Cash		1,050	1,348	1,010	1,106
Sch. 7 cl. 6(1), Sec. 269(7)(a)		Receivables	10	16,005	14,519	3,547	4,244
Sch. 7 cl. 6(1)		Investments	11	155	—	155	—
Sch. 7 cl. 6(1)		Inventories	12	12,991	9,855	3,224	2,652
Sch. 7 cl. 6(1)		Other	13	485	452	96	93
Sch. 7 cl. 6(1)		TOTAL CURRENT ASSETS		30,686	26,174	8,032	8,095
Sch. 7 cl. 6(1), Sec. 269(7)(c)		NON-CURRENT ASSETS					
Sch. 7 cl. 6(1), Sec. 269(7)(a)		Receivables	10	1,942	1,697	2,942	2,197
Sch. 7 cl. 6(1)		Investments	11	3,055	2,740	14,688	13,338
Sch. 7 cl. 6(1)		Inventories	12	1,045	870	1,045	870
Sch. 7 cl. 6(1)		Property, plant and equipment	14	29,618	21,047	7,024	6,759
Sch. 7 cl. 6(1)		Intangibles	15	2,460	1,195	225	260
Sch. 7 cl. 6(1)		Other	16	5,330	4,973	1,855	1,016
Sch. 7 cl. 6(1)		TOTAL NON-CURRENT ASSETS		43,450	32,522	27,779	24,440
Sch. 7 cl. 6(1)		TOTAL ASSETS		74,136	58,696	35,811	32,535

continued over ...

App. B

Sch. 7 cl. 6(1)	CURRENT LIABILITIES					
Sch. 7 cl. 6(1)	Creditors and borrowings	17	12,525	15,144	4,035	3,269
Sch. 7 cl. 6(1)	Provisions	18	3,037	3,924	506	883
Sch. 7 cl. 6(1)	Other	19	—	—	845	180
Sch. 7 cl. 6(1)	TOTAL CURRENT LIABILITIES		15,562	19,068	5,386	4,332
Sch. 7 cl. 6(1)	NON-CURRENT LIABILITIES					
Sch. 7 cl. 6(1)	Creditors and borrowings	17	23,126	17,050	13,450	13,425
Sch. 7 cl. 6(1)	Provisions	18	2,920	2,073	413	378
Sch. 7 cl. 6(1)	Other	19	—	—	1,000	1,000
Sch. 7 cl. 6(1)	TOTAL NON-CURRENT LIABILITIES		26,046	19,123	14,863	14,803
Sch. 7 cl. 6(1)	TOTAL LIABILITIES		41,608	38,191	20,249	19,135
Sch. 7 cl. 6(1)	NET ASSETS		32,528	20,505	15,562	13,400
Sch. 7 cl. 6(1)	SHAREHOLDERS' EQUITY					
Sch. 7 cl. 6(1)	Share capital	20	7,250	6,750	7,250	6,750
Sch. 7 cl. 6(1)	Reserves	7	12,942	5,147	2,747	1,889
Sch. 7 cl. 6(1)	Retained profits		10,661	7,287	5,565	4,761
Sch. 7 cl. 6(1)	Shareholders' equity attributable to members of the holding company		30,853	19,184	15,562	13,400
Sch. 7 cl. 6(1)	Minority shareholders' interest in subsidiaries		1,675	1,321	—	—
Sch. 7 cl. 6(1)	TOTAL SHAREHOLDERS' EQUITY		32,528	20,505	15,562	13,400
Sch. 7 cl. 21 Sch. 7 cl. 22	Commitments and contingent liabilities	21				

D1.1(39)   The balance sheets are to be read in conjunction with the notes to and forming part of the accounts set out on page 249ff.

Sch. 7 cl. 6(1), D1.1(39)   *(Notes:)*

- The references to commitments, contingencies and the notes are not included in the prescribed format of Sch. 7 and are included in the above balance sheets as a matter of best practice.

Sch. 7 cl. 6(2) and (3)
Sch. 7 cl. 5(5)

- The headings and subheadings set out in Sch. 7 shall be used to the extent they are relevant. The headings and subheadings shown comprise all of the headings and subheadings contained in Sch. 7 and are shown in the sequence specified.

- The NCSC issued a Class Order on 3 August 1988 relieving any company limited by guarantee which does not have a share capital from the requirements of cl. 6 of Sch. 7 in so far as cl. 6 requires disclosure in the balance sheet of information relating to share capital and shareholders, providing that the corresponding information relating to the company's capital and members is disclosed. Accordingly, the financial statements of a company limited by guarantee must disclose the total number of members and the amount of each member's guarantee in the event that the company goes into liquidation as at balance date, in accordance with the company's memorandum.)

App. B

EXAMPLE PUBLIC COMPANY LIMITED
AND SUBSIDIARIES

NOTES TO AND FORMING PART OF THE ACCOUNTS
FOR THE YEAR ENDED 30 JUNE 19X9

ASRB 1001.20,
ASRB 1001.30

1. STATEMENT OF SIGNIFICANT ACCOUNTING POLICIES

The accounts of the holding company and the group have been drawn up in accordance with the accounting standards and disclosure requirements of the Australian accounting bodies, applicable Approved Accounting Standards, the provisions of Schedule 7 to the Companies Regulations, and the requirements of law. They have been prepared on the basis of historical costs and do not take into account changing money values or, except where stated, current valuations of non-current assets. Except as stated in Note 2, the accounting policies have been consistently applied.

In addition, supplementary equity financial statements (set out in Note 48) have been prepared using the equity method of accounting for the group's investment in associated companies. A summary of accounting policies adopted in the preparation of these financial statements is set out in Note 48.

Set out below is a summary of the significant accounting policies adopted by the group in the preparation of the principal accounts.

(Note: The statement of accounting policies note should include explanations of all significant accounting policies adopted by the group. The following examples are illustrations of the more common notes encountered in practice and may not be significant in all cases. They do not necessarily represent the only accounting treatments that may be adopted.)

(a) Principles of Consolidation

Sch. 7 cl. 38(1)

The group accounts comprise the accounts of the holding company and all subsidiary companies as defined by sec. 7 of the Companies Code. All inter-company balances and transactions have been eliminated.

Where a subsidiary has been sold (or acquired) during the year, its result has been included in the group profit up to the date of sale (from the date of acquisition). The effective date for this purpose is determined in accordance with ASRB 1015.

(b) Goodwill

ASRB 1013.35
ASRB 1015.20
ASRB 1013.70

Goodwill, representing the excess of the purchase consideration over the fair value of the identifiable net assets acquired arising upon the acquisition of a business entity, is amortised on a straight-line basis. The period of amortisation is the period of time during which benefits are expected to arise, which period varies from 10 to 20 years.

(Notes:
- *ASRB 1013 is effective for balance dates ending on or after 19 June 1988.*
- *ASRB 1015 is effective for balance dates ending on or after 31 December 1988.)*

App. B

(c) Foreign Currency

ASRB 1012.60 — Foreign currency transactions are translated to Australian currency at the rates of exchange ruling at the dates of the transactions. Amounts receivable and payable in foreign currencies are translated at the rates of exchange ruling at balance date.

ASRB 1012.12 — Exchange differences relating to amounts payable and receivable in foreign currencies are brought to account in the profit and loss account in the financial year in which the exchange rates change, as exchange gains or losses.

ASRB 1012.20 — The balance sheets of the overseas subsidiary companies (being self-sustaining foreign operations) are translated at the rates of exchange ruling at their balance dates. The profit and loss accounts are translated at a weighted average rate for the year. The translation adjustments are taken directly to the foreign currency translation reserve.

(Note: The other information required to be disclosed by ASRB 1012.60 is shown in Notes 4 and 6 (Profit and Loss), 7 (Reserves) and 44 (Amounts Payable/Receivable in Foreign Currencies).)

(d) Income Tax
ASRB 1020

The group adopts the liability method of tax-effect accounting.

The group has raised a provision for withholding tax on dividends proposed by overseas subsidiaries. No provision has been made for the balance of unremitted profits.

(Note: Following the introduction of Australia's Foreign Tax Credit System, provision for income tax less a credit for foreign tax paid should be raised in respect of income expected to be remitted to a resident holding company. Reference should be made in the contingent liability note (refer Note 21) to the outstanding income tax liability that would arise on the receipt of remaining overseas dividends.)

(e) Investments

Related Corporations

Investments in related (subsidiary) corporations are valued in the holding company's accounts at cost less amounts written off to recognise any permanent diminution in value. Dividends are brought to account in the profit and loss account when they are proposed by the related corporations.

Associated Corporations

Investments in associated corporations are valued at cost less any amounts written off to recognise permanent diminutions in value. Dividends are brought to account in the profit and loss account as they are received.

ASRB 1016.20 — Supplementary equity financial statements have been drawn up using the equity method to account for the group's interest in associated corporations. These statements are contained in Note 48.

An associated corporation is one in which the group's beneficial interest in the issued capital of that corporation is not less than 20% and does not exceed 50%, and where:

EXAMPLE CONSOLIDATED FINANCIAL STATEMENTS

- the group exercises significant influence over that corporation, and
- the investment is long-term.

(Note: ASRB 1016 is effective for balance dates ending on or after 31 December 1988.)

Other Corporations

Investments in corporations other than related and associated corporations are valued at the lower of cost or Directors' valuation. Dividends and interest are brought to account as they are received.

D1.1(28) **(f) Partnership**

The group's interest in the partnership is carried at its share of the net assets of the entity. The group's share in the result for the year of the partnership is included in the group profit.

(Note: Where a company or group has majority interests in partnerships which are material to the company or group's operations, which are not consolidated in the accounts or group accounts, details of those interests should be disclosed. This is recommended as best practice.)

ASRB 1019.10 **(g) Inventories**

Inventories are valued at the lower of cost and net realisable value.

Manufacturing Activities

Cost is based on the first-in first-out principle and includes expenditure incurred in acquiring the inventories and bringing them to their existing condition and location. In the case of manufactured inventories and work-in-progress, cost includes an appropriate share of both variable and fixed costs. Fixed costs have been allocated on the basis of normal operating capacity.

Mining Activities

Cost is allocated on an average basis and includes direct material, labour, related transportation costs to the point of sale and other fixed and variable overhead costs directly related to mining activities.

Net Realisable Value

Net realisable value is determined on the basis of each company's normal selling pattern. Expenses of marketing, selling and distribution to customers are estimated and are deducted to establish net realisable value.

(h) Land Held for Resale

Valuation

Development properties are valued at the lower of cost and net realisable value. Cost includes the cost of acquisition, development, holding the property and interest expense incurred, up to the date of completion of development, on funds borrowed specifically to finance the acquisition and development of the property.

App. B

Recognition of Income

Income from sales is not recognised until unconditional contracts are exchanged and at least 10% of the contract sale price is received.

A portion of the income on sale contracts having a term of less than five years is deferred by using the Rule of 78 method. The income deferred on contracts having a term of five years or greater is calculated by other actuarial methods.

The methods used for deferral have the effect of apportioning an "interest element" in the sales price over the term of each contract.

(i) Construction Work in Progress

Valuation

ASRB 1009.20 — Construction work in progress is valued at cost plus profit recognised to date based on the value of work completed, less provision for foreseeable losses. Provision for the total loss on a contract is made as soon as the loss is foreseeable.

Cost includes both variable and fixed costs directly related to specific contracts, and those which can be attributed to contract activity in general and which can be allocated on a reasonable basis. Those costs which are expected to be incurred under penalty clauses and warranty provisions are also included.

Recognition of Profit

ASRB 1009.11 — Profit is recognised using the percentage of completion method, but is not taken up until projects are 30% complete. However, due to the inherent risks associated with construction contracts, only 90% of the contract profit capable of being recognised is taken up. The final 10% of profit is recognised in the financial year in which the contract is completed.

(j) Property, Plant and Equipment

Property, Plant and Equipment Acquired by the Group

Items of property, plant and equipment are capitalised at historical cost and depreciated as outlined below.

ASRB 1010.40 — Land and buildings are independently valued every three years and, where considered appropriate by the Directors, included in the financial statements at the revalued amounts.

AGR 8(10), (11) — In revaluing land and buildings during the year, the potential capital gains tax in relation to such assets acquired after 19 September 1985 has not been taken into account as the Directors believe the company will not ultimately be liable to this tax (refer also Note 14).

The cost of property, plant and equipment constructed by group companies includes the cost of materials and direct labour and an appropriate proportion of fixed and variable overheads.

Disposal of Revalued Assets

ASRB 1010.30 — The gain or loss on disposal of revalued assets is calculated as the difference between the carrying amount of the asset at the time of disposal and the proceeds of disposal, and is included in the result of the group in the year of disposal.

App. B

EXAMPLE CONSOLIDATED FINANCIAL STATEMENTS

Any realised revaluation increment relating to the disposed asset standing in the asset revaluation reserve at the time of disposal is transferred to the capital profits reserve.

Depreciation and Amortisation of Property, Plant and Equipment

ASRB 1021.10 — Items of property, plant and equipment, including buildings and leasehold property but excluding freehold land, are depreciated/amortised over their estimated useful lives ranging from three to 30 years. The straight-line method is used except in the case of two subsidiary companies where the reducing balance method is used in respect of buildings.

Assets are first depreciated or amortised in the year of acquisition or, in respect of internally constructed assets, from the time an asset is held ready for use.

ASRB 1021.70 — (Note: When depreciation of buildings is introduced for the first time the method used to account for prior years' depreciation should be disclosed.)

ASRB 1008 — *Leased Plant and Equipment*

Leases of plant and equipment under which the company assumes substantially all of the risks and benefits of ownership, and which meet the criteria set out in Approved Accounting Standard ASRB 1008, are classified as finance leases. Refer also Note 2. Other leases are classified as operating leases.

Finance leases are capitalised; a lease asset and liability equal to the present value of the minimum lease payments, excluding executory costs, are recorded at the inception of the lease. Contingent rentals are written off as an expense of the accounting period in which they are incurred. Capitalised lease assets are amortised on a straight-line basis against the income of the accounting periods which are expected to benefit from their use, not exceeding 10 years.

Minimum lease payments made under operating leases are charged against profits in equal instalments over the accounting periods covered by the lease term, except in those circumstances where an alternative basis would be more representative of the pattern of benefits to be derived from the leased property.

AGR 5(3) — **(k) Intangibles**

Debenture issue costs are amortised over a period corresponding to the issue period of the debentures. The cost of patents and trademarks is amortised against profits earned from those assets, but over a period not exceeding seven years.

The carrying values of intangibles are reviewed annually.

ASRB 1022 — **(l) Exploration Expenditure**

Exploration, evaluation and development costs are accumulated in respect of each separate area of interest. Such costs are carried forward where they are expected to be recouped through successful development and exploitation of the area of interest or where activities in the area of interest have not yet reached a stage which permits reasonable assessment of the existence of economically recoverable reserves.

App. B

ASRB 1022.71   The ultimate recoupment of costs related to areas of interest in the exploration and/or evaluation phase is dependent on the successful development and commercial exploitation or sale of the relevant areas. Costs related to areas of interest in the development stage are amortised upon the commencement of production.

Each area of interest is reviewed annually to determine whether costs should continue to be carried forward in respect of that area of interest.

Where it is decided to abandon an area of interest, costs carried forward in respect of that area are written off in full in the year in which the decision is taken. Otherwise such costs are amortised over the life of the area of interest based on the rate of depletion of the economically recoverable reserves. Provision for cost of restoration of sites is made at the relevant stages and included in the cost of each stage.

AAS 9(9)   **(m) Deferred Expenditure**

Expenditure of a material amount is carried forward to the extent it is recoverable out of future revenue, where it does not relate solely to revenue which has already been brought to account, and where it contributes to the future earning capacity of the group.

Deferred expenditure is amortised over the period in which the related benefits are expected to be realised, not exceeding three years. Expenditure deferred in a previous period is reviewed annually to determine the amount (if any) that is no longer recoverable and any amount so determined is written off.

(n) Research and Development Costs

Expenditure is expensed as incurred except to the extent that its recoverability is assured beyond any reasonable doubt.

ASRB 1011.60   Deferred research and development costs are amortised over the future accounting periods during which the related benefits are expected to be realised, not exceeding five years.

(o) Provisions

Provision for Employee Entitlements

The provision made in the accounts for amounts expected to be paid to employees by way of long service and sick leave is based on assessments having regard to experience of staff departures and leave utilisation. The dissection between current and non-current is also based on a past experience assessment. Employees are paid on termination for untaken sick leave. Accrued annual leave is included in trade creditors.

Current wage rates are used in the calculation of the provisions.

Provision for Doubtful Debts

The collectability of debts is assessed at year end and provision is made for any specific doubtful accounts. In addition a general provision of 3% of debtors outstanding is maintained.

Provision for Warranties

Provision is made for the group's estimated liability on all products still under warranty, including claims already received. The estimate is based on the group's warranty costs experience over previous years.

App. B

(p) Superannuation Fund

The group contributes to an employee superannuation fund to match contributions to the fund made by employees. Such group contributions are charged against income. Refer also Note 21.

(q) Joint Venture

ASRB 1006.10   The group's interest in the unincorporated joint venture is brought to account by including in the respective balance sheet classes the amount of:

- the group's interest in each of the individual assets employed in the joint venture,
- liabilities incurred by the group in relation to the joint venture, and
- the group's interest in the expenses incurred in relation to the joint venture.

Refer also Note 41.

ASRB 1001.40   ## 2. CHANGE IN ACCOUNTING POLICY

As from 1 July 19X8, the group has adopted the policy of capitalising finance leases of plant and equipment since this accounting treatment more correctly reflects the nature of the transactions entered into (refer Note 1(j)).

The effect of this change in accounting policy on the accounts for the year ended 30 June 19X9 is that at balance date the value of property, plant and equipment increased by $2,426,000, non-current liabilities increased by $2,126,000 and current liabilities by $300,000. There is no material effect on the group profit for the year from the change in accounting policy, as the amount of amortisation and interest expense approximates the rentals paid.

ASRB 1001.41   *(Notes:*

- *The nature and reason for a change in accounting policy materially affecting the financial statements of subsequent periods should also be disclosed.*

APS 1(6)
- *If there has been a material departure from an accounting standard, the reasons for the departure and its financial effect should be disclosed.)*

App. B

		Consolidated		Holding Company	
		19X9	19X8	19X9	19X8
		$000	$000	$000	$000

3. OPERATING REVENUE

ASRB 1004.10 SE 3C(3)(a)	Included in operating revenue are the following items entering into the determination of operating profit:				
ASRB 1004.10	Sales revenue	80,531	66,977	5,740	5,216
Sch. 7 cl. 8(1)(a)(i)	Other revenue —Dividends received or due and receivable from:				
Sch. 7 cl. 10(c)	Related corporations	—	—	546	331
Sch. 7 cl. 10(d)	Other corporations	152	56	118	34
Sch. 7 cl. 8(1)(a)(ii)	—Interest received or due and receivable from:				
Sch. 7 cl. 10(c)	Related corporations	2	—	15	2
	Other related parties	2	2	2	2
Sch. 7 cl. 10(d)	Other corporations	112	95	73	60
ASRB 1004.10	—Gross proceeds from sale of property, plant, equipment and investments*	2,018	212	102	207
Sch. 7 cl. 8(1)(a)(v)	—Write-back of provision for stock obsolescence no longer required	—	187	—	187
		82,815	67,529	6,596	6,039
Sch. 7 cl. 8(1)(a)(iii)	Profit from sale of property, plant, equipment and investments*	55	102	—	25

* Schedule 7, cl. 8 requires the separate disclosure of material profits arising from the sale of non-current assets and Approved Accounting Standard 1004 requires the disclosure of gross proceeds.

ASRB 1022.72 (Notes:

• Government subsidies received and receivable in respect of extractive activities should be disclosed.

Sch. 7 cl. 8(2) • Profits on the sale of non-current assets, increments from the revaluation of non-current assets (see Note 7) and transfers from provisions are required to be disclosed only where they are material.

Sch. 7
cl. 8(1)(a)(vi)
Sch. 7 cl. 8(1)(c)
• Schedule 7 also requires the disclosure of any abnormal item credited as revenue. The amount derived by the application of equity accounting is also to be disclosed.)

App. B

EXAMPLE CONSOLIDATED FINANCIAL STATEMENTS

		Consolidated		Holding Company	
		19X9	19X8	19X9	19X8
		$000	$000	$000	$000

4. OPERATING PROFIT

Included in operating profit are the following items of expense:

Expense

— Interest paid or due and payable to:

		Consolidated		Holding Company	
Sch. 7 cl. 10(c) ASRB 1017.11	Related corporations	—	—	50	24
Sch. 7 cl. 10(d) ASRB 1008.50	Other persons	1,460	1,173	1,239	1,082
	Finance charges on capitalised leases	207	—	—	—
	— Less: Capitalised				
	Related corporations	—	—	(18)	(12)
	Other persons	(28)	(20)	(24)	(18)
Sch. 7 cl. 8(1)(b)(i)		1,639	1,153	1,247	1,076
Sch. 7 cl. 8(1)(b)(ii)	Bad trade debts written off to profit and loss account	26	24	2	4
Sch. 7 cl. 8(1)(b)(iii)	Loss on sale of property, plant and equipment*	50	24	12	—
Sch. 7 cl. 8(1)(b)(v) ASRB 1011.60	Amortisation of: Research and development costs	16	9	10	4
Sch. 7 cl. 8(1)(b)(v)(E)	Deferred expenditure	20	18	6	4
ASRB 1022.70	Exploration expenditure	46	15	23	—
ASRB 1013.70	Goodwill	242	209	—	—
Sch. 7 cl. 8(1)(b)(v)(D)	Other intangibles	165	53	45	31
ASRB 1008.50	Leased assets capitalised	182	—	—	—
Sch. 7 cl. 8(1)(b)(v)(C)	Leasehold property	23	20	4	4
Sch. 7 cl. 8(1)(b)(v)(C)	Depreciation of property, plant and equipment	2,679	1,652	1,112	632
Sch. 7 cl. 8(1)(b)(v)(B)	Write-down in value of inventories	105	92	51	47
	Amounts set aside to provision for:				
Sch. 7 cl. 8(1)(b)(ii)	Doubtful trade debts	64	50	10	9
Sch. 7 cl. 8(1)(b)(ii)	Doubtful term debts	6	3	6	3
Sch. 7 cl. 8(1)(b)(vi)	Employee entitlements*	461	382	84	56
Sch. 7 cl. 8(1)(b)(vi)	Repairs and maintenance*	11	124	37	41

App. B

Sch. 7 cl. 8(1)(b)(vi)	Warranties*	306	143	—	—
ASRB 1018.30 Sch. 7 cl. 8(1)(b)(vii) ASRB 1022.70	Abnormal Item — Exploration expenditure written off in respect of areas of interest abandoned during the year (Income tax benefit of $372,000)	953	—	—	—
ASRB 1012.60	Foreign exchange losses	92	41	15	4
ASRB 1008.51	Lease rental expense—				
	Operating leases	209	146	22	16
	Finance leases	—	282	—	—
ASRB 1011.60	Research and development costs written off	3,677	2,257	795	395
Sch. 7 cl. 26	Remuneration of auditors: —Amounts received or due and receivable for audit services by:				
Sch. 7 cl. 26(3)	Auditors of the holding company	79	70	22	17
	Other auditors	4	5	—	—
	—Amounts received or due and receivable for other services by:				
Sch. 7 cl. 26(3)	Auditors of the holding company	21	19	16	13
	Other auditors	3	3	—	—

Sch. 7 cl. 8(1)(b) * *Losses from the sale of non-current assets, decrements arising from the revaluation of non-current assets and transfers to provisions are required to be disclosed only where they are material.*

Sch. 7 cl. 8(1)(b)(v)(A) (Notes):
- Schedule 7 also requires the disclosure of amounts charged for the diminution in value of investments.

Sch. 7 cl. 8(1)(c) • The amount derived by the application of equity accounting is also to be disclosed.

		Consolidated		Holding Company	
		19X9 $000	19X8 $000	19X9 $000	19X8 $000
	5. TAXATION				
Sch. 7 cl. 9(1) ASRB 1020.10	**Income Tax Expense** Prima facie income tax expense calculated at 39% (19X8 — 49%) on the operating profit	2,461	2,485	479	388
	Increase in income tax expense due to non-tax deductible items:				
	Depreciation of buildings	259	214	51	29
	Amortisation of goodwill	94	102	—	—

App. B

EXAMPLE CONSOLIDATED FINANCIAL STATEMENTS

AGR 6(4)	Loss of non-resident subsidiary company not carried forward as future income tax benefit	21	7	—	—
	Fringe benefits tax	41	—	9	—
	Sundry items (including entertainment)	23	47	3	24
		2,899	2,855	542	441
	Decrease in income tax expense due to:				
	Rebate on dividend income	59	28	259	179
	Research and development allowance	727	558	160	101
	Recovery of tax losses of subsidiary company not previously brought to account	—	96	—	—
ASRB 1020.16	Abnormal Item: Future tax benefit due to tax losses of previous years not previously brought to account	276	—	—	—
		1,062	682	419	280
	Income tax expense on operating profit	1,836	2,173	123	161
Sch. 7 cl. 9(2)	Add: Income tax under/(over) provided in prior year	(126)	(52)	(33)	(5)
	Total income tax expense	1,710	2,121	90	156
	Total income tax expense is made up of:				
	Current income tax expense	1,646	2,501	136	221
Sch. 7 cl. 9(2)	Deferred income tax expense	64	(380)	(46)	(65)
		1,710	2,121	90	156

Sch. 7 cl. 9(1) *(Notes:*

- *Where prima facie tax payable on operating profit differs by more than 15% from income tax provided, a reconciliation is required. Schedule 7 allows compensatory items to be taken into account in calculating the 15% variance.*
- *The amounts shown for income tax under/(over) provided in prior years appearing in the reconciliation of prima facie tax to income tax expense shall relate only to permanent differences.*
- *Clauses 12(k)(ii) and 16(4)(c) of Sch. 7 require the balances of the provision for current income tax and the provision for deferred income tax to be disclosed. The following details of movements in the provision for current income tax and the composition of the provision for deferred income tax and future income tax benefit may be disclosed if considered appropriate.)*

App. B

		Consolidated		Holding Company	
		19X9 $000	19X8 $000	19X9 $000	19X8 $000
	Provision for Current Income Tax				
	Movements during the year were as follows:				
	Balance at beginning of year	2,864	2,478	401	129
	Income tax paid	(2,738)	(2,426)	(368)	(124)
	Addition through acquisition of subsidiary company	152	136	—	—
	Current year's current income tax expense on operating profit	1,772	2,553	169	226
Sch. 7 cl. 9(2)	Under/(over) provision in prior year	(126)	(52)	(33)	(5)
	Current income tax expense on extra-ordinary items	(159)	175	(159)	175
		1,765	2,864	10	401
	Provision for Deferred Income Tax				
	Provision for deferred income tax comprises the estimated expense at current income tax rates on the following items:				
	Difference in depreciation and amortisation of property, plant and equipment for accounting and income tax purposes	111	96	—	—
	Expenditure currently deductible but deferred and amortised for accounting purposes	766	359	102	108
	Sundry items	33	17	28	9
		910	472	130	117
	Future Income Tax Benefit				
	Future income tax benefit reflects the future benefit at current income tax rates of the following items:				
	Provisions and accrued employee entitlements not currently deductible	1,362	1,096	256	236
ASRB 1020.12	Tax losses carried forward	405	440	—	—

App. B

EXAMPLE CONSOLIDATED FINANCIAL STATEMENTS

Difference in depreciation and amortisation of property, plant and equipment for accounting and income tax purposes	1,048	943	275	232
Sundry items	51	13	—	4
	2,866	2,492	531	472

ASRB 1020.15 **Future Income Tax Benefit Not Taken to Account**

The future income tax benefit in a subsidiary company arising from tax losses and timing differences has not been recognised as an asset because recovery is not virtually certain:

ASRB 1020.15

Tax losses carried forward	272	506	—	—
Timing differences	38	35	—	—
	310	541	—	—

ASRB 1020.15 The future income tax benefit which has not been recognised as an asset will only be obtained if:

(i) the relevant subsidiary company derives future assessable income of a nature and an amount sufficient to enable the benefit to be realised, or the benefit can be utilised by another group company in accordance with sec. 80G of the *Income Tax Assessment Act 1936*;

(ii) the relevant subsidiary company and/or the group continues to comply with the conditions for deductibility imposed by the law; and

(iii) no changes in tax legislation adversely affect the relevant subsidiary company and/or the group in realising the benefit.

SE 3C(2)(b)   The holding company is taxed as a public company.

AGR 7(6)   **Dividend Franking Account**

As at 30 June 19X9 the holding company's Dividend Franking Account had a surplus of $327,000 (19X8 — $249,000). The extent to which dividends paid or provided for during the year have been franked is contained in Note 8.

AGR 7(7), (9)   *(Note: Where the dividend franking account has a deficit at the end of a tax year, the franking deficit tax payable in respect of the deficit should be recognised as a liability in the financial statements of that year. To the extent that it is assured beyond reasonable doubt the company will have its income tax liability reduced as a result of paying the franking deficit tax, an asset equivalent to the amount of the franking deficit tax should be recognised (such an amount forming part of the future income tax benefit).*

Where over-franked dividends have been paid during the year and franking additional tax is payable, this amount should be included in the year's income tax expense and separately detailed in the income tax expense reconciliation for the year.)

App. B

	Consolidated		Holding Company	
	19X9	19X8	19X9	19X8
	$000	$000	$000	$000

Sch. 7
cl. 8(1)(d)
ASRB 1018.40
ASRB 1018.41
ASRB 1018.06

6. EXTRAORDINARY ITEMS

Insurance proceeds received for loss of assets resulting from fire (assets written down to nil value subsequent to fire in a prior year)	—	656	—	356
Income tax expense	—	(321)	—	(175)
Surplus arising from liquidator's distribution out of post-acquisition capital profits of subsidiary company (no income tax applicable) (Note 31)	—	—	155	401
Loss on closure of a significant business (no income tax applicable)	(249)	—	—	—
	(249)	335	155	401

Sch. 7 cl. 12(n)

7. RESERVES

Capital

Sch. 7
cl. 12(n)(i)
Sec. 119

Share premium	985	490	985	490
Asset revaluation	9,107	2,677	1,709	1,322
Capital profits	1,200	400	27	27
Revenue				
General	1,514	1,480	26	50

ASRB 1012.60

Foreign currency translation	136	100	—	—
	12,942	5,147	2,747	1,889

(Notes:

* *Clause 12(n) of Sch. 7 requires the classification of reserves under the following headings:*
  * *— share premium account*
  * *— capital redemption reserve*
  * *— other reserves other than capital reserve arising on consolidation.*

D1.1(11),
D1.1(9)

* *The headings "Capital" and "Revenue" are not mandatory, nor is the classification of the share premium and asset revaluation reserve as capital reserves. These disclosures are regarded as best practice.)*

EXAMPLE CONSOLIDATED FINANCIAL STATEMENTS

		Consolidated		Holding Company	
		19X9	19X8	19X9	19X8
		$000	$000	$000	$000

Sch. 7 cl. 12(n)
ASRB 1018.51
Sch. 7 cl. 15

Movements During the Year*

Sch. 7 cl. 15	Share premium				
	Balance at beginning of year	490	—	490	—
	Add: Premium on ordinary shares issued during the year (Note 20)	495	490	495	490
	Balance at end of year	985	490	985	490
Sch. 7 cl. 15	Asset revaluation**				
	Balance at beginning of year	2,677	2,677	1,322	1,322
	Add: Revaluation increment on freehold land and buildings (Note 14)	7,230	—	387	—
	Less: Prior year revaluation increment realised on sale of building during the year transferred to capital profits reserve	(800)	—	—	—
	Balance at end of year	9,107	2,677	1,709	1,322
Sch. 7 cl. 15	Capital profits				
	Balance at beginning of year	400	400	27	27
	Add: Realised increment on building sold during the year transferred from asset revaluation reserve	800	—	—	—
	Balance at end of year	1,200	400	27	27
Sch. 7 cl. 15	Foreign currency translation				
	Balance at beginning of year	100	75	—	—
ASRB 1012.60	Add: Translation adjustment on overseas subsidiaries' financial statements	36	25	—	—
	Balance at end of year	136	100	—	—
Sch. 7 cl. 15	General				
	Balance at beginning of year	1,480	1,861	50	216
	Transfer from (to) retained profits	34	(381)	(24)	(166)
	Balance at end of year	1,514	1,480	26	50
	Total reserves	12,942	5,147	2,747	1,889

Sch. 7 cl. 15   * Details of transfers to or from any class of reserves need only be disclosed where such transfers are material.

ASRB 1010.25   ** Increments arising from the revaluation of non-current assets are taken direct to reserves except to the extent such increments reverse revaluation decrements previously charged to the profit and loss account in respect of the same class of asset. Revaluation decrements are debited to the profit and loss account except to the extent such decrements reverse revaluation increments previously credited to asset revaluation reserves, in respect of the same class of asset.

App. B

	Consolidated		Holding Company	
	19X9	19X8	19X9	19X8
	$000	$000	$000	$000

8. DIVIDENDS PAID AND PROPOSED

AGR 7(6)

The amounts paid or declared by way of dividend by the holding company are:

(i) an interim ordinary fully franked dividend of 8 cents per share (19X8: 7.5 cents) was paid on 31 January 19X9	230	201	230	201
(ii) a final ordinary fully franked dividend of 8 cents per share (19X8: 8 cents) is recommended by the Directors	250	230	250	230
(iii) a preference fully franked dividend of 3.5% per share (19X8: 3.5% per share) is recommended by the Directors	35	35	35	35
	515	466	515	466

* *Details of dividends paid or proposed are required to be disclosed in the Directors' Report but are not required to be disclosed in the notes. Such details are disclosed as a matter of best practice.*

EXAMPLE CONSOLIDATED FINANCIAL STATEMENTS

			Note	Consolidated 19X9 $000	Consolidated 19X8 $000	Holding Company 19X9 $000	Holding Company 19X8 $000
	9. OTHER APPROPRIATIONS						
	Retained earnings of a subsidiary company de-consolidated as a consequence of an issue of shares by the subsidiary causing it to be no longer a subsidiary			—	425	—	—
	10. RECEIVABLES						
	Current						
Sch. 7 cl. 11(2)	Short-term deposits			8,180	8,250	120	1,225
Sch. 7 cl. 12(a)(i)	Trade debtors		22, 46	7,285	5,809	2,707	2,439
Sch. 7 cl. 11(2)	Term debtors		22	540	460	540	460
Sch. 7 cl. 17(2) ASRB 1017.11	Loans to subsidiary companies			—	—	180	120
				16,005	14,519	3,547	4,244
	Non-Current						
Sch. 7 cl. 11(2)	Term debtors		23	1,660	1,447	1,660	1,447
Sch. 7 cl. 17(2) ASRB 1017.11	Loans to subsidiary companies			—	—	1,250	750
Sch. 7 cl. 11(2)	Other loans		24	282	250	32	—
				1,942	1,697	2,942	2,197

App. B

		Note
	11. INVESTMENTS	
	Current	
Sch. 7 cl. 12(b)(iii)	Shares — other corporations	29
	Non-Current	
	Shares	
Sch. 7 cl. 12(e)(iii) Sch. 7 cl. 17(1)	— related corporations	29, 30, 31
Sch. 7 cl. 12(e)(iii) Sch. 7 cl. 17(1)	— associated corporations	29, 48
Sch. 7 cl. 12(e)(iii)	— other corporations	29
Sch. 7 cl. 12(e)(ii)	Debentures	29
Sch. 7 cl. 12(e)(v)	Interest in business undertaking — partnership	32
ASRB 1019.60	**12. INVENTORIES**	
	Current	
Sch. 7 cl. 12(c)(i)	Raw materials and stores	
Sch. 7 cl. 12(c)(ii)	Work in progress	
Sch. 7 cl. 12(c)(iii)	Finished goods	
Sch. 7 cl. 16(1)	— at cost	
	— at net realisable value	
	(Note: Schedule 7 cl. 13 also requires the separate disclosure of any provisions by the classes of inventories indicated.)	
Sch. 7 cl. 12(c)(iv)	Land held for resale	25
Sch. 7 cl. 12(c)(ii)	Construction work in progress	26
	Non-Current	
Sch. 7 cl. 12(f)(iv)	Land held for resale	25
	13. OTHER CURRENT ASSETS	
Sch. 7 cl. 11(2)	Prepayments	
Sch. 7 cl. 11(2)	Deferred expenditure	27
Sch. 7 cl. 11(2)	Research and development costs	28

App. B

EXAMPLE CONSOLIDATED FINANCIAL STATEMENTS

	Consolidated		Holding Company	
	19X9 $000	19X8 $000	19X9 $000	19X8 $000
	155	—	155	—
	—	—	12,089	11,033
	1,990	1,621	1,590	1,221
	305	642	249	607
	20	—	20	—
	740	477	740	477
	3,055	2,740	14,688	13,388
	4,442	3,735	1,202	1,073
	1,417	1,085	427	231
	4,750	3,230	1,250	793
	310 5,060	527 3,757	115 1,365	375 1,168
	10,919	8,577	2,994	2,472
	230	180	230	180
	1,842	1,098	—	—
	12,991	9,855	3,224	2,652
	1,045	870	1,045	870
	444	426	77	81
	23	20	7	4
	18	6	12	8
	485	452	96	93

App. B

		Consolidated		Holding Company	
		19X9	19X8	19X9	19X8
		$000	$000	$000	$000

14. PROPERTY, PLANT AND EQUIPMENT

Sch. 7 cl. 12(g)(i)	Freehold land				
	At cost	200	1,482	—	164
	At Directors' valuation 19X7	—	1,605	—	1,193
Sch. 7 cl. 31	At independent valuation 19X9	4,815	—	1,457	—
		5,015	3,087	1,457	1,357
Sch. 7 cl. 12(g)(i)	Buildings				
	At cost	600	4,931	—	1,662
Sch. 7 cl. 16(1)(c)	Accumulated depreciation	4	1,456	—	475
Sch. 7 cl. 13(a) Sch. 7 cl. 13(b)		596	3,475	—	1,187
	At Directors' valuation 19X7	—	4,300	—	1,494
Sch. 7 cl. 31	At independent valuation 19X9	13,208	—	3,106	—
		13,208	4,300	3,106	1,494
Sch. 7 cl. 16(1)(c)	Accumulated depreciation	679	1,269	151	428
Sch. 7 cl. 13(a) Sch. 7 cl. 13(b)		12,529	3,031	2,955	1,066
	Net book value — buildings	13,125	6,506	2,955	2,253
	Leasehold property — at cost	485	460	74	74
Sch. 7 cl. 13(a)	Accumulated amortisation	123	100	26	22
Sch. 7 cl. 13(b)		362	360	48	52
Sch. 7 cl. 12(g)(ii)	Plant and equipment — at cost	17,675	16,963	5,778	5,619
Sch. 7 cl. 13(a)	Accumulated depreciation	10,034	8,816	3,214	2,522
Sch. 7 cl. 13(b)		7,641	8,147	2,564	3,097
ASRB 1008.50 Sch. 7 cl. 16(4)(d)	Leased plant and equipment capitalised	2,426	—	—	—
Sch. 7 cl. 13(a)	Accumulated amortisation	182	—	—	—
Sch. 7 cl. 13(b)		2,244	—	—	—
Sch. 7 cl. 11(2)	Capital works in progress — at cost	1,231	2,947	—	—
	Total property, plant and equipment — net book value	29,618	21,047	7,024	6,759

App. B

EXAMPLE CONSOLIDATED FINANCIAL STATEMENTS

Sch. 7
cl. 16(1)(a)
ASRB 1010.40

The independent valuation in 19X9 was carried out as at 31 March 19X9 by Mr R. Perrin, F.A.I.V., and is on the basis of the open market value of the properties concerned in their existing use. This valuation is in accordance with the company's policy of obtaining an independent valuation of land and buildings every three years. Land and buildings valued at cost were purchased after 31 March 19X9.

In revaluing freehold land and buildings the Directors have not taken into account the potential impact of capital gains tax on the grounds that such assets are an integral part of the group's operations and there is no intention to sell the assets. If the land and buildings had been disposed of at balance date at its revalued amount, a capital gains tax liability of $2,480,000 (holding company $340,000) would have arisen.

(Notes:

- *Generally, in a revaluation all assets in a class should be revalued. It is necessary to disclose the reasons for not revaluing an entire class of assets when an asset in that class has been revalued.*

ASRB 1010.20
Sch. 7 cl. 31(2)

- *The accounts of a company and of a group beginning with the third financial year commencing on or after 1 October 1986, and each successive financial year, shall include a note specifying the current values of interests in land and buildings. Current value means the most recent valuation made within the last three years. Typically, the first years affected will be 31 December 1989 and 30 June 1990 for December and June balance dates respectively. The requirement applies to listed corporations, borrowing corporations and large corporations other than exempt proprietary companies.*

Sch. 7 cl. 29(2)

Wholly owned subsidiaries of Australian corporations do not need to disclose the information in their own accounts.

- *Schedule 7 cl. 12 only requires an analysis by "land and buildings; plant or equipment". The additional disclosure is considered necessary to calculate depreciation/amortisation and as a matter of best practice.)*

		Consolidated		Holding Company	
		19X9	19X8	19X9	19X8
		$000	$000	$000	$000
	15. INTANGIBLES				
Sch. 7 cl. 12(h)(i)	Goodwill	1,342	1,140	—	—
Sch. 7 cl. 13(a) ASRB 1013.70	Accumulated amortisation	641	399	—	—
Sch. 7 cl. 13(b)		701	741	—	—
Sch. 7 cl. 12(h)(ii)	Patents and trade marks	1,880	410	220	210
Sch. 7 cl. 13(a)	Accumulated amortisation	230	80	82	50
Sch. 7 cl. 13(b)		1,650	330	138	160
	Debenture issue costs	150	150	120	120
Sch. 7 cl. 13(a) Sch. 7 cl. 13(b)	Accumulated amortisation	41	26	33	20
		109	124	87	100
		2,460	1,195	225	260

(Note: ASRB 1013 is effective for balance dates ending on or after 19 June 1988.)

App. B

		Note	Consolidated 19X9 $000	Consolidated 19X8 $000	Holding Company 19X9 $000	Holding Company 19X8 $000
	16. OTHER NON-CURRENT ASSETS					
Sch. 7 cl. 11(2) ASRB 1020.11	Future income tax benefit	5	2,866	2,492	531	472
Sch. 7 cl. 11(2) ASRB 1022.71	Exploration expenditure	33	2,148	2,227	1,224	478
Sch. 7 cl. 11(2)	Deferred expenditure	27	247	210	58	38
Sch. 7 cl. 11(2)	Research and development costs	28	69	44	42	28
			5,330	4,973	1,855	1,016
	17. CREDITORS AND BORROWINGS					
	Current					
Sch. 7 cl. 12(1)(v)	Trade creditors	46	8,295	10,808	2,685	2,074
Sch. 7 cl. 12(j)(i) Sch. 7 cl. 16(2)	Bank overdraft — secured	34	680	1,561	400	570
Sch. 7 cl. 12(j)(ii)	Bank loans — secured	35	2,700	2,300	500	250
	— unsecured		300	225	300	225
Sch. 7 cl. 12(1)(iii)	Debentures — secured	36	250	250	150	150
Sch. 7 cl. 12(j)(vi) ASRB 1008.50	Lease liabilities — secured	37	300	—	—	—
			12,525	15,144	4,035	3,269
	Non-Current					
Sch. 7 cl. 12(1)(i) Sch. 7 cl. 16(2)	Bank loans — secured	35	11,450	8,400	8,250	8,250
Sch. 7 cl. 12(1)(i)	— unsecured		3,750	2,400	1,200	1,025
Sch. 7 cl. 12(1)(ii)	Debentures — secured	36	6,000	6,250	4,000	4,150
Sch. 7 cl. 12(1)(v) ASRB 1008.50	Lease liabilities — secured	37	1,926	—	—	—
			23,126	17,050	13,450	13,425

(Note: It may be desirable to include "Creditors" and "Borrowings" under separate headings in the balance sheet.)

App. B

		Note	Consolidated 19X9 $000	Consolidated 19X8 $000	Holding Company 19X9 $000	Holding Company 19X8 $000
	18. PROVISIONS					
	Current					
Sch. 7 cl. 12(k)(i)	Dividends	8	285	265	285	265
Sch. 7 cl. 12(k)(ii)	Income tax	5	1,765	2,864	10	401
Sch. 7 cl. 12(k)(iii)	Employee entitlements		329	272	118	112
Sch. 7 cl. 11(2)	Repairs and maintenance		120	163	36	57
Sch. 7 cl. 11(2)	Warranties		538	360	57	48
			3,037	3,924	506	883
	Non-Current					
Sch. 7 cl. 12(m)	Employee entitlements		1,337	1,130	134	124
Sch. 7 cl. 16(4)(c)	Deferred income tax	5	910	472	130	117
Sch. 7 cl. 11(2)	Repairs and maintenance		395	321	149	137
Sch. 7 cl. 11(2)	Warranties		278	150	—	—
			2,920	2,073	413	378
	19. OTHER LIABILITIES					
	Current					
Sch. 7 cl. 17(2) ASRB 1017.11	Other loans — related corporations		—	—	845	180
	Non-Current					
Sch. 7 cl. 17(2) ASRB 1017.11	Other loans — related corporations		—	—	1,000	1,000
	20. SHARE CAPITAL					
Sch. 7 cl. 14(1)(a)(i) Sch. 7 cl. 14(2)(b)	**Authorised Capital** 5,000,000 (19X8 — 5,000,000) ordinary shares of $2.00 each		10,000	10,000	10,000	10,000
	1,000,000 (19X8 — 1,000,000) 3.5% redeemable non-participating cumulative preference shares of $2.00 each		2,000	2,000	2,000	2,000
			12,000	12,000	12,000	12,000

App. B

		Consolidated		Holding Company	
		19X9	19X8	19X9	19X8
		$000	$000	$000	$000

Sch. 7 cl. 14(1)(a)(ii)	**Issued and Paid-Up Capital** 3,125,000 (19X8 — 2,875,000) ordinary shares of $2.00 each, fully paid	6,250	5,750	6,250	5,750
Sch. 7 cl. 14(1)(c)	500,000 (19X8 — 500,000) 3.5% redeemable non-participating cumulative preference shares of $2.00 each, fully paid	1,000	1,000	1,000	1,000
		7,250	6,750	7,250	6,750

Sch. 7 cl. 14(1)(d)	During the year the holding company issued 250,000 ordinary shares of $2.00 each to provide additional working capital. 200,000 were issued at a premium of $2.00 per share and 50,000 were issued at a premium of $1.90 per share.
Sch. 7 cl. 14(1)(c)	The holding company's preference shares are redeemable at par value at the holder's option at any time after 1 July 20Y0. The company has the power to redeem any of the shares before 1 July 20Y0 at a premium of 25 cents per share.
Sch. 7 cl. 21, 22	**21. COMMITMENTS AND CONTINGENT LIABILITIES*** The estimated maximum amount of commitments and contingent liabilities not provided for in the accounts of the group as at 30 June 19X9 are set out below:
Sch. 7 cl. 21(2), 22(1)	* *Commitments for expenditure and contingent liabilities need only be disclosed where they are material.* A. COMMITMENTS
Sch. 7 cl. 32	**Superannuation Commitments**** The holding company and other group corporations contribute to a group employee superannuation fund, matching contributions to the fund made by employees. Employees' contributions are based on various percentages of their gross salaries. After serving a qualifying period, all employees are entitled to benefits on retirement, disability or death.
Sch. 7 cl. 32	The fund provides defined benefits based on years of service and final average salary. The company and other group corporations are under no legal obligation to make up any shortfall in the fund's assets to meet payments due to employees. An actuarial assessment of the fund as at 30 June 19X9 was carried out by Mr. W.A. Smith, F.I.A.A. on 31 July 19X9. The assessment concluded that the assets of the fund are sufficient to meet all benefits payable in the event of the fund's termination, or the voluntary or compulsory termination of employment of each employee of the holding company and other group corporations.
Sch. 7 cl. 29	** *Details of superannuation commitments are only required to be disclosed by listed corporations, borrowing corporations and large corporations other than exempt proprietary companies. Wholly owned subsidiaries of Australian corporations need not disclose the information in their own accounts.*

App. B

EXAMPLE CONSOLIDATED FINANCIAL STATEMENTS

		Consolidated		Holding Company	
		19X9	19X8	19X9	19X8
		$000	$000	$000	$000
Sch. 7 cl. 21	**Capital Expenditure Commitments***				
	Plant and equipment purchases:				
	Not later than one year	864	576	768	374
	Later than one year but not later than two years	254	306	118	207
	Capital expenditure projects:				
	Not later than one year	1,081	825	—	—
	Later than one year but not later than two years	189	202	—	—
		2,388	1,909	886	581
	Business Undertaking Commitments*				
	Future contributions to partnership, due not later than one year	1,087	1,210	1,087	1,210

Sch. 7 cl. 21(2)   * Where relevant, the dissection required by Schedule 7 is:
    (a) not later than one year;
    (b) later than one year but not later than two years;
    (c) later than two years, but not later than five years; and
    (d) later than five years.

		Consolidated		Holding Company	
		19X9	19X8	19X9	19X8
		$000	$000	$000	$000
Sch. 7 cl. 21	**Lease Rental Commitments**				
ASRB 1008.52	Future operating lease rentals of plant and equipment: Due:				
	Not later than one year	125	177	28	19
	Later than one year but not later than two years	110	141	24	25
	Later than two years but not later than five years	350	477	76	64
	Later than five years	178	207	74	—
		763	1,002	202	108
	Future finance lease rentals of plant, equipment and motor vehicles: Due:				
	Not later than one year	—	225	—	—
	Later than one year but not later than two years	—	149	—	—
	Later than two years but not later than five years	—	985	—	—
	Later than five years	—	521	—	—
		—	1,880	—	—

App. B

		Consolidated		Holding Company	
		19X9	19X8	19X9	19X8
		$000	$000	$000	$000

Sch. 7 cl. 22   **B. CONTINGENT LIABILITIES**

In respect of related corporations:

(i) Secured guarantee by the holding company of bank accommodation of related corporations   —   —   724   566

(ii) Under the terms of the Class Order issued by the National Companies and Securities Commission on 9 August 1988 which relieves certain wholly owned subsidiaries from specified accounting and financial reporting requirements, the holding company has entered into approved deeds of indemnity for the cross-guarantee of liabilities with each of the following subsidiaries:

Example Public Company (Construction) Pty. Limited

Example Public Company (Manufacturing) Pty. Limited

(iii) The potential tax liability arising from a full distribution of the retained distributable earnings of foreign subsidiary companies, including distributions made out of share premium accounts, and asset revaluation reserves, is estimated to amount to   71   61   —   —

The Directors are of the opinion that the amount set aside for the tax liability arising from anticipated dividend distributions by foreign subsidiary companies is sufficient having regard to the proposed dividend distribution policies of those companies.

App. B

EXAMPLE CONSOLIDATED FINANCIAL STATEMENTS

		Consolidated		Holding Company	
		19X9	19X8	19X9	19X8
	In respect of other persons:	$000	$000	$000	$000
Sch. 7 cl. 22(3)	(i) A claim has been lodged against Example Public Company (Hardware) Pty. Limited in respect of a product warranty. Liability is not admitted and the claim will be defended	100	—	—	—
SE 3C(2)(d)	(ii) Retirement benefits payable, on termination, in certain circumstances to Directors under service agreements	149	128	149	128
	In respect of business undertakings:				
	(i) The holding company as a 50% partner in Property Development Partnership is jointly and severally liable for 100% of all liabilities incurred by that partnership. The assets of the partnership are sufficient to meet such liabilities. The partnership's liabilities not included in the group accounts as at 30 June 19X9 amounted to	80	57	80	80
ASRB 1006.22	(ii) Under the provisions of the agreement for the joint venture in which the holding company has a 33% interest, the holding company is jointly and severally liable for all liabilities incurred by the joint venture. As at 30 June 19X9 the assets of the joint venture were sufficient to meet such liabilities. The joint venture's liabilities not included in the group accounts as at 30 June 19X9 amounted to	220	150	220	150

App. B

Sch. 7 cl. 22 (Note: Clause 22(3) of Sch. 7 requires that the group accounts shall include a note specifying in respect of all corporations in the group, so far as is practicable, the total amount (or an estimate) of any contingent liabilities of those corporations where the total amount is material to the group. Prior to the September 1987 Sch. 7 amendments, materiality was determined on the basis of an individual corporation rather than the group. Such a note is to be specified under subheadings similar to the above, plus corporations and undertakings over which the subsidiary or another group company exerts significant influence.)

		Consolidated		Holding Company	
		19X9	19X8	19X9	19X8
		$000	$000	$000	$000
	22. DEBTORS (CURRENT)				
Sch. 7 cl. 12(a)(i)	Trade debtors	7,619	6,063	2,850	2,554
Sch. 7 cl. 13(a)	Less: Provision for doubtful trade debtors	334	254	143	115
Sch. 7 cl. 13(b)		7,285	5,809	2,707	2,439
Sch. 7 cl. 11(2)	Term debtors	605	510	605	510
Sch. 7 cl. 19	Less: Deferred income	65	50	65	50
		540	460	540	460
	23. DEBTORS (NON-CURRENT)				
Sch. 7 cl. 11(2)	Term debtors	1,890	1,640	1,890	1,640
Sch. 7 cl. 19	Less: Deferred income	210	179	210	179
		1,680	1,461	1,680	1,461
Sch. 7 cl. 13(a)	Less: Provision for doubtful non-current term debtors	20	14	20	14
Sch. 7 cl. 13(b)		1,660	1,447	1,660	1,447

24. OTHER LOANS

Sch. 7 cl. 17(3)
ASRB 1017.16
SE 3C(3)(d)

Included in other loans is an amount of $32,000 (19X8 — $nil) being a loan made by the holding company to Mr K. Johns, a Director of that company. Interest is payable monthly at a flat rate of 6% per annum. The principal is repayable on 30 June 19Y0. The loan is secured by a registered first mortgage over the Director's residence.

(Notes:
• Alternatively, where approval has been received from the Stock Exchange, abridged details of directors' loans may be disclosed.
• Non-listed companies only need to disclose the total amount of all loans to directors, without reference to interest, repayment dates or security details.)

App. B

EXAMPLE CONSOLIDATED FINANCIAL STATEMENTS

		Consolidated		Holding Company	
		19X9	19X8	19X9	19X8
		$000	$000	$000	$000
Sch. 7 cl. 18	**25. LAND HELD FOR RESALE***				
	Cost of acquisition	506	506	506	506
	Development costs	558	382	558	382
	Holding costs	104	87	104	87
	Interest expense	107	75	107	75
		1,275	1,050	1,275	1,050
	Classified as: Non-current	1,045	870	1,045	870
	Current	230	180	230	180
		1,275	1,050	1,275	1,050

* *Separate analysis of holding costs and interest expense is provided as a matter of best practice.*

Sch. 7 cl. 16   Land held at valuation should be separately disclosed.
Sch. 7 cl. 13   Any provisions for diminution in value should also be disclosed, as between cost and valuation.

26. CONSTRUCTION WORK IN PROGRESS

		Consolidated		Holding Company	
		19X9	19X8	19X9	19X8
		$000	$000	$000	$000
ASRB 1009.50	Cost	2,584	1,827	—	—
	Profit recognised to date	598	411	—	—
	Less: Provision for losses	(140)	(140)	—	—
		3,042	2,098	—	—
	Less: Progress billings	1,200	1,000	—	—
		1,842	1,098	—	—
ASRB 1009.51	Cash received and receivable as progress billings (including retention allowances) and advances	1,300	1,100	—	—

27. DEFERRED EXPENDITURE

	Gross	362	302	87	58
Sch. 7 cl. 13(a)	Less: Accumulated amortisation	92	72	22	16
Sch. 7 cl. 13(b)		270	230	65	42
	Classified as: Non-current	247	210	58	38
	Current	23	20	7	4
		270	230	65	42

App. B

		Consolidated		Holding Company	
		19X9	19X8	19X9	19X8
		$000	$000	$000	$000
ASRB 1011.60	**28. RESEARCH AND DEVELOPMENT COSTS**				
	Expenditure brought forward	71	50	50	34
	Add: Deferred costs	53	21	28	16
		124	71	78	50
Sch. 7 cl. 13(a)	Less: Accumulated amortisation	37	21	24	14
Sch. 7 cl. 13(b)		87	50	54	36
	29. INVESTMENTS				
	Current				
Sch. 7 cl. 17(1)(d)	*Investments in Other Corporations*				
	Shares (unquoted) — at cost	155	—	155	—
	Non-Current				
Sch. 7 cl. 17(1)(c)	*Shares in Related Corporations* (unquoted)				
	At cost	—	—	12,279	11,223
	Less: Amount written off	—	—	190	190
		—	—	12,089	11,033
	Refer Note 30 for particulars in relation to related corporations				
Sch. 7 cl. 17(1)(d) Sch. 7 cl. 34(2)(e) ASRB 1016.22	**Shares in Associated Corporations**				
	Unquoted — at cost	870	501	870	501
	Less: Amount written off	80	80	80	80
		790	421	790	421
	Refer Note 48 for particulars in relation to associated corporations				
Sch. 7 cl. 16(3)(b) Sch. 7 cl. 34(2)(e)	Quoted — at cost	1,200	1,200	800	800
	Quoted market value: Consolidated 19X9 — $1,309,000 19X8 — $1,292,000 Holding company 19X9 — $872,667 19X8 — $861,333	—	—	—	—
		1,990	1,621	1,590	1,221

AGR 8(12) No capital gains tax would be payable if the quoted shares in associated corporations were sold at balance date at the disclosed market values since the shares were acquired prior to 19 September 1985.

App. B

EXAMPLE CONSOLIDATED FINANCIAL STATEMENTS

		Consolidated		Holding Company	
		19X9	19X8	19X9	19X8
		$000	$000	$000	$000

Sch. 7 cl. 17(1)(d) — **Investments in Other Corporations**

Sch. 7 cl. 16(3)(b) — Shares — quoted

	19X9	19X8	19X9	19X8
At cost	205	542	149	507
At Directors' valuation 19X7	100	100	100	100

Sch. 7 cl. 16(3)(b) — Quoted market value:
Consolidated
  19X9 — $371,000
  19X8 — $751,000
Holding company
  19X9 — $264,000
  19X8 — $710,000

AGR 8(12) — The amount of capital gains tax that would be payable if the quoted shares in other corporations were sold at balance date at the disclosed market values should not exceed:

Consolidated
  19X9 — $24,300
  19X8 — $2,150
Holding company
  19X9 — $5,800
  19X8 — $1,000

Sch. 7 cl. 12(e)(ii) — Debentures (unquoted) — at cost

	20	—	20	—
	325	642	269	607

Sch. 7 cl. 16(3)(a) — The quoted shares comprise investments in industrial and mining corporations.

(Notes:

- *Schedule 7 only requires a dissection of shares between Related Corporations (i.e. subsidiaries, the holding company and fellow subsidiaries) and Other Corporations. The analysis between Associated Corporations and Other Corporations is shown as a matter of best practice.*

- *Schedule 7 cl. 34 requires disclosure of detailed information where a company has an interest in a corporation that is material to the company, or the group has an interest in a company that is material to the group. An interest includes shares, convertible notes, loans and advances.)*

App. B

	30. **PARTICULARS IN RELATION TO CORPORATIONS IN THE GROUP**				
Sch. 7 cl. 10 Sch. 7 cl. 37(2) ASRB 1017.11	Name	Note	Class of Share	Holding 19X9 %	19X8 %
	Example Public Company Limited				
	Related Corporations				
	Example Public Company (Construction) Pty. Limited	2	Ord	100	100
	Example Public Company (Manufacturing) Pty. Limited	2	Ord	100	95
	Example Public Company (Mining and Exploration) Pty. Limited		Ord	80	80
	Subsidiary Company Example Public Company (Useless) Pty. Limited	3	Ord		
	Example Public Company (Hardware) Pty. Limited (formerly Hardware Distributors Pty. Limited)		Ord	76	—
	Example Public Company (Singapore) Pte. Limited	4	Ord	100	100
	Example Public Company (Caribbean) Ltd.	4	Ord	56	56
	Example Public Company (Dormant) Pty. Limited	1	Ord	—	100
	Example Public Company (Holdings) Pty. Limited		Ord	—	100

(Note:

Reg. 58(3) 1. *Investments eliminated when rounded to the nearest thousand dollars are:*

	Amount of Investment	
	19X9 $	19X8 $
Example Public Company (Dormant) Pty. Limited	—	100

2. *Example Public Company (Construction) Pty. Limited and Example Public Company (Manufacturing) Pty. Limited have each entered into a cross-guarantee with Example Public Company Limited in respect of relief granted from specified accounting and financial reporting requirements in accordance with the Class Order issued by the National Companies and Securities Commission on 9 August 1988.*

App. B

EXAMPLE CONSOLIDATED FINANCIAL STATEMENTS

Amount of Investment		Dividends Received or Receivable		Contribution to Group Profit	
19X9	19X8	19X9	19X8	19X9	19X8
$000	$000	$000	$000	$000	$000
				844	642
4,724	4,724	190	110	1,198	684
5,093	4,739	187	160	1,255	637
1,280	1,280	109	61	419	279
				(31)	(6)
782	—	60	—	165	—
80	80	—	—	28	12
130	130	—	—	45	35
—	—	—	—	—	—
—	—	—	80	—	—
12,089	11,033	546	331	3,923	2,283

3. Example Public Company (Useless) Pty. Limited, an Australian subsidiary, is not audited by KPMG Peat Marwick.

4. Example Public Company (Caribbean) Ltd. was incorporated in and carries on business in Barbados, and Example Public Company (Singapore) Pte. Limited was incorporated in and carries on business in Singapore. All other companies are incorporated in Australia.

Sch. 7
cl. 37(2)(c)

Where the financial year of a subsidiary does not coincide with that of the holding company, the date on which the financial year of the subsidiary ends needs to be stated.)

App. B

31. ACQUISITION/DISPOSAL OF SUBSIDIARIES

Sch. 7 cl. 36

The following subsidiary companies were acquired or disposed of during the financial year:

	Consideration $000	Net Tangible Assets at Date of Acquisition/ Disposal $000	Holding Company's Profit/Loss on Disposal $000	Holding Company's Interest %
Company Acquired Example Public Company (Hardware) Pty. Limited (formerly Hardware Distributors Pty. Limited)	782	654	—	76

Sch. 7 cl. 36(1)
ASRB 1015.41

ASRB 1015.41 — The company was acquired on 1 April 19X9 and the operating results of the company from that date have been included in the consolidated operating profit. The purchase consideration for the acquisition was in the form of cash.

Sch. 7 cl. 36(2)

Companies Disposed of by Sale				
Example Public Company (Dormant) Pty. Limited	*	*	*	100

Sch. 7 cl. 36(2)

Companies Disposed of by Liquidation				
Example Public Company (Holdings) Pty. Limited	484	80	155	100

Reg. 58(3)

* Amounts eliminated when rounded to the nearest thousand dollars are:

Companies Disposed of by Sale

App. B

EXAMPLE CONSOLIDATED FINANCIAL STATEMENTS

	Consideration	Net Tangible Assets	Profit on Disposal
Example Public Company (Dormant) Pty. Limited	$350	$100	$250

(Notes:
- ASRB 1015 is effective for balance dates ending on or after 31 December 1988.
- The analysis between companies disposed of by sale and by liquidation is shown as a matter of best practice.)

Sch. 7 cl. 33
ASRB 1017.16

32. HOLDING COMPANY'S INTEREST IN BUSINESS UNDERTAKING — PARTNERSHIP*

Name of Undertaking	Principal Activities	Nature of Interest	Interest 19X9 %	Interest 19X8 %	Share of Net Assets 19X9 $000	Share of Net Assets 19X8 $000	Contribution to Operating Profit 19X9 $000	Contribution to Operating Profit 19X8 $000
Property development partnership	Property development and investment	Tenant-in-common in various properties	50	50	740	477	21	24

ASRB 1017.10 The value of products or services directly received by the company/group from the partnership after allowing for costs incurred by the company/group in receiving those products or services was $10,000 (19X8 — $10,000).

Sch. 7 cl. 20 The partnership assets include a holding of 100,000 units of $1 each in the XYZ Property Trust included in the partnership accounts at $100,000. The par value of the units is unconditionally guaranteed by the Manager of the Trust, ABC Management Limited. At balance date the estimated realisable value of the units, if not supported by the guarantee, totalled $50,000.

Sch. 7 cl. 29 * Details of interests in business undertakings are only required to be disclosed by listed corporations, borrowing corporations and large corporations other than exempt proprietary companies. Wholly owned subsidiaries of Australian corporations do not need to disclose the information in their own accounts.

Note: The interest in the business undertaking constitutes an interest in land and buildings under cl. 31 of Sch. 7. The valuation of the interest would need to be stated in accordance with that clause even if cl. 20 did not apply. Refer commentary to Note 14.)

App. B

284 ACCOUNTING FOR BUSINESS CONSOLIDATIONS

		Consolidated		Holding Company	
		19X9 $000	19X8 $000	19X9 $000	19X8 $000
ASRB 1022.71	**33. EXPLORATION EXPENDITURE**				
	Costs carried forward in respect of areas of interest in:				
	Exploration and/or evaluation phase	861	618	405	260
	Development phase	606	1,347	472	218
		1,467	1,965	877	478
	Production phase	866	401	370	—
Sch. 7 cl. 13(a)	Less: Accumulated amortisation	185	139	23	—
Sch. 7 cl. 13(b)		681	262	347	—
		2,148	2,227	1,224	478

Sch. 7 cl. 16(2) **34. BANK OVERDRAFT**

The bank overdrafts of related corporations are secured by guarantees from the holding company.

The bank overdraft of the holding company is secured by a registered first mortgage over certain of the holding company's land and buildings.

Sch. 7 cl. 23 The group has access to bank overdraft facilities to a maximum of $5 million, leaving an unused facility of $4,320,000.

(Note: Details of standby arrangements, unused credit facilities, etc. only apply to borrowing or guarantor corporations or corporations to which the Financial Corporations Act 1974 applies.)

Sch. 7 cl. 16(2) **35. BANK LOANS**

The bank loans are secured by registered first mortgages over certain properties of the holding company to the extent of $4 million (19X8 — $4 million), and certain of its related companies' properties for the remainder.

		Consolidated		Holding Company	
		19X9 $000	19X8 $000	19X9 $000	19X8 $000
	36. DEBENTURES				
Sch. 7 cl. 12(j)	**Current**				
	Holding company	150	150	150	150
	Example Public Company (Manufacturing) Pty. Limited	100	100	—	—
		250	250	150	150
Sch. 7 cl. 12(1)	**Non-Current**				
	Holding company	4,000	4,150	4,000	4,150
	Example Public Company (Manufacturing) Pty. Limited	2,000	2,100	—	—
		6,000	6,250	4,000	4,150
		6,250	6,500	4,150	4,300

App. B

EXAMPLE CONSOLIDATED FINANCIAL STATEMENTS

			Consolidated		Holding Company	
			19X9 $000	19X8 $000	19X9 $000	19X8 $000
D1.1(21)	**Details**					
	Maturity Dates	Interest Rate				
	1 December 19X8	13.50	—	250	—	150
	1 December 19X9	13.50	100	100	—	—
	30 June 19Y0	14.00	150	150	150	150
	30 June 19Y1	12.25	4,000	4,000	2,000	2,000
	30 June 19Y2	13.00	2,000	2,000	2,000	2,000
			6,250	6,500	4,150	4,300

Sch. 7 cl. 16(2)   All debentures are held by persons outside the group, and are secured by floating charges over the assets of the group.

ASRB 1008.50

37. LEASE LIABILITIES

Included as lease liabilities are the present values of future rentals for leased assets capitalised

		Consolidated		Holding Company	
		19X9	19X8	19X9	19X8
Sch. 7 cl. 12(j)(vi)	Current	300	—	—	—
Sch. 7 cl. 12(l)(v) ASRB 1008.50	Non-current	1,926	—	—	—
		2,226	—	—	—

ASRB 1008.50
Sch. 7 cl. 21(2)

Lease commitments in respect of capitalised finance leases are payable as follows:

Not later than one year		365	—	—	—
Later than one year but not later than two years		344	—	—	—
Later than two years but not later than five years		1,011	—	—	—
Later than five years		795	—	—	—
		2,515	—	—	—
Deduct: Future finance charges		289	—	—	—
Total lease liability		2,226	—	—	—

App. B

38. DIRECTORS' AND EXECUTIVES' REMUNERATION

Remuneration of Directors

		Consolidated		Holding Company	
		19X9 $000	19X8 $000	19X9 $000	19X8 $000
Sch. 7 cl. 24(2)	The number of Directors of the holding company, including Executive Directors, who received or in respect of whom income is due and receivable, from the holding company and related corporations, excluding amounts included under retirement payments, within the following bands is:				
	$ 0-$ 9,999			1	—
	$ 20,000-$ 29,999			1	2
	$ 60,000-$ 69,999			3	4
	$ 90,000-$ 99,999			2	2
	$100,000-$109,999			1	1
	$110,000-$119,999			1	—
Sch. 7 cl. 24(2), (4) ASRB 1017.15	Total income received, or due and receivable (including Directors' fees of $100,000; 19X8 — $90,000), by the Directors, including Executive Directors, from the holding company and related corporations, excluding amounts included under retirement payments	724	658	615	582

Remuneration of Executives*

Sch. 7 cl. 28(2)	The number of Executive Officers who received, or in respect of whom income is due and receivable, which equals or exceeds $85,000, from the holding company and related corporations, excluding amounts included under retirement payments, within the following bands is:				
	$ 85,000-$ 94,999	3	3	2	2
	$ 95,000-$104,999	2	1	1	1
	$105,000-$114,999	1	—	1	—

App. B

EXAMPLE CONSOLIDATED FINANCIAL STATEMENTS

		Consolidated		Holding Company	
		19X9	19X8	19X9	19X8
		$000	$000	$000	$000
Sch. 7 cl. 28(3)	Total income received, or due and receivable, by these Executives from the holding company and related corporations, excluding amounts included under retirement payments	602	385	405	293

* This information is only required to be disclosed by listed corporations.

(Notes:
- The NCSC issued a Class Order on 3 April 1987 relieving borrowing corporations from the requirement to disclose details of directors' remuneration and executives' remuneration in their half-yearly accounts. A similar Class Order for guarantor corporations was issued on 15 May 1987.
- The NCSC issued a Class Order on 11 March 1988 which provides that, for non-resident directors of an Australian subsidiary of a foreign holding company, any income received by such non-resident directors from wholly owned foreign subsidiaries of the foreign holding company in the non-resident director's capacity as a director or employee of that wholly owned foreign subsidiary is excluded from the income to be disclosed under cl. 24(2) and 24(4) of Sch. 7.)

		Consolidated		Holding Company	
		19X9	19X8	19X9	19X8
		$000	$000	$000	$000
	Superannuation and Retirement Payments				
Sch. 7 cl. 25(1) ASRB 1017.17	Amounts paid to superannuation funds in connection with the retirement of the Directors and Principal Executive Officers of the holding company and subsidiary companies. The amounts are disclosed in aggregate only as the Directors believe that the provision of full particulars would be unreasonable	41	32	27	19
Sch. 7 cl. 25(1)	Retirement allowance paid by the holding company to one of its former Directors, Mr R. Stephens, in connection with his retirement from the office of Director			20	—
Sch. 7 cl. 25(2)	Retiring allowances paid in connection with the retirement of persons from the offices of Director and Principal Executive Officer of the holding company				

App. B

and subsidiary companies. The amounts are disclosed in aggregate only as the Directors believe that the provision of full particulars would be unreasonable	32 15

Sch. 7 cl. 23 **39. FINANCING ARRANGEMENTS***

In addition to the bank overdraft facility outlined in Note 34, the group has access to the following financing arrangements:

Credit Standby Arrangement

The group has been granted a standby letter of credit facility of $5 million available to be drawn down over the next five years. Annual draw-downs are not permitted to exceed $2 million. No draw-downs against this facility had been made as at the 19X9 balance date.

Bill Acceptance Facility

The group has access to a bill acceptance facility to a limit of $7.5 million, available for the next two years. This facility was unused as at the 19X9 balance date.

* *Disclosure of details of standby arrangements, unused credit facilities, etc. available to or provided by a company is only applicable to borrowing or guarantor corporations or corporations to which the Financial Corporations Act 1974 applies.*

Sch. 7 cl. 30 **40. ECONOMIC DEPENDENCY***

Significant volumes of PVC and polyethylene used in the building products' manufacturing operations are supplied by Rubber Industries (Singapore) Pte. Limited. This company is the major supplier of these materials in the world, there being no other supplier of the products in Australia.

ASRB 1006.21
ASRB 1017.16
Sch. 7 cl. 33

41. INTEREST IN JOINT VENTURE*

The holding company holds an interest of 33% (19X8 — 33%) in a joint venture named Large Mining Venture whose principal activity is coal mining. During the year ended 30 June 19X9 the holding company together with the other venturers were tenants-in-common in various areas of mining interest. For the year ended 30 June 19X9 the contribution of the joint venture to the operating profit of the holding

ASRB 1017.10

company and the group was $100,000 (19X8 — $80,000). The value of the holding company's 33% share of the coal mined during the year was $500,000 (19X8 — $100,000, 33%), after allowing for costs incurred by the holding company in receiving those products.

ASRB 1006.20
Sch. 7 cl. 33

Included in the assets and liabilities of the holding company and the group are the following items which represent the holding company's and the group's interest in the assets and liabilities employed in the joint venture, recorded in accordance with the accounting policies described in Note 1.

Sch. 7
cl. 29(1), (2)
Sch. 7 cl. 30
Sch. 7 cl. 33

* *These details are only required to be disclosed by listed corporations, borrowing corporations and large corporations other than exempt proprietary companies, and where such details are material. Wholly owned subsidiaries of Australian corporations do not need to disclose the information in their own accounts.*

EXAMPLE CONSOLIDATED FINANCIAL STATEMENTS

	Consolidated		Holding Company	
	19X9	19X8	19X9	19X8
	$000	$000	$000	$000
CURRENT ASSETS				
Cash	10	100	10	100
Trade debtors	150	—	150	—
Less: Provision for doubtful trade debtors	20	—	20	—
	130	—	130	—
Prepayments	10	—	10	—
TOTAL CURRENT ASSETS	150	100	150	100
NON-CURRENT ASSETS				
Freehold land				
At directors' valuation 19X5	—	400	—	400
At independent valuation 19X9	400	—	400	—
	400	400	400	400
Buildings				
At directors' valuation 19X5	—	180	—	180
At independent valuation 19X9	180	—	180	—
	180	180	180	180
Less: Accumulated depreciation	5	10	5	10
	175	170	175	170
Plant and equipment				
At cost	340	210	340	210
Less: Accumulated depreciation	25	8	25	8
	315	202	315	202
Exploration expenditure carried forward in respect of areas of interest in:				
Exploration and/or evaluation phase	405	260	405	260
Development phase	472	218	472	218
	877	478	877	478
Production phase	370	—	370	—
Less: Accumulated amortisation	23	—	23	—
	347	—	347	—
TOTAL NON-CURRENT ASSETS	2,114	1,250	2,114	1,250
TOTAL ASSETS	2,264	1,350	2,264	1,350

continued over ...

App. B

CURRENT LIABILITIES				
Trade creditors	110	75	110	75
TOTAL CURRENT LIABILITIES	110	75	110	75
TOTAL LIABILITIES	110	75	110	75

Refer Note 21 for details of commitments and contingent liabilities.

ASRB 1002.22

42. EVENT SUBSEQUENT TO BALANCE DATE

Since 30 June 19X9 the holding company has entered into a contract to purchase for cash all of the issued shares in Super Tiles Pty. Limited, a manufacturer of indoor and outdoor tiles. The cost of purchase is $890,000.

	Consolidated		Holding Company	
	19X9	19X8	19X9	19X8
	$000	$000	$000	$000

Sch. 7 cl. 27

43. DEBTS RECEIVABLE AND PAYABLE*

Sch. 7 cl. 27(10)(a)

Debts receivable				
Not later than one year	17,055	15,867	4,557	5,350
Later than one year but not later than two years	680	447	680	447
Later than two years but not later than five years	782	650	1,782	1,150
Later than five years	500	600	500	600
	19,017	17,564	7,519	7,547

Sch. 7 cl. 27(1)(b)

Amounts payable				
Not later than one year	15,825	18,769	5,389	4,284
Later than one year but not later than two years	8,146	250	4,210	150
Later than two years but not later than five years	3,979	9,057	2,283	6,286
Later than five years	14,154	9,900	8,403	8,388
	42,104	37,976	20,285	19,108

* This information is only required in respect of borrowing or guarantor corporations.

EXAMPLE CONSOLIDATED FINANCIAL STATEMENTS

44. AMOUNTS PAYABLE/RECEIVABLE IN FOREIGN CURRENCIES

ASRB 1012.60 The Australian dollar equivalents of amounts payable or receivable in foreign currencies, calculated at year end exchange rates, are as follows:

	Consolidated		Holding Company	
	19X9	19X8	19X9	19X8
	$000	$000	$000	$000
United States dollars:				
Amounts payable				
Current	1,273	1,032	41	27
Non-current	222	187	64	51
	1,495	1,219	105	78
Amounts receivable:				
Current	624	555	24	15
Non-current	59	39	51	38
	683	594	75	53
Singapore dollars:				
Amounts payable				
Current	708	651	73	40
Non-current	421	382	138	120
	1,129	1,033	211	160
Amounts receivable				
Current	489	427	152	117
Non-current	108	101	50	26
	597	528	202	143

None of the above amounts are effectively hedged.

(Notes:

• *ASRB 1012.60(d) requires separate disclosure, in aggregate for each foreign currency, of the amounts payable or receivable in a foreign currency. Under ASRB 1012 such disclosure only applies where the amounts are material and where the amounts payable or receivable are not effectively hedged for a period of at least 12 months after balance date.*

• *The NCSC issued a Class Order on 2 June 1988 relieving a company which is an Authorised Foreign Exchange Dealer from the disclosure of amounts payable or receivable in a foreign currency, in respect of speculative dealings, to the extent they are not effectively hedged (ASRB 1012.60). Relief under the Class Order applies for financial years ending before 1 July 1989 and is conditional upon certain disclosures being made in the accounts. Reference should be made to the detailed provisions of the Class Order.)*

App. B

45. STATEMENT OF OPERATIONS OF SEGMENTS*

		Manufacture of Building Products		Mining		Construction		Property Development		Other Industries		Eliminations		Consolidated	
		19X9	19X8	19X9	19X8	19X9	19X8	19X9	19X8	19X9	19X8	19X9	19X8	19X9	19X8
		$000	$000	$000	$000	$000	$000	$000	$000	$000	$000	$000	$000	$000	$000
ASRB 1005.10	INDUSTRY SEGMENTS														
	Revenue outside the group	24,176	18,298	16,734	13,008	25,788	20,124	8,159	12,074	7,958	4,025	—	—	82,815	67,529
	Inter-segment revenue	2,807	2,098	—	—	—	—	—	—	—	—	(2,807)	(2,098)	—	—
ASRB 1005.24	Total revenue	26,983	20,396	16,734	13,008	25,788	20,124	8,159	12,074	7,958	4,025	(2,807)	(2,098)	82,815	67,529
	Segment operating profit	2,865	1,996	852	749	2,555	1,990	1,084	1,310	387	194	(210)	(178)	7,533	6,061
	Unallocated expenses and income tax expense													(2,933)	(3,110)
	Operating profit after tax													4,600	2,951
	Segment assets	19,116	16,987	11,579	8,897	20,390	15,201	8,897	8,076	3,849	3,061	(87)	(52)	63,744	52,170
	Unallocated assets													10,392	6,526
	Total assets													74,136	58,696

The major products/services from which the above segments derive revenue are:

Industry Segments	Products/Services
Manufacture of building products	Bricks, pipes and windows
Mining	Iron ore and coal
Construction	Construction of commercial buildings
Property development	Development of commercial and housing sites

ASRB 1005.24 Inter-segment pricing is determined on an arm's-length basis.

ASRB 1005.22 **Geographical Segments**

The group operates predominantly in Australia. More than 90% of revenue, operating profit and segment assets relate to operations in Australia.

*ASRB 1005 only applies to listed companies and companies which are subsidiaries of foreign listed corporations. The standard provides for disclosure only in group accounts where presented by a holding company.

46. OTHER RELATED PARTY DISCLOSURES
Related Party Transactions

ASRB 1017.10   During the year Example Public Company Limited purchased building materials from its wholly owned subsidiary, Example Public Company (Manufacturing) Pty. Limited, and purchased hardware products from its 76% owned subsidiary, Example Public Company (Hardware) Pty. Limited. In addition, Example Public Company Limited earned consulting fees from its wholly owned subsidiary, Example Public Company (Construction) Pty. Limited in relation to the provision of design and construction advice. All transactions with related corporations are on normal commercial terms and conditions.

Example Public Company Limited has made loans to two subsidiary companies, Example Public (Manufacturing) Pty. Limited and Example Public Company (Hardware) Pty. Limited (refer Note 10). Example Public Company Limited has received a loan from Example Public Company (Construction) Pty. Limited (refer Note 19). Interest is payable at commercial rates on all inter-company loans.

Amounts Receivable or Payable

ASRB 1017.11   Included in trade debtors of the holding company is an amount receivable from a related corporation of $227,000 (19X8 — $195,000).

Included in trade creditors of the holding company are amounts payable to related corporations of $421,000 (19X8 — $386,000).

Directors

ASRB 1017.15   The names of each person holding the position of Director of Example Public Company Limited during the financial year are Messrs W. Michael, G. Andrews, H. James, K. Johns, D. Marks, S. Martin, A. Stewart and R. Thomas (Alternate Director for Mr D. Marks). Mr R. Stephens retired as a Director during the year.

Holding Company

ASRB 1017.18   The immediate and ultimate holding company of Example Public Company Limited is believed to be Example Holdings PLC, a company incorporated in the United Kingdom.

ACCOUNTING FOR BUSINESS CONSOLIDATIONS

				19X9	19X8
SE 3C(3)(b) ASRB 1007.10	**47. CONSOLIDATED SUMMARY OF SOURCES AND APPLICATIONS OF FUNDS**		Note	$000	$000
	SOURCES OF FUNDS				
ASRB 1007.20	Funds from operations:		(i)		
	Inflows of funds from operations				
	Sales revenue			80,531	66,977
	Other revenue				
	Proceeds from sale of property, plant, equipment and investments			2,018	212
	Other			266	153
				82,815	67,342
	Less: Outflows of funds from operations			69,065	59,417
				13,750	7,925
	Extraordinary item — insurance proceeds received for loss of assets resulting from fire			—	356
	Proceeds from share issue			995	2,187
	Increase in:				
	Bank loans			4,400	2,400
	Liability in respect of capitalised leases			2,226	—
	Other items			36	21
	Provisions in related corporation acquired			287	164
	Minority interest in subsidiary company acquired		(ii)	206	190
				21,900	13,243

The consolidated summary of sources and applications of funds is to be read in conjunction with the notes to and forming part of the summary set out on pages 295-296.

SE 3C(3)(b)
ASRB 1007.10

(Note: ASRB 1007 sets out the requirements for the preparation of a "Summary of Sources and Applications of Funds" and applies to all companies other than exempt proprietary companies.

In the Example Public Statements gross proceeds from the disposal of non-current assets have been included, and shown separately, as an inflow of funds from operations in accordance with ASRB 1007.

The book written-down value of assets disposed of is added to the profit on disposal of non-current assets included in the reconciliation of operating profit to funds from operations, as in our opinion the item does not constitute an outflow of funds.

In the illustrative example to ASRB 1007, the book value of non-current assets disposed of is included in outflows of funds (though not shown separately) and added back later in the summary. Commentary xiv in ASRB 1007 states that any profit or loss on disposal needs to be excluded in determining funds from operations.)

App. B

EXAMPLE CONSOLIDATED FINANCIAL STATEMENTS

	Note	19X9 $000	19X8 $000
ASRB 1007.20 **APPLICATIONS OF FUNDS**			
Expenditure on:			
Property, plant and equipment		3,475	5,141
Interest in business undertaking		263	812
Exploration		920	560
Investments		389	309
Land held for resale		445	248
Intangible assets		1,470	12
Deferred research and development		53	21
Leased assets capitalised		2,426	—
Increase in:			
Deferred expenditure		60	55
Other non-current assets		245	184
Redemption of debentures		250	250
Extraordinary item — Settlement of a legal action relating to a former subsidiary company		408	—
Dividends paid		495	437
Income tax paid		2,738	2,426
Amounts paid out of provisions		415	322
Minority interest in related corporation bought during the year		280	—
Goodwill on acquisition of interests in subsidiary companies	(ii)	202	300
Increase in working capital	(iii)	7,366	2,166
		21,900	13,243

The consolidated summary of sources and applications of funds is to be read in conjunction with the notes to and forming part of the summary set out below.

ASRB 1007.10 **NOTES TO AND FORMING PART OF THE CONSOLIDATED SUMMARY OF SOURCES AND APPLICATIONS OF FUNDS**

	19X9 $000	19X8 $000
(i) Funds from Operations		
Reconciliation of funds from operations with operating profit before tax is as follows:		
Funds from operations	13,750	7,925
Add/(subtract) non-fund items:		
Amortisation	(452)	(115)
Amounts set aside to provisions	(881)	(750)
Book value of property, plant, equipment and investments disposed of	(2,013)	(134)
Costs previously capitalised now brought to account	(220)	(180)
Depreciation	(2,679)	(1,652)

continued over ...

App. B

		19X9	19X8
Exploration expenditure written off		(953)	—
Goodwill amortisation		(242)	(209)
Write-back of provision*		—	187
		(7,440)	2,853)
Operating profit before income tax		6,310	5,072
Reconciliation of inflows of funds from operations:			
Inflows of funds from operations		82,815	67,342
Add: Write-back of provision		—	187
Operating revenue		82,815	67,529

* The write-back of the provision affects both operating profit and operating revenue as the write-back is included to comply with Sch. 7 cl. 8(1)(a)(v).

		19X9	19X8
		$000	$000

ASRB 1007.30 **(ii) Acquisition and Disposals of Interests in Subsidiary Companies**

	19X9	19X8
Net assets acquired and disposed of		
Property, plant and equipment	1,379	760
Future income tax benefit	60	200
Other non-current assets	100	980
Inventories	1,287	2,076
Trade debtors	942	1,847
Loans	(1,300)	(500)
Trade creditors	(1,121)	(570)
Bank overdraft	—	(15)
Provisions	(287)	(164)
	1,060	4,614
Less: Minority interest at date of acquisition	206	190
	854	4,424
Goodwill on consolidation	202	300
	1,056	4,724

The acquisition was made entirely out of cash.

(iii) Increase in Working Capital

	19X9	19X8
Increase/(decrease) in current assets		
Inventories	3,086	1,320
Investments	155	—
Prepayments	18	(56)
Debtors	1,556	1,009
Short-term deposits	(70)	580
Cash	(298)	—
	4,447	2,853
Less: Increase/(decrease) in current liabilities		
Bank loans	475	326
Bank overdraft	(881)	(80)
Trade creditors	(2,513)	441
	(2,919)	687
Net increase in working capital	7,366	2,166

App. B

EXAMPLE CONSOLIDATED FINANCIAL STATEMENTS

48. SUPPLEMENTARY EQUITY FINANCIAL STATEMENTS PROFIT AND LOSS ACCOUNT FOR THE YEAR ENDED 30 JUNE 19X9

	Note	19X9 $000	19X9 $000	19X8 $000	19X8 $000
Operating profit					
Holding company and subsidiary companies	(ii)	6,220		5,061	
Share of associated companies		551	6,771	376	5,437
Income tax attributable to operating profit					
Holding company and subsidiary companies		1,710		2,121	
Share of associated companies		190	1,900	129	2,250
Operating profit after income tax			4,871		3,187
Profit/(loss) on extraordinary items		(408)		(160)	
Income tax attributable to profit or loss on extraordinary items		(159)		175	
Profit/(loss) on extraordinary items after income tax					
Holding company and subsidiary companies		(249)		(335)	
Share of associated companies		—	(249)	—	(335)
Operating profit and extraordinary items after income tax					
Holding company and subsidiary companies		4,261		2,605	
Share of associated companies [ASRB 1016.22]		361	4,622	247	2,852
Minority interests in operating profit and extraordinary items after income tax			428		333
Operating profit and extraordinary items after income tax attributable to members of the holding company			4,194		2,519
Retained profits at the beginning of the year					
Holding company and subsidiary companies		7,287		5,525	
Share of associated companies [ASRB 1016.22]		4,568	11,855	4,321	9,846

App. B

Aggregate of amounts transferred from reserves		—		381
Total available for appropriation		16,049		12,746
Dividends paid and proposed		515		466
Aggregate of amounts transferred to reserves	34		—	
Other appropriations	—	549	425	891
Retained profits at the end of the financial year				
Holding company and subsidiary companies	10,661		7,287	
Share of associated companies	4,839		4,568	
		15,500		11,855

ASRB 1016.22

The supplementary equity profit and loss account is to be read in conjunction with the notes to and forming part of the supplementary equity financial statements set out on pages 300-301.

Balance Sheet as at 30 June 19X9

	Note	19X9 $000	19X8 $000
CURRENT ASSETS			
Cash		1,050	1,348
Receivables		16,005	14,519
Investments		155	—
Inventories		12,991	9,855
Other		485	452
TOTAL CURRENT ASSETS		30,686	26,174
NON-CURRENT ASSETS			
Receivables		1,942	1,697
Investments			
Associated companies [ASRB 1016.22]	(iii)	6,854	6,189
Other corporations and business undertakings		1,065	1,119
Inventories		1,045	870
Property, plant and equipment		29,618	21,047
Intangibles		2,460	1,195
Other		5,330	4,973
TOTAL NON-CURRENT ASSETS		48,314	37,090
TOTAL ASSETS		79,000	63,264
CURRENT LIABILITIES			
Creditors and borrowings		12,525	15,144
Provisions		3,037	3,924
TOTAL CURRENT LIABILITIES		15,562	19,068
NON-CURRENT LIABILITIES			
Creditors and borrowings		23,126	17,050
Provisions		2,920	2,073
TOTAL NON-CURRENT LIABILITIES		26,046	19,123
TOTAL LIABILITIES		41,608	38,191
NET ASSETS		37,392	25,073
SHAREHOLDERS' EQUITY			
Share capital		7,250	6,750
Reserves	(iv)	12,967	5,147
Retained profits		10,571	7,287
Equity in retained profits of associated companies [ASRB 1016.22]		4,929	4,568
Shareholders' equity attributable to members of the holding company		35,717	23,752
Minority shareholders' interest in subsidiaries		1,675	1,321
TOTAL SHAREHOLDERS' EQUITY		37,392	25,073

The supplementary equity balance sheet is to be read in conjunction with the notes to and forming part of the supplementary equity financial statements set out on pages 300-301.

App. B

Notes to and Forming Part of the Supplementary Equity Financial Statements for the year ended 30 June 19X9

SE 3C(4)*

(i) STATEMENT OF ACCOUNTING POLICIES

The supplementary financial statements have been prepared on the same bases as the principal accounts, except for the application of the equity method in the supplementary financial statements to account for the group's investment in associated companies.

An associated company is one in which the group's beneficial interest in the issued capital of that company is not less than 20% and does not exceed 50%, and where:

- the group exercises significant influence over that company, and
- the investment is long-term.

Under the equity method, the carrying value of the group's investment in an associated company is initially recorded at cost, and adjusted for the group's interest in any subsequent profits or losses of the associated company, after eliminating unrealised inter-company transactions.

This adjusted share of the associated company's subsequent profits or losses is included in the group's profits or losses; dividends received or receivable from the associated company are brought to account as deductions from the carrying value of the investment.

Post-application movements in the reserves of an associated company not recognised in its profit and loss account are taken directly to the carrying value of the investment and to the equivalent group reserve accounts.

There are no major differences in accounting policies adopted by associated companies and those by the group.

	19X9 $000	19X8 $000
(ii) OPERATING PROFIT		
Operating profit per consolidated financial statements	6,310	5,072
ASRB 1016.22 Less: Dividends received from associated companies	(90)	(11)
Operating profit — holding and subsidiary companies (per supplementary equity profit and loss account)	6,220	5,061

App. B

EXAMPLE CONSOLIDATED FINANCIAL STATEMENTS

Sch. 7 cl. 34
ASRB 1016.50
ASRB 1017.11

(iii) ASSOCIATED COMPANIES

Details of interests in associated companies are as follows*:

Name	Principal Activities	Place of Incorporation	Class of Share	Group Interest 19X9 %	Group Interest 19X8 %	Investment Carrying Amount Consolidated 19X9 $000	Investment Carrying Amount Consolidated 19X8 $000	Equity 19X9 $000	Equity 19X8 $000	Contribution to Equity Profit 19X9 $000	Contribution to Equity Profit 19X8 $000	Dividends Received/Receivable Consolidated 19X9 $000	Dividends Received/Receivable Consolidated 19X8 $000	Dividends Received/Receivable Holding Co. 19X9 $000	Dividends Received/Receivable Holding Co. 19X8 $000
Example Public Company Assoc. (Listed) Limited	Investment	N.S.W.	Ord.	49	49	1,200	1,200	3,064	2,915	149	113	25	4	17	3
Example Public Company Assoc. (Transport) Pty. Limited	Transport	Vic.	Ord.	40	25	790	421	3,790	3,274	212	134	65	7	65	7
Example Public Company Assoc. Participacoes Ltda.	—	Brazil	Ord.	25	25	—	—	—	—	—	—	—	—	—	—
						1,990	1,621	6,854	6,189	361	247	90	11	82	10

ASRB 1016.50   The balance dates of all associated companies is 30 June 19X9.

The use of the equity method has been discontinued in respect of Example Public Company Assoc. Participacoes Ltda. due to the inability of the group to exercise significant influence over the company. The company incurred losses in previous years and a permanent diminution in value has occurred. The investment was written off in full in a previous year.

ASRB 1016.50   (Notes:
- Any significant events or transactions which have occurred after the balance date which could materially affect the financial position or operating performance of an associated company should be disclosed.
- Where adjustments to eliminate dissimilar accounting policies cannot be made, the nature of the dissimilarities should be disclosed.)

SE 3C(4)**   (iv) RESERVES
ASRB 1016.22   Included in reserves is an amount of $25,000 being the group's share of a post-acquisition revaluation increment transferred to the asset revaluation reserve of an associated company.

Sch. 7 cl. 29(1), (2)
Sch. 7 cl. 34(2)

* The details of interests in corporations not being subsidiaries as required by cl. 34 of Sch. 7 are only required to be disclosed by listed corporations, borrowing corporations and large corporations (other than exempt proprietary companies) and where such interests are material. Wholly owned subsidiaries of Australian corporations do not need to disclose the information in their own accounts.

**First year requirements only.

App. B

STATEMENT BY DIRECTORS

Sec. 269(9), (9A)
Sec. 269(10), (10A)

In the opinion of the Directors of Example Public Company Limited:

(a) The accompanying accounts of the company and the group as set out on pages ...... to ...... are drawn up so as to give a true and fair view of the result for the year ended 30 June 19X9, and the state of affairs as at 30 June 19X9, of the company and the group so far as they concern members of the company.

(b) At the date of this statement, there are reasonable grounds to believe that the company will be able to pay its debts as and when they fall due.

(c) At the date of this statement, there are reasonable grounds to believe that the company will be able to meet any obligations or liabilities that may arise from any guarantees or undertakings given pursuant to approved deeds of indemnity for the cross guarantee of liabilities to wholly owned subsidiaries granted relief from specified accounting and financial reporting requirements in accordance with the Class Order issued by the National Companies and Securities Commission on 9 August 1988. The subsidiaries so relieved are listed in Note 30.

The accompanying accounts of the company and the group are made out in accordance with applicable Approved Accounting Standards.

Dated at [City] this..........................day of 19X9

Signed in accordance with a resolution of the Directors:

....W. Michael

:Directors

.... G. Andrews

AUDITORS' REPORT TO THE MEMBERS OF EXAMPLE PUBLIC COMPANY LIMITED

Sec. 269(5)
Sec. 285

We have audited the accounts set out on pages ...... to ...... in accordance with Australian Auditing Standards.

In our opinion the accounts of Example Public Company Limited, and group accounts, are properly drawn up in accordance with the provisions of the Companies [State] Code and so as to give a true and fair view of:

(i) the state of affairs of the company and the group as at 30 June 19X9 and of the results of the company and the group for the year ended on that date so far as they concern members of the company; and

(ii) the other matters required by sec. 269 of that Code to be dealt with in the accounts and in group accounts;

and are in accordance with applicable Approved Accounting Standards.

The only Australian subsidiary for which we have not acted as auditor is Example Public Company (Useless) Pty. Limited.

KPMG PEAT MARWICK
[City] .... CHARTERED ACCOUNTANTS
..............19X9   [Name] ....
                                                              PARTNER

(Note: On 9 August 1988 the NCSC issued a Class Order relieving the auditor of an Australian company with overseas subsidiaries from the following requirements:

(i) to state in the auditors' report the names of the overseas subsidiaries for which he has not acted as auditor provided the auditor has examined the auditors' report of the overseas subsidiary or group accounts and is satisfied that the auditors' report is based on Australian Auditing Standards and applicable Approved Accounting Standards;

(ii) to give particulars in relation to a qualification or comment contained in an overseas subsidiary's auditors' report on condition that the abovementioned provisions occur, the qualification/comment relates solely to departures from the auditing or accounting standards of the overseas country and those departures do not involve a failure to comply with Australian Auditing Standards or applicable Approved Accounting Standards.

However, there is a continuing requirement to disclose in the auditors' report the names of domestic subsidiaries not audited by the Firm.)

SUPPLEMENTARY INFORMATION

SE 3C(3)(c)
SE 3C(2)(d)

DIRECTORS' INTERESTS

The maximum contingent liability of the group for termination benefits under service agreements with Directors and persons who take part in the management of the holding company amounted to $148,560 at 30 June 19X9. Provision has not been made in the accounts for this contingent liability.

SE 3C(3)(e)

SHAREHOLDINGS*

Substantial Shareholders

The number of shares held by the substantial shareholders listed in the holding company's register as at 31 August 19X9 were:

Shareholder	Ordinary	Preference
Example Holdings PLC	1,600,000	—
Substantial Investor Limited	—	250,000
Large Investments Limited	—	250,000

Class of Shares and Voting Rights

At 31 August 19X9 there were 7,802 holders of the ordinary shares of the holding company. The voting rights attaching to the ordinary shares, set out in Article 54 of the holding company's Articles of Association, are:

"Subject to any rights or restrictions for the time being attached to any class or classes of shares—
(a) at meetings of members or classes of members each member entitled to vote may vote in person or by proxy or attorney; and
(b) on a show of hands every person present who is a member has one vote, and on a poll every person present in person or by proxy or attorney has one vote for each ordinary share he holds."

At 31 August 19X9 there were two holders of the preference shares of the holding company. There are no voting rights attached to the preference shares.

* The shareholdings component of a listed company's Annual Report is to be made up to a date not earlier than six weeks from the date of the issue of the annual audited accounts.

App. B

Distribution of Shareholders (as at 31 August 19X9)

Category	Number Ordinary	Preference
1-1,000	3,522	—
1,001-5,000	2,982	—
5,001-10,000	877	—
10,000 and over	421	2
	7,802	2

20 Largest Shareholders* (as at 31 August 19X9)

Name	Number of Ordinary Shares Held
Example Holdings PLC	1,600,000
Aust. Nominees Limited	150,200
New Life Association Limited	95,400
Queens Trustee Limited	82,800
Australian Assurance Co. Limited	78,905
JTD Nominees Pty. Limited	72,700
S & K Mutual Limited	62,450
Bank Insurance Co. Limited	61,320
The Life Assurance Company Limited	61,300
Superannuation Trustee Pty. Limited	59,750
PLC Superannuation Fund Limited	59,720
Regal Insurance Pty. Limited	48,400
Fund Managers Limited	40,100
Investment Placements Pty. Limited	38,295
Credit Union Investments Limited	35,600
Employees Trust Fund Pty. Limited	34,800
Securities Investment Pty. Limited	32,480
Employee Pension Fund Pty. Limited	31,290
Institutional Investor Limited	29,800
Investment Management Limited	28,240
	2,703,550

Name	Number of Preference Shares Held
Substantial Investor Limited	250,000
Large Investments Limited	250,000
	500,000

The 20 largest shareholders hold 86% of the ordinary shares of the holding company, and 100% of the preference shares.

* *The list of the 20 largest shareholders may be excluded if a separate statement is lodged with the Home Exchange with the annual report.*

OFFICES AND OFFICERS

Company Secretary
Mr David Bruce, A.C.A., A.C.I.S.

Principal Registered Office
Example Public Company House,
20 Sydney Street,
Sydney,
New South Wales, 2000.
Telephone: (02) 20 2020.

Locations of Registers of Securities
Example Public Company House,
20 Sydney Street,
Sydney,
New South Wales, 2000.

500 Melbourne Street,
Melbourne,
Victoria, 3000.

(Note: If applicable, details of the following matters should also be disclosed:

- *deferred shares issued;*
- *classification of receivables and basis for calculation of deferred income, where the ordinary business of the company is lending money;*
- *a statement in the annual report of any material variations in results from those contained in the preliminary final report;*
- *material contracts involving directors' interests still subsisting at the end of the financial year or, if not then subsisting, entered into since the end of the previous year and before year-end;*
- *in the case of a mining company, securities issued to vendors;*
- *in the case of mining exploration companies, a list of mining tenements held together with the percentage interest held therein;*
- *in the case of a mining company, statements contained in the annual report should comply with Listing Requirements in Section 3M.)*

Index

References are to paragraph (¶) numbers and Appendixes.

Paragraph

A

AAS — see under **Accounting standards**

Accounting Guidance Releases (AGR)
  disclosure requirements; example
  financial statements .... App. B

Accounting methods
  cross holdings 2402
  equity accounting 802
  foreign currency translation 2201
  goodwill 301

Accounting periods, divergent 2312

Accounting policies
  change
  – example note .... App. B (Note 2)
  consistency within group 203
  – adjustments 206
  example note .... App. B (Note 1)

Accounting standards
  acquisition of assets
    (ASRB 1015/AAS 21) 706
  approved accounting standards (ASRB)
  – group accounts; statutory
    requirements 2301
  consolidated financial statements 1802
  disclosure requirements
  – example financial statements ...... App. B
  equity accounting (ASRB 1016/
    AAS 14) 801; 802; 1301
  foreign currency translation
    (ASRB 1012/AAS 20) 2201
  funds statement (ASRB 1007/
    AAS 12) 2101
  goodwill (ASRB 1013/AAS 18) 301;
                    304; 307; 402; 1607
  holding/subsidiary relationship 905
  inventory valuation (AAS 2) 1107
  preparation of accounts 201

Paragraph

  related party disclosures
    (ASRB 1017) 1007
  revaluations (ASRB 1010/
    AAS 10) 707; 1802
  significant influence 801
  tax-effect accounting
    (ASRB 1020/AAS 3) 703

Acquisitions — see also
  Intra-group investments;
  Piecemeal or creeping acquisition
  date not relevant to minority 907
  determination of date 401
  – long-term effect 402
  example note .... App. B (Note 31)
  foreign subsidiary 2203
  funds statement 2103
  holding company shares by
    subsidiary 2306
  negative shareholders' funds
    at acquisition 1802
  part acquisitions 307
  Sch. 7 disclosure requirements 2312

Adjustments 204
  asset values 707
  carrying value of investment
    and goodwill 804
  disclosure adjustments 206
  discount on acquisition
  – adjustment on sale of
    adjusted assets 310
  dissimilar accounting policies 203; 206
  inventory at value higher
    than cost 1101
  preparation of group
    accounts 103; 207
  – methodology 702; 703
  profit and loss account
    items 501; 502

Adj

ACCOUNTING FOR BUSINESS CONSOLIDATIONS

Adjustments — continued   **Paragraph**
  to pre-acquisition situation 2001
  – post-acquisition recognition of future
    income tax benefits not recognised
    at acquisition date 2003
  – pre-acquisition inventory and
    fixed asset sales 2002

After balance date events
  example note ....App. B (Note 42)

Aggregation 103; 707
  consolidation journal entries 205
  consolidation worksheets 207

AGR (Accounting Guidance Releases)
  disclosure requirements; example
    financial statements .... App. B

Amortisation
  goodwill 303; 304
  – accounting standards 304; 402
  – companies legislation 402
  – depreciation charges 307
  – equity accounting 804
  – example accounting policy
    note ....App. B (Note 1(b))
  – maximum period 303; 304; 402
  – "straight-line" basis 305

Annual leave provision
  movements 2102

Appropriations
  example note ....App. B (Note 9)

Approved accounting standards (ASRB)
  — see under **Accounting standards**

**APS (Statements on Conformity
with ... Accounting Standards)**
  disclosure requirements; example
    financial statements .... App. B

Arm's length
  intra-group inventory sales at
    arm's length prices 1107

ASRB — see under **Accounting standards**

Asset revaluation reserve
  bonus issue by subsidiary 1607
  subsidiary's; post-acquisition
    reduction 1805

Asset sales — see **Fixed asset movements**

**Assets understated at
acquisition date** 2001

Audit of group accounts 2311

Auditor's report
  example .... App. B

                      Paragraph
Australian accounting standards (AAS)
  — see under **Accounting standards**

B

Balance sheet
  example .... App. B
  minority interest 910

"Balancing figures" 204

Bank loans
  example note ....App. B (Note 34)

Bank overdrafts
  example note ....App. B (Note 34)

Bills of exchange
  intra-group debt 602

Bonus share issue by subsidiary 1606
  from intra-group asset
    revaluation reserve 1607

Business undertaking interests
  example note ....App. B (Note 32)

C

Change in accounting policy
  example note ....App. B (Note 2)

Checklist
  consolidation review 208

Class orders
  wholly owned subsidiaries 2307

Classification
  profit and loss account items 501

Commitments
  example note ....App. B (Note 21)

Companies legislation
  amounts owing to related
    corporations 1007
  cross holdings 2401
  disclosure requirements; example
    financial statements .... App. B
  goodwill; amortisation 402
  group accounts; statutory
    requirements 2301–2312
  holding/subsidiary relationship 905
  minority interest disclosure 502; 902
  preparation of accounts 201
  share premium 706

Company
  interpretation 101

Computerisation 207; 208

Aft

INDEX 309

                                          Paragraph

Consistency
  group accounting policies and reporting format 203
  – adjustments 206

Consolidated accounts
  group accounts defined 2304

Consolidation 101
  example accounting policy note ....App. B (Note 1(a))
  general application 101
  inter-entity transactions 103
  "notional entity" concept 102
  process
  – consolidation adjustments 204
  – disclosure adjustments 206
  – elimination entries 205
  – entities to be consolidated 201
  – example ....App. A
  – information from entities 203
  – journal book – see Consolidation journal book
  – review checklist 208
  – "rules" to be followed 201
  – stages 202
  – worksheet – see Consolidation worksheet

Consolidation journal book 204
  aggregation entries 205
  consolidation review checklist 208
  elimination entries 205
  example ....App. A
  minority interest disclosure 207
  "one-sided journal entries" 501; 703
  permanent record 205
  prior year information 205
  profit and loss account items 501
  separate components 204
  – allocation to group entity 205
  share sales 1502
  standing entries 205
  summarisation 205

Consolidation worksheet 202; 207
  computerisation 207; 208
  disclosure adjustments 206
  example ....App. A
  memorandum notes 204

Construction work in progress
  example note ....App. B (Note 26)
  – accounting policy ....App. B (Note 1(i))

Contingent debt 603

Contingent liabilities
  example note ....App. B (Note 21)

                                          Paragraph

Control 201; 905

Cost based equity method 802

Cost method (equity accounting) 802

Creditors and borrowings
  example note ....App. B (Note 17)

Creeping or piecemeal acquisition 1401
  purchase of further shares from minority shareholders 1402

Cross holdings 2401
  accounting methods 2402
  summary 2403

Current assets
  example note ....App. B (Note 13)

Current rate method of foreign currency translation 2201

D

D1.1 (Statement on Accounting Practice: Presentation of Balance Sheet)
  disclosure requirements; example financial statements .... App. B

Date of acquisition
  determination 401
  – long-term effect 402

Debentures
  example note ....App. B (Note 36)

Debt – see **Intra-group debt**

Debtors, current
  example note ....App. B (Note 22)

Debtors, non-current
  example note ....App. B (Note 23)

Debts receivable and payable
  example note ....App. B (Note 43)

Deferred expenditure
  example note ....App. B (Note 27)
  – accounting policy ......App. B (Note 1(m))

Definitions
  Australian holding companies 2303
  bill of exchange 602
  bonus 1606
  fair value 707
  funds 2101
  group accounts 2304
  holding company 905; 2303
  income tax expense 703
  intermediate holding company 2303
  related corporations 2303
  share 2312

Def

Definitions — continued **Paragraph**	**Paragraph**
significant influence 801	**Double counting** 205; 208; 707
subsidiary company 905; 2303	**Double entry bookkeeping** 501; 703
ultimate holding company 2303	**Doubtful debt provision**
Depreciation — see **Amortisation**	movements 2102
Depreciation charges 307	
fixed asset movements 1201; 1204	**E**
Directors' interests	**Economic dependency**
supplementary information;	example note ....App. B (Note 40)
example .... App. B	**Economic entity concept**
Directors' remuneration	of consolidation 901; 903
example note ....App. B (Note 38)	**Eliminations**
Directors' report 2309	discount on acquisition against
example .... App. B	fixed assets 309
Directors' statement 2308	equity accounting 806
example .... App. B	inter-entity transactions 103
Disclosures	— involving minority interest 903
adjustments 206	intra-group debt 601
dividends paid/proposed by	investments in subsidiaries 204;
subsidiaries 1003	205; 208; 703
example financial statements	— in subsequent years 704
and notes .... App. B	— involving indirect interests 1904
group accounts; Sch. 7 2312	journal entries 204; 205
minority interest 207; 902; 905; 910	methodology 702; 703
Discount on acquisition 307	preference shares; consolidation
adjustment on sale of	principles 1702
adjusted assets 310	Sch. 7 requirements 2312
elimination against fixed assets 309	subsidiary dividends 1003
equity accounting 804	**Entity**
future periods 308	group entities — see Member entities
share sales 1501	"notional entity" concept 102
Discounted bills of exchange 602	use of "company" 101; 103
Disposal of subsidiary	**Equity accounting** 801
example note ....App. B (Note 31)	accounting policy
Sch. 7 disclosure requirements 2312	— example note ....App. B (Note 1(e))
Dissimilar accounting policies 203; 206	carrying value of investment
Divergent accounting periods 2312	and goodwill 804
Dividend franking account	illustration 806
example taxation note ......App. B (Note 5)	methods 802
Dividends	prior to consolidation 1301
all subsidiary dividends to be	— piecemeal acquisition 1401
eliminated 1003	realisation argument 805
example note ....App. B (Note 8)	subsequent to sale of part
from other reserves 1002	of subsidiary 1507
from profits 1001	supplementary financial statements,
paid from post-acquisition profits 1005	example ....App. B (Note 48)
paid from pre-acquisition profits 1004	unrealised profits 806
proposed; pre-acquisition and	use 801; 805
post-acquisition 1006	when to discontinue 803
proposed by subsidiary, not recognised	**Example financial**
by holding company 1007	**statements** .... App. B
to minority shareholders 1003	**Executives' remuneration**
	example note ....App. B (Note 38)

Dep

INDEX

                                  Paragraph

Exploration expenditure
    example note .... App. B (Note 33)
    – accounting policy .... App. B (Note 1(l))

Extraordinary items
    example note .... App. B (Note 6)

F

Fair value
    asset values at date of acquisition 707
    – funds statement, note 2103
    definition 707
    share issue for acquisition 706

Financial periods, divergent 2312

Financial statements,
    example .... App. B

Financial years 2305

Financing arrangements
    example note .... App. B (Note 39)

First **journal entry** 702; 906
    netting *first* and *second* entries 909

Fixed asset movements 1201
    funds statement 2102
    – foreign subsidiaries 2103
    pre-acquisition sales 2002
    sale from holding company to
        subsidiary 1202
    sale from subsidiary to
        another subsidiary 1204
    sale from subsidiary to
        holding company 1203
    summary of procedures 1205

Foreign currency amounts
    example note .... App. B (Note 44)

Foreign currency translation
    – see also **Overseas subsidiaries**
    example accounting policy
        note .... App. B (Note 1(c))

Format of accounts
    consistency within group 203
    – adjustments 206

Format of consolidation
    worksheet 207

Funds from operations 2102

Funds statement
    accounting standards 2101
    consolidated funds statement 2103
    – example .... App. B (Note 47)
    purpose 2102

                                  Paragraph

Future income tax benefits
    example taxation note ...... App. B (Note 5)
    inventory movements
    – minority interest 1103
    – sale outside group 1104
    post-acquisition recognition 2003

G

Geometric progression
    accounting for cross holdings 2402

Goodwill 301
    accounting policy note;
        example .... App. B (Note 1(b))
    accounting standards 301;
                            304; 307; 402; 1607
    acquisition of foreign subsidiary 2203
    acquisition of wholly owned
        subsidiary 703–705
    amortisation 304
    – accounting standards 304; 402
    – companies legislation 402
    – maximum period 303; 304; 402
    – "straight-line" 305
    depreciation charges 307
    discount on acquisition
        (negative goodwill) 307
    – adjustment on sale of
        adjusted assets 310
    – elimination against fixed assets 309
    – equity accounting 804
    – future periods 308
    dividend paid out of pre-acquisition
        profits 1002; 1004
    equity accounting 804
    fair value of assets
        acquired 707; 2103
    funds statement 2103
    future benefits 301
    internally generated goodwill 1607
    part acquisitions 307
    post-acquisition recognition of
        future income tax benefits 2003
    share sales 1501–1504
    valuation 302
    write-off 306

Group accounts
    audit 2311
    definition 2304
    directors' report 2309
    directors' statement 2308
    form and content 2304; 2312
    presentation; Schedule 7 2312
    statutory requirements 2301–2312
    true and fair view 2310

Paragraph

H

Historical cost accounting
  decrease in ownership through
    share issue 1605
  internally generated goodwill 1607

Holding companies
  "Australian" holding companies 2302
  definition 905; 2303
  form of accounts 2312
  preparation of accounts 2302

Holding/subsidiary
  relationship 905; 2303
  investment in preference shares 1701

I

Income tax
  example note ....App. B (Note 5)
  – accounting policy ....App. B (Note 1(d))
  funds statement 2102
  inventory sale to overseas
    subsidiary 2204
  tax consequences
  – inventory movements; minority
    interest 1103

Income tax expense
  acquisition of wholly owned
    subsidiary 703
  example note ....App. B (Note 5)
  inventory movements
  – minority interest 1103
  – sale outside group 1104

Indirect interests
  examples 1903
  holding/subsidiary relationship 2303
  partly owned subsidiaries 1902
  summary of procedures 1904
  wholly owned subsidiaries 1901

Intangibles
  example note ....App. B (Note 15)
  – accounting policy ....App. B (Note 1(k))

Inter-company/inter-entity
  transactions
  elimination 103; 205

Intermediate holding company 2303

Internally generated goodwill 1607

Intra-group debt 601
  commercial bills 602
  contingent debt 603

Intra-group inventory movements
  cost of inventory 1101
  entry in subsequent year if not
    sold outside group 1105

Paragraph

  intra-group sales at arm's
    length prices 1107
  inventory valuation 1107
  minority interest 1103
  overseas subsidiaries 2204
  profit effect 1102
  subsequent sale outside group 1104
  write-downs 1106

Intra-group investments 701
  acquisition during a year 705
  asset values at date of acquisition 707
  elimination 204; 205; 208
  – in subsequent years 704
  first journal entries 702; 906
  indirect – see Indirect interests
  non-corporate entities 708
  non-wholly owned subsidiary 908
  share issue for acquisition 706
  wholly owned subsidiary; acquisition
    at balance date 703
  – *see also* **Equity accounting**

Intra-group transactions
  elimination 103; 205

Inventories – see also
  Intra-group inventory movements
  example note ....App. B (Note 12)
  – accounting policy ....App. B (Note 1(g))
  pre-acquisition inventory sales 2002

Investments – see also **Cross holdings;**
  Intra-group investments
  example notes .... App. B (Notes 11, 29)
  – accounting policy ....App. B (Note 1(e))

Issued capital
  acquisition of wholly owned
    subsidiary 703

J

Joint venture interests
  example note ....App. B (Note 41)
  – accounting policy ....App. B (Note 1(q))

Journal entries – see
  Consolidation journal book

L

Land held for resale
  example note ....App. B (Note 25)
  – accounting policy ....App. B (Note 1(h))

Lease liabilities
  example note ....App. B (Note 37)

Liabilities
  example note ....App. B (Note 19)
  understated at acquisition date 2001

INDEX

Paragraph

Listing Rules
disclosure requirements; example
  financial statements .... App. B
preparation of accounts 201

Loans
example note .... App. B (Note 24)
– bank loans .... App. B (Note 35)

Loss-making subsidiaries 1801
  loss in a particular year 1803
  negative shareholders' funds
    at acquisition 1802
  post-acquisition reduction to
    pre-acquisition asset revaluation
    reserve of subsidiary 1805
  return to positive share-
    holders' funds 1804

M

Matching concept
accounting for goodwill 301; 304; 307

Member entities
accounting policies 203; 206
entities to be consolidated 201
information for group accounts 203
non-corporate entities, acquisition 708
particulars
– example note .... App. B (Note 30)
reporting format 203; 206

Mining companies
supplementary information .... App. B

Minority interest 901
  acquisition date not relevant
    to minority 907
  acquisition of non-wholly
    owned subsidiary 908
  allocation not to be combined with
    investment elimination 909
  direct interests 904; 1904
  disclosure 902; 910
  – adjusting entries 206
  – profit and loss account 502
  fixed asset movements 1201–1204
  funds statement 2103
  indirect interests 904; 1902–1904
  indirect relationships 2303
  inventory movements 1103
  – sale outside group 1104
  – subsequent year entry if not sold
    outside group 1105
  loss-making subsidiaries 1801
  – loss in a particular year 1803
  – negative shareholders' funds
    at acquisition 1802

Paragraph

– post-acquisition reduction to
  pre-acquisition asset revaluation
  reserve of subsidiary 1805
– return to positive share-
  holders' funds 1804
piecemeal acquisition 1402
preference shares; consolidation
  principles 1702
second journal entry 906; 910;
    1005; 1103; 1105; 1201; 1803
subsidiary dividends 1003; 1005
transactions not realised 903
when minority owns majority 905
worksheet column 207

Movements in reserves
minority interest 502
– indirect 1904
payment of dividends 1002

N

**National Companies and Securities
Commission (NCSC)**
class order; wholly owned
  subsidiaries 2307

Negative goodwill — see
Discount on acquisition

Negative minority interest 1802

Net assets of group
acquisition of wholly owned
  subsidiary 703; 704

Non-corporate entities
acquisition 708

Non-current assets
example note .... App. B (Note 16)
funds statement
– foreign subsidiaries 2103

Notes to the accounts
example .... App. B

"Notional entity" concept 102; 1802

O

**"One-sided journal
entries"** 501; 703

Operating profit
acquisition of wholly owned
  subsidiary 703
example note .... App. B (Note 4)

Operating revenue
example note .... App. B (Note 3)

Ope

	Paragraph
Overdrafts	
example note	App. B (Note 34)
Overseas subsidiaries	2201
acquisition elimination entry	2203
funds statement	2103
inter-company balances	2202
inter-company inventory sale	2204
Ownership	905
— see also **Share issues by subsidiary**	

P

Parent entity concept of consolidation	903
Part acquisitions	307
Partly owned subsidiaries	
indirect interests	1902
sale	1504
— part sale; no longer a subsidiary	1506
— part sale; still a subsidiary	1505
Partnership agreements	
preparation of accounts	201
Partnership interests	
example note	App. B (Note 32)
— accounting policy	App. B (Note 1(f))
Permanent difference	1103
Piecemeal or creeping acquisition	1401
purchase of further shares from minority shareholders	1402
Preference shares	1701
consolidation principles	1702
preference dividends in arrears	1703
Profit and loss account	501
acquisition of wholly owned subsidiary	703–705
example	App. B
minority interest	502; 910
Property, plant and equipment	
example note	App. B (Note 14)
— accounting policy	App. B (Note 1(j))
Proposed post-acquisition dividends	1001; 1006
Proposed pre-acquisition dividends	1001; 1006
Proprietary concept of consolidation	903
Provisions	
example note	App. B (Note 18)
— accounting policy	App. B (Note 1(o))
funds statement	2102

	Paragraph
Pure equity method	802

R

Receivables	
example note	App. B (Note 10)
Reciprocal shareholdings	2401
accounting methods	2402
summary	2403
Related company, definition	2303
Related party disclosures	
example note	App. B (Note 46)
Relief from preparation of accounts	
group accounts	2302
wholly owned subsidiaries	2307
Research and development costs	
example note	App. B (Note 28)
— accounting policy	App. B (Note 1(n))
Reserves	
acquisition of wholly owned subsidiary	703
asset revaluation reserve	
— bonus issue by subsidiary	1607
— subsidiary's; post-acquisition reduction	1805
example note	App. B (Note 7)
transfers — see **Movements in reserves**	
Retained earnings	
acquisition of wholly owned subsidiary	703; 704
Review of consolidation	208

S

Sale of fixed assets	
— see **Fixed asset movements**	
Sale of shares — see **Share sales**	
Schedule 7	2301; 2304
disclosures in group accounts	2312
— example financial statements	App. B
Second journal entry	906; 910; 1005; 1103; 1105; 1201; 1803
Segment information	
example note	App. B (Note 45)
Share, definition	2312
Share capital	
example note	App. B (Note 20)

INDEX

	Paragraph
Share issue for acquisition of subsidiary	706
Share issues by subsidiary	1601
bonus issue	1606
– from intra-group asset revaluation reserve	1607
degree of ownership	
– decrease; no longer a subsidiary	1605
– decrease; still a subsidiary	1604
– increase	1603
– no change	1602
Share sales	1501
journal entry components	1502
part sale	
– partly owned subsidiary, no longer a subsidiary	1506
– partly owned subsidiary, still a subsidiary	1505
sale	
– all of partly owned subsidiary	1504
– all of wholly owned subsidiary	1503
subsequent equity accounting	1507
Shareholders' funds of subsidiary	
reduction — see Loss-making subsidiaries	
Shareholders' interests	
disclosure	905
Shareholdings	
supplementary information; example	App. B
Significant influence	801
factors indicating existence	801
Simultaneous equations	
accounting for cross holdings	2402
Sources and applications of funds — see **Funds statement**	
Statutory requirements for group accounts	2301
acquisition of holding company shares by subsidiary	2306
audit	2311
definitions	2303
directors' report	2309
directors' statement	2308
financial years	2305
form and content	2304; 2312
preparation	2302
relief from preparation of accounts	2307
Schedule 7	2312
true and fair view	2310

	Paragraph
Stock Exchange Listing Rules — see **Listing Rules**	
Straight-line amortisation of goodwill	305
Subsidiaries	
acquisition — see Acquisitions	
definition	905; 2303
disposal	
– example note	App. B (Note 31)
– Sch. 7 disclosure requirements	2312
foreign; funds statement	2103
form of accounts	2312
holding company shares	2306
investment in — see Intra-group investments	
loss-making — see Loss-making subsidiaries	
overseas — see Overseas subsidiaries	
sale; funds statement	2103
sale of partly owned subsidiary	1504
– part sale; no longer a subsidiary	1506
– part sale; still a subsidiary	1505
sale of wholly owned subsidiary	1503
Sch. 7 disclosure requirements	2312
Superannuation fund	
example accounting policy note	App. B (Note 1(p))
Supplementary equity financial statements	App. B (Note 48)
Supplementary information to financial statements	App. B

T

Tax — see **Income tax; Income tax expense**	
Temporal method of foreign currency translation	2201
Tests of consolidation results	208
Third journal entry	906
Timing difference	1103; 1105
True and fair view	2310
Trust deeds	
preparation of accounts	201
Trusts	
acquisition	708
Twenty largest shareholders	
supplementary information; example	App. B

Paragraph

U

Ultimate holding company 2303

Understatement of assets or liabilities
   at acquisition date 2001

V

Valuation
   goodwill 302

W

Wholly owned subsidiaries
   acquisition
   – at balance date 703

Paragraph

– during a year 705
– in subsequent years 704
indirect interests 1901
relief from preparation
   of accounts 2307
sale 1503

Worksheet — see **Consolidation worksheet**

Write-downs
   inventory 1106

Write-off
   goodwill 306